The Communicator's Commentary

Hebrews

THE COMMUNICATOR'S COMMENTARY SERIES

Lloyd J. Ogilvie
—— General Editor ——

The Communicator's Commentary

Hebrews

Louis H. Evans, Jr.

WORD BOOKS, PUBLISHER • WACO, TEXAS

Library of Congress Cataloging in Publication Data
Main entry under title:

The Communicator's commentary.

  Includes bibliographical references.
  Contents: v. 10. Hebrews/Louis H. Evans, Jr.
  1. Bible, N.T.—Commentaries—Collected works.
I. Ogilvie, Lloyd John. II. Evans, Louis H., Jr.
BS2341.2.C65   225.7'7   81–71764
ISBN 0–8499–0163–4   AACR2
567898 FG   987654321
Printed in the United States of America

Dedication

Four teachers come readily to my mind as I think about this epistle. Professor John Wicke Bowman of San Francisco Theological Seminary first stimulated me to see the rich Hebraic background to the New Testament. His wealth of knowledge in Semitic and Indo-Germanic languages was intriguing and captivating. He made me hunger for more of that knowledge in order to understand the person of Jesus Christ. A student of his from India, Surjit Singh, came to be our Visiting Professor of Systematic Theology in 1952–53. Professor Singh's vast understanding of epistemology, systematics, and Christian philosophy stimulated me to a thrilling comprehension of the movement of history. As I prepared to leave the seminary, a word of affirmation and painful challenge from President Jesse Baird of San Francisco Theological Seminary challenged me to go on. He said, "Louie, you are a man of inspiration; you need to become a man of discipline."

These three, sensing my hunger for better exegetical tools for clarification of some Christological problems I had and for an understanding of how New Testament writers used Old Testament material, encouraged me to take postgraduate study at the University of Edinburgh under Professors James S. Stewart, William Manson, and Matthew Block. It was under Professor Stewart's tutelage that I took up this study. During those two years of 1953–55, I faced an agonizing personal struggle, and the preaching of Professor Stewart became sustaining manna for me in the midst of my wilderness.

I thank God for the stimulation and modeling which these four giants of the faith provided and so dedicate this work to them.

Contents

Editor's Preface

God has called all of His people to be communicators. Everyone who is in Christ is called into ministry. As ministers of "the manifold grace of God," all of us—clergy and laity—are commissioned with the challenge to communicate our faith to individuals and groups, classes and congregations.

The Bible, God's Word, is the objective basis of the truth of His love and power that we seek to communicate. In response to the urgent, expressed needs of pastors, teachers, Bible study leaders, church school teachers, small group enablers, and individual Christians, the Communicator's Commentary is offered as a penetrating search of the Scriptures of the New Testament to enable vital personal and practical communication of the abundant life.

Many current commentaries and Bible study guides provide only some aspects of a communicator's needs. Some offer in-depth scholarship but no application to daily life. Others are so popular in approach that biblical roots are left unexplained. Few offer impelling illustrations that open windows for the reader to see the exciting application for today's struggles. And most of all, seldom have the expositors given the valuable outlines of passages so needed to help the preacher or teacher in his or her busy life to prepare for communicating the Word to congregations or classes.

This Communicator's Commentary series brings all of these elements together. The authors are scholar-preachers and teachers outstanding in their ability to make the Scriptures come alive for individuals and groups. They are noted for bringing together excellence in biblical scholarship, knowledge of the original Greek and Hebrew, sensitivity to people's needs, vivid illustrative material from biblical, classical, and contemporary sources, and lucid communication by the use of clear outlines of thought. Each has been selected to contribute to this series because of his Spirit-empowered ability to help people live in the skins of biblical characters and provide a "you-are-there" intensity to the drama of events of the Bible which have so much to say about our relationships and responsibilities today.

The design for the Communicator's Commentary gives the reader an overall outline of each book of the New Testament. Following the introduction, which reveals the author's approach and salient background on the book, each chapter of the commentary provides the Scripture to be exposited. The New King James Bible has been chosen for the Communicator's Commentary because it combines with integrity the beauty of language, underlying Greek textual basis, and thought-flow of the 1611 King James Version, while replacing obsolete verb forms and other archaisms with their everyday contemporary counterparts for greater readability. Reverence for God is preserved in the capitalization of all pronouns referring to the Father, Son, or Holy Spirit. Readers who are more comfortable with another translation can readily find the parallel passage by means of the chapter and verse reference at the end of each passage being exposited. The paragraphs of exposition combine fresh insights to the Scripture, application, rich illustrative material, and innovative ways of utilizing the vibrant truth for his or her own life and for the challenge of communicating it with vigor and vitality.

It has been gratifying to me as Editor of this series to receive enthusiastic progress reports from each contributor. As they worked, all were gripped with new truths from the Scripture—God-given insights into passages, previously not written in the literature of biblical explanation. A prime objective of this series is for each user to find the same awareness: that God speaks with newness through the Scriptures when we approach them with a ready mind and a willingness to communicate what He has given; that God delights to give communicators of His Word "I-never-saw-that-in-that-verse-before" intellectual insights so that our listeners and readers can have "I-never-realized-all-that-was-in-that-verse" spiritual experiences.

The thrust of the commentary series unequivocally affirms that God speaks through the Scriptures today to engender faith, enable adventuresome living of the abundant life, and establish the basis of obedient discipleship. The Bible, the unique Word of God, is unlimited in its resource for Christians in communicating our hope to others. It is our weapon in the battle for truth, the guide for ministry, and the irresistible force for introducing others to God. In the New Testament we meet the divine Lord and Savior whom we seek to communicate to others. What He said and did as God with us has been faithfully recorded under the inspiration of the Spirit of God. The cosmic implications of the Gospels are lived out in Acts and spelled out in the Epistles. They have stood the test of time because the eternal Communicator, God Himself, communicates through them to those who would be communicators of grace. His essential nature is exposed, the plan of salvation is explained, and the Gospel for all of life, now and for eternity, is proclaimed.

A biblically rooted communication of the Gospel holds in unity and oneness what divergent movements have wrought asunder. This commentary series courageously presents personal faith, caring for individuals, and social responsibility as essential, inseparable dimensions of biblical Christianity. It seeks to present the quadrilateral Gospel in its fullness which calls us to unreserved commitment to Christ, unrestricted self-esteem in His grace, unqualified love for others in personal evangelism, and undying efforts to work for justice and righteousness in a sick and suffering world.

A growing renaissance in the church today is being led by clergy and laity who are biblically rooted, Christ-centered, and Holy Spirit-empowered. They have dared to listen to people's most urgent questions and deepest needs and then to God as He speaks through the Bible. Biblical preaching is the secret of growing churches. Bible study classes and small groups are equipping the laity for ministry in the world. Dynamic Christians are finding that daily study of God's Word allows the Spirit to do in them what He wishes to communicate through them to others. These days are the most exciting time since Pentecost. The Communicator's Commentary is offered to be a primary resource of new life for this renaissance.

Over the years, my conversations with pastors and teachers about their expository communication of the New Testament has revealed that the Epistle to the Hebrews has been overlooked. It is one of the least appreciated and utilized books of the New Testament for comprehensive, thematic, or verse-by-verse study and preaching. Some preachers have found individual verses or favorite chapters propitious for powerful preaching, but they seldom take their congregations through the entire epistle in a prolonged series of messages. Teachers of Bible classes or small group discussion leaders frequently quote from the rich store of truth in the epistle, but few tackle it as a whole. Yet Hebrews is a treasure chest brimming over with spiritual power for the preacher and teacher. However, help is needed to examine these jewels and utilize them in a way that not only exposes the separate texts in depth, but the context of the epistle as a whole.

We have needed a contemporary commentary on Hebrews that explains the sweep of its deeper meaning and that exemplifies how to develop a series of messages or classes for preaching and teaching today. I believe this commentary on Hebrews accomplishes both—and so much more.

When I carefully and prayerfully considered the persons who might most creatively write the commentary on Hebrews, I wanted an author who had made the epistle a major focus of his study, research, and expository preaching and teaching through the years. That choice was not difficult. One scholar-preacher who has become distinguished for his work in Hebrews over the years is Dr. Louis H. Evans, Jr., Pastor of the National Presbyterian Church, Washington, D.C.

Dr. Evans's concentration on Hebrews began during his postgraduate studies at New College, University of Edinburgh, Scotland. His research and writing on Hebrews at that time has been further refined and deepened in application in preaching and teaching to congregations, classes, and conferences through the years. His distilled insights into the text, as well as his magnificent outline of the contents of the epistle as a whole, offer the communicator a ready guide for the development of sermons and study plans for classes and group discussions. In a very viable way, Dr. Evans has given Hebrews back to the contemporary church as a basis for dynamic preaching and teaching of Christ, our High Priest, Prophet and King.

This stunning commentary of Hebrews provides a stimulating resource for preachers and teachers. The author's etymological exposure of the deeper meaning of the Greek, along with his interpretation of the Old Testament roots of the phrases, images, and concepts of the epistle make this commentary a rich source of material for the communicator. The work stands on its own as an excellent scholarly treatment of Hebrews, but it is done in a way that will enable the reader to approach his or her own preaching and teaching with new depth and freshness. The essential research and exposition has been done. The contemporary and personal illustrations and anecdotes used to clarify introduce us to the author's mind and heart; they also show us how to draw on our own experiences and observations of life in our teaching and preaching of Hebrews. I predict that this volume will become one of the most cherished and used commentaries for the exposition of the epistle today.

Dr. Evans is one of the finest biblical preachers in America today. As Pastor of the strategic National Presbyterian Church in Washington, he is also a distinguished, pivotal leader of church renewal in the nation. Admired and emulated by pastors and church leaders, he is noted for his forthright preaching and the way he exemplifies the implementation of the Gospel in his own life and in his leadership of his parish. He is a frontiersman, constantly breaking new ground with new forms of ministry to meet the deepest needs of people and to confront the urgent issues of our society. In his personal life, he puts his money, energy, and influence where his preaching is. He has become a front-runner in the most crucial issues gripping us today. Hunger, poverty, and human rights, as well as the spiritual needs of people, are all urgent concerns of his life and ministry. Dr. Evans's leadership is a magnificent blend of a call to personal faith and social responsibility. For that reason, his writing, preaching, and innovative churchmanship result in solidly converted, deeply committed, and energetically involved laity who can share their faith and work for justice and righteousness in the structures of society. And at the source of it all is the quality of biblical research and exposition you will appreciate in this volume. All this has made him a revered pastor and friend of both the top leaders of the nation who depend on his counseling and care and the disadvantaged who have been helped by his practical compassion and concern.

One added personal word. Dr. Evans is a valued covenant brother of mine. Over the years we have been part of a covenant group of men and women who meet consistently for study, prayer, and mutual encouragement, as well as to strategize for the renewal of the church in America. As my friend, "Lou" has been a faithful prayer partner who has shared the joys and challenges of the adventure of discipleship.

Thus, it is with profound gratitude that I commend to you this outstanding treatment of Hebrews and rejoice with you as you enjoy the new delight of communicating Christ's authority, power, and redemption from this epistle.

LLOYD OGILVIE

Introduction

Expositional works are usually written in a nonpersonal style, either without reference to the author or, if any is made, in the third person. My editor, good friend, and covenant brother Lloyd Ogilvie, has asked me in his own quiet but graciously persistent manner to make a personal statement introducing this study to you. At first I hesitated, but realize that any work is an expression of the person and experience of the writer. After many years of reading scholarly works, I am convinced that the claim for utterly objective and scholastic approach is a false one. Therefore I may as well tell you who I am and why I have approached this work in the manner I have. You will discover it sooner or later anyway.

My family background has two main streams, one Calvinistic and the other Anabaptist. On my father's side, Presbyterianism and Calvinism were my strong diet and environment as long as I can remember. My grandfather William, an early convert of D. L. Moody, and the first graduate from Moody Bible Institute, was one of America's great scholar-preachers. He knew the New Testament by heart in several English versions and major portions of the Greek. He was a master of memorization and wrote a book on the subject, *How to Memorize,* published by Moody Press in 1909. His lecturing and preaching skills led him around the country in the great movement of Chatauquas and tabernacle meetings in every corner of the nation and across the seas. He was a Welshman, native born, and always a colonialist and Britisher at heart. I remember his saying in his great elocutionary style, "Son, there will always be an England. The sun never sets on the British Empire." He was a disciplined scholar, spending six to eight hours each working day in scriptural studies and writing.

My father, Louis H. Evans, Sr., was one of the nation's great pastors and preachers. Honored several times as one of America's ten great preachers, he brought the stirring combination of fine athlete, musician, and forceful presence to all his ministries. Collegians thronged university auditoriums to hear him; men hung on his words at large church rallies and responded to his powerful challenges for the Kingdom of God. He served the Presbyterian denomination as president of the Board of National Missions, the pastor of its largest congregation, Hollywood, California, and finally as Minister-at-Large for the Board of National Missions.

On my mother's side the Anabaptist stream ran rich. My great-grandfather, Bishop Henry Egly, an Amishman of Swiss descent, discovered Christ in a life-changing evangelical encounter. He preached the Christian experience until an evangelical movement among the Amish became so significant it was named the Egly Amish. Pressed out of that fellowship over this matter, he became the founder of the Defenseless Mennonites, later to become the Evangelical Mennonite Church of America.

My grandfather Joseph Egly moved from Berne, Indiana, the center of the Defenseless Mennonites, to begin a Missionary and Alliance congregation in Phoenix, Arizona, where my mother was raised.

Mother is one of those radiant, solid Christian women whose strong piety has always been touched with realism and practicality. Her life has been an example par excellence for the servant, always strong and filled with a love for Jesus Christ.

My own pilgrimage has had perhaps four phases. The first I can remember is that of traditional and institutional Christianity as expressed in the life of the Presbyterians in Pittsburgh, Pennsylvania. I was conscious of a socially oriented congregation of Pittsburgh's wealthy, whose people vacationed in Miami and Lake Placid. Smooth sophistication, nonenthusiastic attitudes toward religion, nonintimate relationships, country club protocol, and the right schools seemed to me the emphases of greatest magnitude. Dad's ministry appeared tangential to the society's main course and few followed him.

My second phase began as my father moved to Hollywood, California, where I experienced evangelical faith for the first time. In 1947 I had a life-transforming experience with Christ and in the ensuing years was disciplined in a mildly fundamental and dispensational theology. Even in this phase, however, I began to struggle with certain doctrines of inspiration that did not appear to correlate with what I was discovering in New Testament studies of ancient manuscripts. Moreover, I was questioning the New Testament writers' use of Old Testament material. Having some background in philosophy and logic, I found it difficult to go along with or understand some of the interpretations made by New Testament authors.

Finishing seminary and wanting to answer some questions I had in Christology and hermeneutics (the art of interpreting the Scriptures), I counseled with Dr. Jesse Baird, President of San Francisco Seminary, and Dr. John Wick Bowman, my New Testament professor, who urged me to do a post-graduate study in Edinburgh with Professors James S. Stewart, Matthew Black, and William Manson. They suggested the Epistle to the Hebrews which would cover both the christological and hermeneutical themes.

The thesis topic was chosen: "A Christological Study of the Epistle to the Hebrews with Special Emphasis on the Writers' Use of Old Testament Material." About that time the Qumran Fragments broke upon the path of the thesis and I found myself involved in a very heavy topic indeed.

Since that time I have taught the epistle many times, always with a deepening sense of appreciation and insight.

The third phase of my Christian growth came during the social justice movement of the sixties and seventies when dear friends of the black community began to share with Colleen and me the painful experiences of being blacks in contemporary America. This led me to a new study of the Scriptures which resulted in a firm conviction that there could be no bifurcation of the faith into the camps of soul-saving or social action. Evangelism and justice were two coordinate themes of the same gospel of our Lord Jesus Christ. The experiences of pastoring in San Diego's suburb of La Jolla and now in Washington, D.C., where we have been active in the inner-city ministry, have convinced me that we have a whole gospel for the whole person in the whole world. In no way can I deny or diminish either emphasis without doing damage to the gospel.

The fourth and present phase of my Christian walk is that of trying to live out my simple role of being a pastor in the latter years of the twentieth century, a member of the rising third party of the church which must be unembarrassingly evangelical and justice-oriented at the same time.

There is another facet of my thinking of which you must be aware: the deep concern I have for our main-line denominations. I love the church of which I am a part and at the same time I agonize for its loss of spiritual vitality in a day of atrophy. Membership of major denominations dwindles from historic peaks; mission efforts wallow in a mixture of theological vagueness, postcolonial guilt, and embarrassment of association with a nation that is a world power. Tragically, in all too many instances the church has been polarized by a dichotomy between the evangelical passion for the souls of people on one hand and the social concern for justice on the other. Issues and power politics, not the Person of Jesus Christ, have become the rallying points at which segments of the church muster for battle. The result is division, distrust, and dissipated energies. The Person and ministry of Jesus Christ have been demythologized of supernatural elements in a milieu of humanistic scientism so that the church's banners are bleached.

In the words of Charles Malik before the Evanston Assembly in 1954, "What is desperately needed, beside the highest political wisdom, is a ringing, positive message, one of reality, of truth, and of hope." Jesus Christ is the center and throbbing core of that reality, truth, and hope. Professor Edmund Schlink said to the same assembly, "The whole point of Christian hope is that we live and act in faith. Christian hope is based in Jesus Christ alone."

Who is this Jesus Christ? Why is hope founded on Him alone? For one simple reason that has many facets: Jesus Christ is the foundation of the church's being. The church's existence is dependent upon its relation to the historical Christ. It is a matter of ontology (the science of being and reality). Without Christ there is no church; without Jesus of Nazareth there is no reality for the church. Because of His identity, because of His life and ministry, because of His atoning death and resurrection, His gift of the Holy Spirit, and His promise of ultimate victory, believers are drawn into a fellowship of hope. To fail to understand Jesus Christ is to fail to understand the church. Cleave the branch from the Vine and the branch *will wither!* There is no way it can be kept alive apart from the Vine.

Renewal in the church depends upon a renewed understanding and a commitment to Jesus Christ as God Incarnate; One of us; Priest, Sacrifice, and Coming Messiah. No other New Testament document so fully explores Him in these dimensions as does the Epistle to the Hebrews. The epistle makes no attempt to prove the existence of Jesus Christ or His atoning death. The author simply makes an exposition of that which he takes as given and so would I. My purpose is to share with you the rich truths and imagery of this passionate and fertile mind of the first century. This author—his (or her) style, thought-form, and urgency—has impacted my life in an inescapable manner and stimulated me to be a different person, a more committed disciple of Jesus my Lord. I trust the same will be true for you, my friend. Needless to say, I am indebted to the teachers and scholars of the centuries who have made their insights available to you and me. Few of these ideas are my own, and even if I should think so, I am sure some saint thought of them long ago. Yet the gracious Holy Spirit permits us the joy of thinking we have made a discovery. So come, share in discovering!

This commentary series is not designed for many footnotes and quotations. Rather, it is to be an aid to those who desire to teach and illustrate the Gospel of our Lord Jesus Christ out of responsible scholarship but without the heavy drapes of academic sophistication. I am excited to do this study with you. My only wish is to be servant to your growth, knowing that you will go far beyond my limited insights into this great epistle. If anything can be a stepping stone or resource for your journey, it is yours. After all, all belongs to Christ.

About the Epistle

The Epistle to the Hebrews is sometimes known as "the forgotten epistle." One might wonder why. I see several possible explanations.

First, the epistle argues strongly from the standpoint of comparative sacrifices, a topic we today are not eager to pursue. Blood sacrifice is no longer practiced, and its liturgical significance has been deemphasized, if not rejected. We tend to turn our backs and minds on that which seems repulsive and some would call uncivilized.

Second, contemporary theology has attempted to demythologize the historical Jesus and those atonement principles that deal with supernatural or nonscientific themes. These thought-forms in Hebrews are not familiar to a technologically oriented society.

Further, much of the church has strongly emphasized social concerns to the detriment of evangelical religious experience. Thus the thrust of Hebrews on a cleansing sacrifice that can make the conscience of a believer clean is not as exciting as street action for social justice. The latter appears more pragmatic than the former. Christian faith is desperately weakened when urgent prophetic social concern is separated from a personal relationship with God. How can we be close to the God of justice and not know His untiring vigilance against oppression? How can we be involved in the draining efforts for the oppressed without being sustained by personal relationship with God?

Finally, the epistle's format makes it a difficult document to study. Its themes weave in and out on the warp of doctrine and the woof of exhortation. So smooth are these transitions that the reader is easily confused by the movement from one to the other.

Now there are fresh reasons for reconsidering this epistle and bringing it out of the "forgotten bin" into the light of study. We have already mentioned the hunger for renewed insights into the study of Christ (Christology) and sacrifice (soteriology). After trying all our human and scientific methods of realizing the good life and having failed so miserably, we are ready to consider our need for some outside help—for salvation from God and on God's terms.

In addition, fresh approaches to the epistle have unraveled its interwoven style and made it excitingly clear and relevant.

Style

The style of the epistle is unique. From the very outset the author runs a race at top speed, not taking time to identify himself or his readers. He thrusts all his energies into the first lines of his argument and does not let up the pace until the end. During the race he changes his stride between doctrine or teaching and exhortation. It is as though he is running against an opponent, cultic Judaism, that will not let go its grasp on previous adherents. Thematically, his style is that of comparison. "Better," "superior," and "more" are words used consistently throughout the arguments. It is obvious that, by showing the superiority of the new covenant to the old and the better sacrifice of Christ to those of the Jewish sacrificial system (cultus), he believes he can pull his readers into the wholehearted acceptance of the uniqueness of Christ's priestly ministry.

In handling the doctrine and exhortation, he differs sharply from Paul. The latter holds his exhortational passages until the end of an epistle or until the doctrinal dissertation is complete. Our author, on the contrary, makes an excursion from the teaching material whenever it reminds him of some characteristic of his readers that demands improvement. The doctrinal and the exhortational are interwoven most smoothly, so that one finds oneself on a different tack within a matter of a few words or lines—now doctrine, now exhortation, now doctrine again. Farther along, we will peruse a schematic diagram of this interweaving; I think it will greatly facilitate and clarify the material we study.

More than any other New Testament writer, our author is classical in his Greek style. Where Paul will use one word, such as "law" in Romans 7, to mean several different types of law, our writer will use several different words for the same thing, showing an immense vocabulary that continues to build all through the epistle.

Among his various peculiarities is his use of what I would call "rhetorical similarity." Using a root word, he will, in order to make a point, choose compound words that have not only rhetorical similarity but contrasting meanings. For example, he uses the root *philo* in three different combinations to form this rhetorical similarity: in Hebrews 13:1, *philadelphia* (brotherly love), verse 2, *philozenias* (hospitality), and in verse 5, *aphilarguros* (not greedy for money). He also enjoys using compounds, beginning with a root word and embellishing it with prefixes (e.g., Heb. 13:2).

Authorship

Perhaps you have heard arguments among your Christian friends over the question, "Who wrote the Epistle to the Hebrews?" "My King James Bible says Paul wrote it, so that must be the case!" is a common response. And yet Origen, a biblical scholar of the second and third centuries, felt that because of style the epistle could not have been the direct work of Paul.[1] Roman Catholics, while wanting to keep the epistle in the Pauline school and yet admitting the differences with Paul, claim the writer was in the company of Paul. Others have even speculated on female authorship, perhaps that of Priscilla, who was undeniably a teacher of no mean ability (Acts 18; Rom. 16:3–5).

These things we can know about the author: He (or she) was a teacher. The thoughtfulness and thoroughness in persuasion marks him (or her) as an instructor in Christian life. Moreover, he (or she) was a second generation Christian, claiming the gospel "was confirmed to us by those who heard Him [Jesus]" (Heb. 2:3).

Our author was most probably a Jew—perhaps an Alexandrian Jew, or one of the *diaspora*, those who had been taken into exile from

Israel but who retained connection with the religion of their father-land. His knowledge of the Old Testament is extensive, not only in the number of Old Testament quotations used but in the manner in which they are used. His method of argument follows Jewish rules of scriptural interpretation, as we shall see later[1] in this Introduction. He interprets with authority as a Jew, not speculatively as a Greek, as some would have him be. The way in which he uses Old Testament material is reminiscent of the *Haggadah* and the *midrash,* two forms of Jewish religious tradition. The *Haggadah* expressed the real-life, flexible, allegorical interpretations of the Torah as would have been expressed by loving and sensitive preachers, rather than *Halakah,* the hard, tight legalism of the Pharisees. It lifted and inspired. Our author is at home in this tradition. The *midrash* was the product of seeking out or searching the Scriptures. This process of investigation would often result in the type of insights represented in the *Haggadah.* Our author uses this peculiar Jewish style with ease and obvious practice. For this reason, some wish to believe the author was Apollos.

The writer of this epistle is aflame with the apostolic message. He has been thoroughly trained in Christian doctrine and can recognize variances from it, which he then attacks with his ability of scriptural interpretation. Like Paul, his heart is alive with the passion for world mission, and he sees his readers growing far too slowly toward their full participation in it. He has little time for speculation, but sees his teaching, sophisticated though it is, as relevant to everyday life and able to move his readers forward. He is most passionate when expressing his deep concern that those who stay too long in one place are in danger of slipping back, refusing to obey God, hesitating to drive forward, or sinking into apostasy. His passion rises to its highest in the face of this possibility (Heb. 5:11—6:8).

Our writer is not afraid of conflict. Although he is a scholar, his garments do not smell of musty books; rather he uses his knowledge as a rapier which takes him out into the streets to meet his foes—lethargy, Jewish possessiveness, and lack of insight and commitment. Then, when his readers are almost lulled into the smoothly flowing stream of quiet scholarship, he inundates them with a cataract of warning and chastisement. He strictly admonishes his readers against taking the message too lightly and possibly drifting away (2:14); he warns them against the hardened heart that rises out of disbelief and disobedience (3:7—4:16); he chastises them into growing in their faith lest they fall in apostasy (5:11—6:20); he encourages them with examples of faith (chap. 11); he prods them to accept God's loving discipline and persevere to the end of the race (chap. 12). Our author is an exhorter! He speaks of his own work as "my word of exhortation" (Heb. 13:22). For this reason some have thought he might be Barnabas, "son of encouragement."

Evidently our author had some contact with the Pauline party, for he speaks of "our brother Timothy" (Heb. 13:23) who has been released, most likely from prison. If this is the same Timothy of whom Paul speaks, it would not surprise us that the same world mission passion that burned in Paul's heart burned in this heart as well. If he is an Alexandrian or a Hellenistic Jew, one raised in the Greek-speaking world, he could easily find himself in step with the Pauline group. He might even have been in prison, for he asks their prayers that "I might be restored to you the sooner" (Heb. 13:19). The restoration may have been from illness, however.

So, who is the writer? From Origen to scholars of the present day, students have despaired of identifying him.

Title and Destination

The one point concerning destination upon which most scholars agree is that the letter was written to a definite group of believers. Even those who have the letter going to the Gentiles would admit this. The writer speaks to those whom he knows well and loves deeply, but whose character causes him specific concerns. Whether the group was a large section of the church in some area, a local congregation, or even a house church is less certain.

In the arguments that follow, we will be dealing with three possible types of readers: Gentile Christians of Greek culture, philosophical background, and religion; Hebraic Jews of the Holy Land; or Hellenistic Jews of Greek-speaking provinces known as the *diaspora* or dispersed ones.

Some would argue for several reasons that the group of readers consisted of Gentile Greeks: no apostasy to Judaism is mentioned; use of the Old Testament does not necessarily mean Jewish readers, since Gentile Christians also used the Old Testament; the epistle turns wholly on ritualistic arguments whereas Judaism of the writer's day was concerned only for the moral law since the temple had been destroyed; and the writer speaks of the mythical tabernacle, not the first-century temple.

I do not think the readers were Gentile Greeks. Even though apostasy to Judaism is not mentioned, the whole ethos of the writing is one of showing that the revelation of God through Jesus Christ is superior to Judaism, not just to religion in general. Prophets were not important to the Greeks, as they were to the Hebrews. Abraham, Moses, Elijah, Isaiah, Jeremiah—these men and others stood in a place of veneration in the Jewish mind that would have been foreign to the Greek mind. The idea of prophets' being filled with the Holy Spirit, having personal contact with God, and functioning as the agents through whom God revealed Himself to the world was a Hebraic, not Greek, concept. The author does not get beyond his first sentence (Heb. 1:1–2) before comparing the Son with the prophets and showing that God is speaking more completely through His Son than through the revered prophets. Such an argument would have been lost on Greek Gentile readers.

Moreover, the argument of Jesus' being superior to the angels would have had little meaning to the Greek mind. Angels were heavenly beings in Jewish theology, not Greek. Although initiated in Persian mythology, angelology developed in Jewish thinking; angels were servants and messengers of God. In earlier mythology they were connected with wind, fire, and other natural elements, and only took on the form of personal beings as the doctrine evolved.

Whatever argument may be advanced with regard to the use of the Old Testament *per se*, I believe the significant factor is the *manner* in which our author has employed it. Study shows that his use of Old Testament material is in complete accord with the Jewish rules of scriptural interpretation, and the expository milieu is thoroughly Hebraic.

To argue that the Jews of the writer's time were not interested in the ritualistic because the temple had been destroyed is fallacious; I believe that the temple was still standing and its sacrificial systems were still in operation, as we will discuss later in connection with the dating of the epistle.

Further, the epistle's argument that Jesus is superior to Moses in the matter of faithfulness because the builder of a house is more important than the house would have been lost on the Greek, who never considered himself a member of the "house" as did the Jews.

The laborious argument of a superior priesthood in Jesus after the order of Melchizedek (Heb. 5:1–10, 7:1–22), together with the interpretation of His name ("king of righteousness") and of Jerusalem ("city of peace"), would have had Gentiles yawning in disinterest. By the same reasoning, the comparison of the old and new covenants would have been boring or nonsensical to the Greek mind, which had no such orientation to God's promises.

Even though the language is Greek and classical, the thought-form and argumentative tracks are thoroughly Hebraic. Nevertheless, many New Testament scholars seem adamant in putting Hellenistic interpretations on New Testament writers. Perhaps the reason is that most come to their knowledge of New Testament Greek (*koinē*)[2] through the classical and are versed in its thought-form long before they make a study, if they do at all, of Hebrew thought-form. Being unfamiliar, or not as familiar, with the Hebraic, they have naturally tended to bring Hellenistic interpretation to bear on New Testament writings.

Because of the extended use of the Septuagint[3] and the references to the tabernacle described in older scriptural writings, I do not believe the readers were Jews of the Holy Land. It is possible that not many of the readers had been to Jerusalem and witnessed the sacrificial system in operation, although many from the *diaspora* did journey to Jerusalem for the holy days.

I therefore believe, in view of all the foregoing, that the readers were Hellenistic Jews, second generation Christians who had been reared in the Jewish religion and its rules of scriptural interpretation according to the standards of the synagogue. Apollos was such a Christian, raised as a Jew in Alexandria, the great Hellenistic center of language and culture, "well-versed in the Scriptures" and the Jewish mode of interpretation. Our writer as well is well-versed in the Jewish rules of interpretation used by the rabbinic schools. By using those principles of argument and interpretation, he hoped to persuade his readers regarding the superiority of Jesus to all the Judaism of his day.

Jewish Principles of Scriptural Interpretation

At this point let us take an excursion to discuss a matter that I feel is very important: the manner in which our author and other New Testament writers use Old Testament material.

Perhaps, you have been a bit uncomfortable, as have I, when at times passages are taken out of context and given an interpretation that seems inconsistent with that context. For instance, Matthew quotes Isaiah 7:14: "A virgin shall conceive and bear a son, and his name shall be called Emmanuel" (1:23). The historical setting is that of the prophet Isaiah telling a terrified and forlorn King Ahaz that the two kings making war against him, Rezin and Remaliah, would be destroyed before a woman (*halmah*, in the Hebrew) could conceive and bear a son and rear him to an age of discernment. *Halmah* means simply a woman of child-bearing years. "Virgin" is only one possible translation of the word and not a good one at that. However, Matthew is quoting from the Septuagint in which the translators used the Greek word *parthenos*, "virgin," when translating the Hebrew word *halmah*.

It is difficult to understand why Matthew would take such a passage out of context and use it as an argument for the virgin birth—or why other New Testament writers might use Old Testament passages in a similar way—until we consider the principles of interpretation used by Jewish teachers and preachers in their exposition of the Scriptures.

Jewish literature was of two main types; the *Halakah* and the *Haggadah*. The *Halakah* (from the Hebrew *halak*, "to walk") signified how to walk; it was a statement of legal rule or prescribed conduct. In later years the exact rules for every situation in life were spelled out in halakic literature like the *Mishnah*. The *Mishnah* was the tradition or teaching of the law handed down through the ages from the 5th century B.C. and was the basis of examination in the temple when a boy came of age for his bar mitzvah, to use our contemporary term. The *Mishnah* (from the Hebrew *shanah*, "repeat, do a second time") was memorized, recited, and interpreted by the teachers (Pharisees) in the synagogue. It was filled with exact detail for almost any circumstance in life. It was a "catwalk" for its narrowness.

The *Halakah* was very important to many Jewish people. Their tradition held that the Torah itself was the result of successive waves of halakic compilation. To the orthodox it was the moral law independent even of the Torah that was transmitted by Moses and the later teachers. Its undisputed place of authority was assured by Nehemiah's actions (Neh. 8). According to the *Universal Jewish Encyclopedia*, "The strict observance of these rules was an absolute necessity for the good Jew; only by this means could he retain that legal purity upon which right relation with Jehovah depends."[4]

Thus the outgrowth of halakic emphasis became what I would call a "cult of Torah." Its basis was a law codified and published by Ezra and Nehemiah, and later by the scribes and the Pharisees who dedicated full time to its observance. It reflected an ideal state that was rigid and inflexible, seeking static perfection. It was believed to contain the absolute and inviolable will of God that was never to be questioned.

No wonder our Lord so often opposed it and was in turn opposed with increasing intensity. He was tampering with the sacred backbone of Jewish life!

The second type of Jewish teaching was the *Haggadah*. In contrast to the rigidity of the *Halakah, Haggadah* was flexible and indicated broad guidelines for action. Although it too was based on the Torah, it offered greater adaptability to life that strict legalism could not allow. More homiletical and allegorical, the method of *Haggadah* was given to parable, legend, and proverb. Its purpose was to bring heaven closer to earth and then to lift man heavenward. Those of mystical bent could find satisfaction and inspiration in *Haggadah;* its sermons were expressed by eloquent preachers who became the beloved teachers of Israel. Preachers drew from the Scriptures that guidance suitable to the day and led their people into satisfying relationships with their fellow human beings. Thus *Haggadah* struck a balance between the will of the Creator and the daily walk of His people.

As mentioned earlier, the *midrash*[5] was the product of seeking out or investigating the Scriptures while arriving at the *Haggadah*. It began in the time of Ezra and Nehemiah, who demonstrated the midrashic method: "So they read distinctly from the book, in the Law of God; and they gave the sense, and helped them to understand the reading" (Neh. 8:8).

Those who expounded the Scriptures by this method were called *sopherim,* interpreters or wise men. The attitude of *midrash* was one of openness and growth. Never could they see the letters of holy writ killing the spirit with rigidity or heaviness. Holy writ was intended to be like a collection of cups, ever to be filled with good vintage, for the Scriptures offered inexhaustible insights. To the *sopherim* the Torah was the sum total of all that was worth knowing and contained everything, *even in germinal form.*

It is this last statement that we want to look at more closely now, for this leads us to the important rules for interpretation that were used by both the rabbinic schools of Judaism and the New Testament writers. The rules for interpretation were called the *middoth.*

The Middoth

The *middoth* were the hermeneutical or expository principles to be used for the proper interpretation of the Scriptures. There were several *middoth* important to our study, and a summary is included here:

1. Inference from the less important to the more important and vice versa. The conclusion is clear when the lesser is like the greater.

2. Inference by similarity. If two scriptural passages have the same words or connotation, both passages, no matter how different in themselves, are subject to the same interpretation.

3. Inference by relationship. If passages are related, any specific regulation found only in one is applied to all others. The principal passage imparts to all the rest a common character that unites them in one family.

4. Deduction from similarity. If two or more passages are similar in their meaning, deduction may be drawn for interpreting other passages with similar conditions. For instance, if a passage says that because a tooth doesn't grow again, the slave can go free, and another passage says that because an eye doesn't grow again, the slave can go free, then the loss of any member that doesn't grow again is basis for the slave's going free.

5. Application of the general to the particular and the particular to the general. Arguments may be decided by comparing the general and the particular.

6. Interpretation by similarity. If one passage has something similar to another, the one may be exposited by means of the other.

7. Deduction from the context. The truth may not be explicitly stated in the passage, but might well be deduced from the context.

8. Interpretation from silence. If a passage is silent on a matter, deduction may be drawn from the silence.

9. If two passages conflict, the conflict may be removed by a third passage.

10. Passages with the same words or same letters may be interpreted similarly. Rabbi Ismael of the first century A.D. rejected this straining interpretation.

As in the case of *Halakah,* the more important the *middoth* became to the interpreters, the more eager they were to claim that the *middoth* had come down from Sinai. The *middoth* carried great weight in deciding arguments and proving points. Our author is thoroughly at home in using these Jewish criteria of interpretation in the hope of swinging the minds of his readers.

As we look at the use of Old Testament passages by New Testament writers and see principles which in some cases we cannot accept by our present criteria, we should not deny the point those writers were trying to prove. In Matthew 1:23, the fact of the Virgin Birth does not depend on the principles of interpretation used by the author of the Gospel; if it was a fact, it was true regardless of the methods used to convince first-century readers. Rather, we have an insight into the patterns of argument and principles of interpretation by which New Testament writers hoped to convince those who held these patterns and principles to be authoritative in proving arguments.

Now we end the excursion and come back to why I think the epistle was written to Jews and not to Gentiles. It will be shown throughout the epistle that the *middoth* find ample application by our author.

Gentiles would find little weight in these *middoth*. Jews, on the other hand, would find them very convincing, as this was the manner in which they argued and decided arguments. This is yet another reason for accepting the title "To the Hebrews" as indicating the readers' identity.

The Date of the Epistle

The latest possible dating for the epistle is A.D. 95–96, at which time Clement of Rome appears to quote from the epistle as though it were before him.

How much earlier might it have been written? Some New Testament scholars would date it rather late in the first century, after the fall of the temple. I do not agree, for two strong reasons.

There is convincing internal evidence for a dating before the fall of the temple in A.D. 70. The writer has used a number of historical allusions and arguments. When trying to prove that the old covenant is obsolete and the new replaces it, would he not use historical argument if it were weighty? In saying the old is about to pass away, because the new is superior, what would have been the greatest argument? That the old *had* passed away and was no more. If the temple had been destroyed and the sacrifices were no longer being made, he would have had his perfect proof. Why then did he not mention it? I believe this was because the temple had not yet been destroyed. The temple fell to the siege of Titus in A.D. 70: therefore the epistle was written sometime prior to that. But how long before?

Here a study of persecutions might give us a clue. Until the time of Nero's burning of Rome in A.D. 64, all incidences of persecution mentioned in Acts were from the Jews, except two that were instigated by local merchants about A.D. 63. The Book of Acts closes with Paul making his appeal to Caesar (25:11), leading us to believe that Paul was convinced he would receive fair treatment at the hand of the emperor, Nero Claudius Caesar. Tradition has it that Nero himself set fire to three of the fourteen sectors of Rome; then, fearing for his life before an angry constituency, he blamed Christians for the burning. The first of the persecutions under Nero began after A.D. 64, shortly after which the practice of Christianity itself became a crime. From that time on any observer could well predict widespread and general persecution of Christians. Already Nero had killed them in his circus games in a manner so brutal that even the Romans took exception.

When our writer prods his readers to courage by saying they "have not yet resisted to the point of shedding their blood," is he indicating he expects such blood-shedding? Is widespread persecution imminent? If so, then the persecutions of Nero had begun and the hostile attitude of the empire toward Christians was growing.

So, it appears probable that the epistle was written somewhere between the fall of the temple in A.D. 70 and the beginnings of Roman persecutions in A.D. 65. Because the siege of Jerusalem was begun in A.D. 66 by Vespasian and the fall of the city was probable, the writer might well have had this in mind when he said, "The old is obsolete and is about to pass away." If the siege were well under way and its outcome clear, which would have been around A.D. 68, this might well be the date of our epistle.

The Difficulty of the Epistle

The literary style of the epistle's interwoven material of doctrine and exhortation makes it a difficult document to study. Luther thought it was "a disorderly mixture of wood and stubble, gold and silver, not representing apostolic levels of thought." E. F. Scott says it is "unable to offer any uniform doctrine." Moffatt says the author seems to wander from point to point without any order or plan.

I experienced the same frustration for the first fifteen months of my studies. Then some insight came! If one were to separate the sections of exhortation from the doctrine, there might be a clearer picture. When I made that separation, a very thrilling clarity of both doctrine and exhortation emerged. The doctrine had a single thrust— the priesthood of Jesus Christ and His ministry of sacrifice. The exhortation passages followed a clear pattern of command, warning, and reasoning. In order to present this most pictorially, I have developed a schematic diagram, reproduced on page 32, which may be of help to you, as it has been to me and a number of students who have studied this epistle with me through the last twenty-five years.

The Purpose of the Epistle

I am strongly convinced that the purpose of this epistle was nurture. Both its main thrusts—teaching and exhortation—are components of nurture. It is quite evident that the writer is aiming at making the superiority and finality of Christ's priesthood and sacrifice certain in the readers' minds. He is equally concerned to goad them on to living out their faith by holding firm what they have believed, moving forward in faith and obedience to God, and growing up to maturity of faith. There is nothing speculative about the work, as if he were writing to philosophically oriented students. Clearly, he is striving for Christian discipleship in the lives of his readers.

Against what odds is he striving? Were his readers being pressured to a loyalty to Judaism with the onset of the Jewish war against the Romans? It would be quite understandable that all Jews would be expected to close ranks in unity and solidarity against the hated Gentile oppressors.

Or was the lack of human priesthood weighing on their desires for a close personal presence and a sanctuary, with all the ceremony that has always been an attraction to religious worshipers? In centuries to come, the church was to hold high its Christian priesthood and even to claim to offer the sacrifice again in the Mass as an indication of the hunger of the human heart for the enacting of the sacrifice. Some liturgists, in fact, argue that the epistle's purpose is to explain the Mass. Since the shape of the liturgy and Mass was hundreds of years in developing, however, this view must be regarded as an anachronism.

Yet another factor may have been holding the readers back from

A SCHEMATIC DIAGRAM OF
THE EPISTLE TO THE HEBREWS

Doctrine			*Exhortation*
I. The Son-Messiah	1:1		
The personal characteristics of the Son	1:14		
		2:1	*Hold Fast Your Confession!* A warning against slipping away
		2:4	
II. The Priest—His Person	2:5		
Four requirements			
A. Identification with the people			
B. Faithfulness to God	3:6		
		3:7	*Trust and Obey!* A warning against the hardened heart
		4:16	
C. Appointment by God after the order of Melchizedek (5:1–10, 7:1–25)	5:1		
	5:10		
		5:11	*Go On to Maturity!* A warning against apostasy
		6:20	
	7:1		
D. Purity	7:26		
	7:28		
III. The Priest—His Ministry			
A. The superiority of the New Covenant	8:1		
	8:13		
B. The sanctuaries and the rituals	9:1		
The earthly sanctuary (vv. 1–5)			
The earthly ritual (vv. 6–10)			
The heavenly ritual (vv. 11–14)			
C. The Mediator of the New Covenant (vv. 15–22)			
D. The Perfect, Single Sacrifice	10:18		
		10:19	*Draw Near with Confidence!* Christian boldness
		11:1	*The Character of Faith* Basic teaching for perseverance
		12:1	*Run with Perseverance!* Christian discipline
		13:1	*Community exhortations*
		13:18	Ending requests and benediction
		13:21	

full commitment to the risen Christ. The old covenant had been established by divine initiative. All the items of the sanctuary and the functions of the priests had been given by divine command. Compare that with the humiliation of a crucified Christ in a Roman culture where crucifixion was repulsive and not even to be mentioned in polite society. It is certainly conceivable that people were tempted to stick with the old and question the validity of the new and untested.

Seen against the backdrop of these possibilities, two emphases of the writer point to a clear purpose. He desperately desired for his readers to see that Christ has become our eternal High Priest and has thereby removed the need for a hierarchy of priests. Moreover, He has opened the way into restored relationship with God. He has accomplished that high purpose of sacrificial religion. He is our exalted priest sitting at the right hand of God, doing His ministry on our behalf in the heavenly sanctuary. Cannot his readers see that the earthly sanctuary is but a copy of the heavenly sanctuary; that the visual aids to worship are all passing and inferior to the eternal Priest and His sacrifice? The way is open; there is no need for any other. Therefore, enter boldly and live in faith, perseverance, and joyful community.

If only he could convince them through sound teaching and urge them to committed discipleship by passionate prodding! What a noble purpose!

A Word about the Outlines

So that you can more easily follow the exposition of this commentary, I have provided two outlines, a brief one in which only the doctrinal portions appear in standard format, with intervening hortatory passages shown in italic type where they interrupt the normal flow of the outline. The number of the commentary chapter corresponding to each outline point is shown in the column at the far right.

In the second and more detailed outline, the main outline points, numbered in Roman capitals, correspond to the chapter titles and numbers. Passages of exhortation are identified by their titles and shown in italic type.

May the study of this magnificent product of the apostolic age nurture your mind and heart to the fullest Christian discipleship. Our world longs for Christians who have a reason for the faith that is within them and a life of courage and integrity to give hope to a cynical world.

NOTES

1. Origen, as found in Eusebius, *Hist. Eccles.* vi, 25.

2. *Koine* or *koinos* signifies that which is common. *Koine* Greek was the language of the marketplace.

3. The Septuagint is a Greek translation of the Old Testament done in the second century B.C. for the library at Alexandria, which desired all major works of all religions and philosophies to be translated into the Greek language. Tradition says that seventy-two scholars laboring under extraordinary circumstances produced the translation in seventy days, thus the name Septuagint, which in Greek means "seventy." The symbol for the Septuagint is LXX.

4. Vol. 5, pp. 172–75.

5. *Midrash* comes from *darash,* which means "to seek out," in this context to seek out a scriptural passage and expound it, or to find something by exposition.

A Brief Outline of Hebrews

An Outline of Hebrews

PART ONE: CHRIST, THE SON-MESSIAH: 1:1—2:4

I. God Has Spoken to Us by a Son: 1:1–2a
II. The Nature of Christ, the Son-Messiah: 1:2–14
    A. Son of God: 1:2a, 5
    B. Heir of All Things: 1:2b
    C. Creator of the World: 1:2c, 10
    D. Radiant Light: 1:3a
    E. The Image of God: 1:3b
    F. Sustainer of the Universe: 1:3c
    G. High Priest of Perfection: 1:3d
    H. Superior to the Angels: 1:4–7, 13–14
    I. Exalted King: 1:3–4, 8a
    J. Lord of Righteousness: 1:8b–9
    K. The Eternal: 1:11–12
    L. Ultimate Conqueror: 1:13
III. The First Exhortation: Hold Fast Your Confession! 2:1–4

PART TWO: THE QUALIFICATIONS OF A HIGH PRIEST 2:5—7:28

IV. A Priest Must Be One with the People: 2:5–18
V. A Priest Must Be Faithful: 3:1–6
VI. A Second Exhortation: Trust and Obey! 3:7—4:16
    A. The Need for Steadfast Belief: 3:7–19
    B. The Rest of God: 4:1–16
VII. A Priest Must Be Appointed by God: 5:1–10; 7:1–25
    A. The Appointment: 5:1–10
    B. After the Order of Melchizedek: 7:1–10

      C. The Need for a New Priesthood: 7:11–19
      D. The Greatness of the New Priest: 7:20–25
VIII. A Priest Must Be Pure: 7:26–28
  IX. *A Third Exhortation: Go On to Maturity! 5:11—6:20*
      A. *Spiritual Immaturity: 5:11–14*
      B. *A Passionate Exhortation: 6:1–3*
      C. *A Warning Concerning Apostasy: 6:4–6a*
      D. *Dramatic Reasoning: 6:6b–8*
      E. *Unexpected Encouragement: 6:9–12*
      F. *The Immutable Promise of God: 6:13–20*

PART THREE: THE MINISTRY OF THE HIGH PRIEST: 8:1—10:18

  X. The Superiority of Christ's Ministry: 8:1–13
      A. The Ritual Elements: 8:1–5
      B. The Covenant Basis: 8:6–13
  XI. The Superiority of the New Covenant: 9:1–28
      A. The Earthly Sanctuary: 9:1–5
      B. The Earthly Ministry: 9:6–10
      C. The Heavenly Ministry: 9:11–15
      D. Ratification by Blood: 9:16–22
      E. The Greatness of Christ's Sacrifice: 9:23–28
  XII. Christ's Perfect Sacrifice: 10:1–18
      A. A Single Sacrifice: 10:1–10
      B. A Complete, Sufficient Sacrifice: 10:11–18

PART FOUR: FINAL EXHORTATIONS AND TEACHING: 10:19—13:25

  XIII. *An Exhortation to Holy Boldness: 10:19–39*
      A. *A Tripartite Invitation: 10:19–25*
      B. *A Fearful Warning: 10:26–31*
      C. *A Statement of Encouragement: 10:32–39*
  XIV. *The Character of Faith—Basic Teaching for Perseverance:*
      11:1–40
      A. *The Substance of Faith: 11:1–2*
      B. *Faith and Epistemology: 11:3*
      C. *Examples in Faith—Abel and Enoch: 11:4–6*
      D. *Faith and Obedience: 11:7–12*
      E. *Faith and Future: 11:13–40*

CHAPTER 1

God Has Spoken to Us by a Son

Hebrews 1:1–2a

1 God, who at various times and in different ways
spoke in time past to the fathers by the prophets,
2 has in these last days spoken to us by His Son,
whom He has appointed heir of all things, through
whom also He made the worlds;

Heb. 1:1–2a

Our author wastes no time in launching into his purpose of nurturing the lives of his readers to mature discipleship. He devotes his entire first chapter to proclaiming and clarifying the doctrine of Jesus Christ, in particular His superiority to all other beings through His nature as Son-Messiah. These introductory phrases draw attention to both the message and Person of Christ by comparison to the prophets. God's message through His Son expresses its superior significance in the relationship of the Speaker to the Author of the message.

The first three words of the epistle in Greek are *Polumerōs kai polutropōs,* *"at various times and in different ways."* God did not reveal all of Himself in any one time. The process of revelation was a continuous one, in which the recipients received ever-increasing revelation of God. At no time in that older process did they have a complete idea of God.

At first they began to understand His creative power. Then they perceived something of His moral demands and His character as Judge as He sent the flood to destroy the evil in the world. Soon they were to see Him as a covenant-making God taking the initiative in establishing a covenant with Noah by means of a rainbow; then establishing a threefold covenant with an old shepherd and his wife, Abram and Sarah, promising them offspring in great number, a land in which their children would dwell, and finally that all nations of the earth would be blessed through their descendants. They perceived Him as a God interested in individuals and families, while yet judging the nations of the earth. Later God revealed that in spite of His judgments, He would always save a remnant and from that remnant bring about a new people. The whole world would discover Him to be a God Who would pay a tremendous price out of redeeming love for the salvation of all people in Jesus Christ.

No, God did not say all about Himself at one time or in one period of revelation. Rather, He spoke in bits and pieces at various times and through different methods—events, prophets, individuals, history. At any point during that process the revelation was not complete, and, in fact, later periods of revelation would clarify and enlarge previously partial and, by themselves, misleading understandings of God. For instance, the judging character of God is a partial understanding that needs the later clarification and enlargement of God's forgiving grace. This is what we mean by progressive revelation.

This idea in Hebrews is made more explicit by the verb forms found in the first two verses. The first form used (*lalēsas*, "spoke") indicates a progressive past, a process that continued over a period of time, largely through the prophets. The second form (*elalēsen*, "has spoken") indicates that the process is finished, completed, not to continue. The process of revelation is perfected in a Son. The old revelation went on and on, incomplete and growing; the new revelation is a completed action, done with, finished, sufficient, never to be added to. The comparison is stunning and clear. Our author will repeat many times the style of comparison used in this first sentence, proving that the ministry of Jesus Christ is superior to that of the older forms. By what means is this new revelation superior to the old? By means of a Son, who is superior to the prophets of old.

There were no more highly regarded persons in the minds of the Jews than the prophets—not only those we think of as the major and minor prophets, but any person through whom God spoke to the people or through whom He did mighty acts. Thus along with the Isaiahs and the Jeremiahs we include Abram, Moses, and all others who had spoken on behalf of God.

The word for prophet, *prophētēs*, comes from the Greek *pros*, "for" or "in front of," and *pherō* or *phōneō*, "to speak in front of or for someone else," as an ambassador. It did not necessarily mean foretelling the future; rather the emphasis was on the spokesmanship, whether speaking to that which had happened, was happening, or would happen in the future. It was through such persons that God spoke of old to the people, telling of Himself and His ways among them.

Now our author strikingly implies a whole different category of being, superior to that of prophet—that of Son. In translation, no article is used, putting the emphasis upon the category or type of Person. The comparison must have been clear and obvious. The Son is superior to the prophets! Although He is in the stream of prophetic utterance and revelation, His Person is in unique relationship to God. With a dash of verbal simplicity, the author draws an essential chasm between the prophets and the Son, while at the same time indicating historical continuity between them both. The revelation is essentially one; Jesus the Son is in the line of the prophets. They were precursors; He is the finality! They preach expectantly of the coming Messiah and divine kingdom of God; the Son is the fulfillment and Messiah-King Himself, who will build the kingdom, and the gates of hell shall not prevail against it (Matt. 16:18).

CHAPTER TWO

The Nature of Christ, the Son-Messiah

Hebrews 1:2–14

Like other New Testament writers, our author not only portrays Jesus Christ as the fulfillment of the prophecies of the Messiah and the kingdom, but as the very foundation of the truth of those prophecies. Before all time and creation, the Word (*logos*) was before God ("in front of" as an expression), was with God, and was God, the One *through* whom all things were created (John 1:3), whether thrones or dominions or principalities or powers, and *for* whom all things are created, being the very foundation of their meaning and purpose (Col. 1:16–17).

2 has in these last days spoken to us by His Son, whom He has appointed heir of all things, by whom also He made the worlds;

3 who being the brightness of His glory and the express image of His person, and upholding all things by the word of His power, when He had by Himself purged our sins, sat down at the right hand of the Majesty on high,

4 having become so much better than the angels, as He has by inheritance obtained a more excellent name than they.

5 For to which of the angels did He ever say:
"You are My Son,
Today I have begotten You"?
  And again:
"I will be to Him a Father,
And He shall be to Me a Son"?

42

6 But when He again brings the firstborn into the
world, He says:
"Let all the angels of God worship Him."
7 And of the angels He says:
"Who makes His angels spirits
And His ministers a flame of fire."
8 But to the Son He says:
"Your throne, O God, is forever and ever;
A scepter of righteousness is the scepter of Your
Kingdom.
9 *You have loved righteousness and hated*
lawlessness;
Therefore God, Your God, has anointed You
With the oil of gladness more than Your
companions."
10 And:
"You, Lord, in the beginning laid the foundation
of the earth,
And the heavens are the work of Your hands;
11 *They will perish, but You remain;*
And they will all grow old like a garment,
12 *Like a cloak You will fold them up,*
And they will be changed.
But You are the same,
And Your years will not fail."
13 But to which of the angels has He ever said:
"Sit at My right hand,
Till I make Your enemies Your footstool"?
14 Are they not all ministering spirits sent forth
to minister for those who will inherit salvation?
Heb. 1:2–14

   With verse 2 our author commences a long listing of the superior
characteristics of the Son, and in doing so states the essential equality
of the Son with the Father. He lists twelve:
   1. Son of God (vv. 2a, 5)
   2. Heir of All Things (v. 2b)
   3. Creator of the World (vv. 2c, 10)
   4. Radiant Light (v. 3a)
   5. The Image of God (v. 3b)
   6. Sustainer of the Universe (v. 3c)
   7. High Priest of Perfection (v. 3d)

8. Superior to the Angels (vv. 4–7, 13–14)
9. Exalted King (vv. 3–4, 8a)
10. Lord of Righteousness (vv. 8b–9)
11. The Eternal (vv. 11–12)
12. Ultimate Conqueror (v. 13)

Son of God

As background to our author's use of the term "Son of God," let us look for a moment at the Old Testament. There the term is used of angels, magistrates, Israelites, the nation of Israel itself, and the theocratic king.

Angels or heavenly beings without clear identity are spoken of in the early accounts as "sons of God [which] came in to the daughters of men and they bore children to them" (Gen. 6:1–4). Job speaks of angelic creatures as the "sons of God [who] came to present themselves before the Lord, and Satan [was] among them" (Job 2:1). The implication is that of beings who were extrahuman and superhuman in character.

Magistrates or princes are also spoken of as "gods, sons of the Most High, all of you; nevertheless you shall die like men, and fall like any prince" (Ps. 82:6, RSV). The context speaks simply of these as members of a divine council who are to judge justly and show no partiality to the wicked.

The Israelites themselves are called "sons of the Lord your God. . . . chosen . . . to be a people for his own possession" (Deut. 14:1–2, RSV). Speaking of some sort of restoration, Hosea says, ". . . where it was said to them, 'You are not My people,' there it shall be said to them, 'You are the sons of the living God' " (Hos. 1:10).

When the Lord was instructing Moses how to warn Pharaoh, the same term, *son*, was used of the nation Israel: "Then you shall say to Pharaoh, 'Thus says the Lord: "Israel is My son, My firstborn. So I say to you, let My son go that he may serve Me. But if you refuse to let him go, indeed I will kill your son, your firstborn" ' " (Exod. 4:22–23). Israel as a nation is also mentioned in Hosea 11:1: "When Israel was a child, I loved him, and out of Egypt I called My son."

And lastly, in 2 Samuel 7:14 the theocratic king is called by this title: "I will be his Father and he shall be My son." The person mentioned here is the progeny of David who will build the temple. Again in Psalm 2:7 the Lord says of the king to be set on the holy hill, ". . . My son, today have I begotten You."

Now let us turn to the use of the term "Son of God" in other New Testament sources, beginning with the synoptic Gospels. How did Jesus look on Himself in reference to this term? What was the meaning of "Son of God," and how unique was the relation between God the Father and this Son; how special was the Son's relation to the Father? What was His essential identity that He could call Himself or be known by others as Son of God?

The Gospel record shows that among Christ's statements there are both direct and implied answers to these questions. The following belong to the latter category.

1. Jesus considered Himself a special envoy of the Father. "All things have been delivered to Me by My Father, and no one knows the Son except the Father. Nor does anyone know the Father except the Son, and he to whom the Son wills to reveal Him" (Matt. 11:27; cf. Luke 10:22).

2. Jesus proclaimed Himself as a unique fulfillment of the law and the prophets; in Him was the fulfillment of the Kingdom of God. "Do not think that I came to destroy the Law or the Prophets. I did not come to destroy but to fulfill" (Matt. 5:17). He took it upon Himself to reinterpret the teaching of the scribes and Pharisees with an authority which implies a primal understanding of the very nature of the law. "Not what goes into the mouth defiles a man; but what comes out of the mouth, this defiles a man" (Matt. 15:11).

3. Jesus claimed the authority to forgive sins, and in so doing incurred the indictment of blasphemy, for only God can forgive sins. "But Jesus, knowing their thoughts, said 'Why do you think evil in your hearts? For which is easier, to say, "Your sins are forgiven you," or to say, "Arise and walk"? But that you may know that the Son of Man has power on earth to forgive sins'—then He said to the paralytic—'Arise, take up your bed, and go to your house' " (Matt. 9:4–6).

4. Jesus stated a unique power to oppose and judge Satan in the last times. "He who sows the good seed is the Son of Man. The field is the world, the good seeds are the sons of the kingdom, but the tares are the sons of the wicked one. The enemy who sowed them is the devil, the harvest is the end of the age, and the reapers are the angels" (Matt. 13:37b–39).

5. Jesus claimed superiority over the angels. "The Son of Man will send out His angels, and they will gather out of His kingdom all things that offend, and those who practice lawlessness, and will cast them into the furnace of fire" (Matt. 13:41–42a).

6. Jesus claimed so unique a relation to the Father that when people recognized or perceived His true identity, they would see the Father.

Surely by these statements Jesus places Himself above the law, the prophets, Satan, and the angels. He claims to be in a category above them all. But how much higher? What is His relation to the Father? What is His essential identity as the Son of God? To answer these questions we turn to the direct statements of Jesus regarding His relation to the Father, as reported in the Gospel of John, the Beloved Disciple. The following, of course, is no way an exhaustive study but should be sufficient for setting some background to our author's use of the term.

1. In John 10:22–39, a scene of near violence catches our attention; Jesus is about to be stoned by an angry group of worshipers at the Feast of Dedication. The location is Solomon's portico. Quite a lively encounter has erupted between Jesus and the Jews who have shown some interest in His teaching; they even seem to be open to the possibility of His being the Messiah and want Him to tell them clearly. He responds that He has told them, but that they do not believe because they are not of His sheep. To His sheep He gives eternal life and none is able to snatch from His hand those whom the Father has given into His hand. Then He speaks the precipitous words: "I and My Father are one" (v. 30).

Given the crowd's passionate monotheism, it is quite understandable that they took up stones to stone Him. But the encounter continues: "Many good works I have shown you from My Father. For which of those works do you stone Me?" (v. 32). Their answer is clearly indicative of His claims. "For a good work we do not stone You, but for blasphemy, and because You, being a Man, make Yourself God" (v. 33). After a quizzical statement/argument quoting Psalm 82:6, which refers to their all being sons of God, Jesus then closes by saying, ". . . the Father is in me, and I in Him" (v. 38). Why all the reaction if He had not been understood to have claimed this special Sonship with God the Father?

2. Jesus speaks of Himself as the Son in a unique relationship to the Father. "The Son can do nothing of Himself, but what He sees

the Father do; for whatever He does, the Son also does in like manner"
(John 5:19).

3. In yet another dialogue (John 8:48–59) which infuriates the Jews,
Jesus claims a kind of pre-existence with God, even using of Himself
a name that is used only of God. After indicating that Abraham
rejoiced to see His day and bearing the anger of the Jews who said
Abraham could not have seen His day because He was not yet fifty
years old, Jesus made a statement that must have chilled their blood:
"Before Abraham, I AM!" We can understand how the Jews felt,
for Jesus used a word which they would not even speak. It was the
four-letter word for God the Eternal—*Jahweh*. When the Jews came
to those holy letters in Scripture, they spoke another word—*Adonai*.
When they wrote the word they cleaned their pens and used fresh
ink. A word that they would not even speak they now hear Jesus
use for Himself! No wonder they tried to stone Him!

4. When speaking to the woman at the well, Jesus tells her that
the water He will give "will become in him a spring of water welling
up to eternal life" (John 4:14, RSV). To the person who believes in
Him He promises eternal life, that this person will not come into
condemnation but already has passed from death to life (John 5:24).
Who is this who claims to dispense eternal life? Is not that a preroga-
tive of God Himself?

5. The Jews believed that the resurrection of the dead in the last
days was to be only by the power and redemption of God. Talking
with Martha before the resurrection of Lazarus, Jesus said, "I am
the resurrection and the life. He who believes in Me, though he
may die, he shall live. And whoever lives and believes in Me shall
never die" (John 11:25–26).

6. Perhaps the most telling of all Jesus' claims to be essentially
one with God is His statement in John 5:26–27 in which He claims
to have the essence of life within Himself even as does the Father.

It is abundantly clear that the Gospel writers were convinced that
Jesus had claimed this unique and essential relationship with the
Father as Son of God. Other apostolic writers concur in their epis-
tles.

Our author uses the term "Son of God" in the same manner. Having
begun his epistle with a simple statement with full apostolic meaning
behind it, our writer now describes the essential identity of this Son
in a number of characteristics.

HEIR OF ALL THINGS

It seems evident in the Creation record in Genesis that God's original plan was for humanity to have an heirdom over that Creation. "And God said to them, 'Be fruitful and multiply; fill the earth and subdue it' " (Gen. 1:28). But alas, in a sinfulness that distorted true identities and relationships, mankind attempted to be like God. Claiming to be wise, our forebears actually lost their wisdom; living in a world of illusory assurances of possessing all things, they lost their God-designed heirdom. What dominion they did exercise became demonic. Their relations with one another were marked by oppression, manipulation, frustration, anger, and war. The whole fabric became unstitched and fell from their shoulders like tattered rags.

The land of Canaan became a fresh symbol of the restoration of God's promised dominion, but again the children lost their opportunity through disbelief, disobedience, and a hardened heart (Heb. 3:7–19). Not until the death and resurrection of Jesus Christ was the victory won nor did those in Christ become heirs once again of the heavenly powers. Paul expresses it eloquently and passionately in the opening verses of his letter to the Ephesians: ". . . that you may know what is the hope of His calling, what are the riches of the glory of His inheritance in the saints, and what is the exceeding greatness of His power toward us who believe, according to the working of His mighty power which He worked in Christ when He raised Him from the dead . . ." (Eph. 1:18–20). The inheritance won by Christ is shared with us as Paul continues: "But God, who is rich in mercy, because of His great love with which He loved us, even when we were dead in trespasses, made us alive together with Christ . . . and made us sit together in the heavenly places in Christ Jesus, that in the ages to come He might show the exceeding riches of His grace in His kindness toward us in Christ Jesus" (Eph. 2:4–7). This was the plan of God for "the fullness of the times He might gather together in one all things in Christ, both which are in heaven and which are on earth" (Eph. 1:10).

When Christ was appointed heir of all things (*klēronomos*), His ultimate authority and possession flowed naturally from His being Son. Both presently and ultimately there is no possession apart from Him. Without Christ we are destitute; we are without those resources which He both controls and distributes to His people.

And how does Christ come about this control, possession, and authority to distribute? There are two reasons: first, He Himself is creator of all things, and second, through His death and resurrection He has been given dominion over all principalities and powers. It is He alone who has defeated the satanic powers and gained the victory over death and the grave. He is indeed Christus Victor!

As we share in His resurrection, we share also in His inheritance. As we fail to share in Him, we are bereft of the inheritance and fail to have the necessary resources for life. As John relates the teaching of Jesus, we are but the branches, He is the Vine; apart from Him, we wither and can do nothing. Without Jesus we are powerless to face a world burgeoning with enemy power; we are but pawns of satanic principalities. When in Christ we are restored, we gain possession again of the inheritance which we lost in the Fall. To Christ alone belongs the ultimate power, dominion, possession, and authority. All of that He shares with those who are His!

CREATOR OF THE WORLD

"By whom also He made the worlds" (v. 2c). Continuing to present the Son as the Exalted, our author adds yet another characteristic, that of Creator. The creation passages in the epistle are 1:2b, 1:3b, 1:10, 2:20, 3:4–5, 4:4, and 11:1. They fall into three categories: (1) those that speak of the Son, (2) those that speak of the Word of God as the agent of creation, and (3) those that speak of God as Creator.

Those passages that speak of the Son as Creator or agent of creation are 1:2b and 1:10. Verse 1:2b sets the Son as the agent or cause of creation, but does not answer the problem of the Son's identity or equality with the Father. Looking at that verse alone, one could argue that He was a middle power like Plato's demiurges that were neither God nor creation but were the powers through which God created the earth and all things. Verse 1:10, however, unashamedly identifies the Son with the Lord: *"You, Lord, in the beginning laid the foundation of the earth, And the heavens are the work of Your hands."* No Jew could miss the point; the quotation is directly from Psalm 102:25–27, and no other than God Himself could be applied to that Psalm.

Those passages that deal with God as the Creator are 2:10, 3:4, 4:4, and 11:10. The phrase "by whom," used in 1:2b in speaking of God as Creator, is used also in 2:10. Verse 4:4 openly states that

God rested on the seventh day from all His works of creation just as verse 3:3 states that God is the Builder of all things. Then the author uses a striking word as though to make bold comparison with Platonic philosophy, stating that not only is God the Builder (*teknitēs*) but also the Maker (*dēmiourgos*). That God should be the one in touch with the creation was appalling and repulsive to the Platonist. God could never touch the physical; that was the task of the *dēmiourgoi*—the middle powers—through whom the Platonists claimed the world was created. And here our writer boldly proposes that God is both designer-builder and the actual artificer. Such a claim flew into the face of popular Platonic philosophy. This is truly a Hebraic concept.

The phrase *"by whom also He made the worlds"* stimulates us to ask, "Is this a Hellenistic thought similar to Plato's?" Could the writer be presenting this "Son" as a being less than God, a *dēmiourgos* or middle power somewhere between God and His created world according to Plato's system, which did not permit the realm of the eternal to be in contact with the realm of the concrete? What similarity is there between the *logos* of the Greek and the epistle's *Logos* as an agent of creation, or is creation a function of God Himself through His Son?

To consider these questions, it might be helpful to peruse the historical uses of the terms *logos* and *rhēma* in Greek writings as compared with our author's use of them. Such a study indicates that our author's thought-forms, in spite of similarities, are in sharp contrast or even confrontation with the established thought-forms of Plato or the emerging forms of Philo of Alexandria. Let us consider the references to *logos* and creation in the works of Heraclitus, Plato, and Philo.

Heraclitus, a sixth-century philosopher, believed the cosmos to be in ceaseless change. This change was both progressive and regressive at the same time, surging forward as burning fire and falling back as when fire dies out. All change, however, is under regulated control of the *logos;* thus the orderliness of the universe. Change must conform to fixed patterns according to *logos,* which subjects all change to orderly law. *Logos* is eternal, intelligent, ultimate reality, but impersonal.

The similarity between *logos* in Heraclitus and the Son in Hebrews is intriguing. However, the dissimilarities are important. First, the writer to the Hebrews does not use the term *logos* for the Son. Moreover, the epistle's concept of creation is quite different from creation under *logos,* which controls change. The first works out of nothing, out of sheer primal and creative energy, "out of that which does not appear," while the latter works with existing material. Whereas Heraclitus's *logos* is impersonal—a force, or neuter entity—characteristics of the Creator in Hebrews are personality, involvement with the created order, and a capacity for feelings based on identification with His own people in empathetic relationship.

The use of *logos* by the philosopher Plato (427–384 B.C.) is not so highly developed. One has the feeling in reading *Crito* or *The Sophist* that a kind of primitive speculation is emerging out of language in a dialogical method. As partners discuss, ideas are discovered rather spontaneously, while following simple logic; these ideas then become the building blocks of reality, a kind of mentalism—"so we think, so it exists." The mental gymnastics of the dialogical method of Plato, based on common language with the resulting opinions and imagination, become the nature of things.

Logos is the philosophical concept in which matter, nature, and being are brought into interrelation. The *logos* of the thinking soul and the *logos* of things have been in a preexistent harmony. The philosophically speculative and the impersonal nature of *logos* in Plato is in marked contrast to the Creator concept of Hebrews, which lacks the speculative and the language-based nature of existence, but instead throbs with personal attributes.

Philo (30 B.C.–A.D. 50) depicts a *logos* that comes closer to the Creator of Hebrews. Using the word some thirteen hundred times in his writing, Philo nevertheless vacillates in his meaning from "divine reason" to "epitome of divine wisdom." His well-known attempt to unite Jewish religion and Greek philosophy resulted in his use of Greek terminology but refashioned with Hebraic texture, new and very different from the Greek development of the concept. *Logos* was not God Himself but a secondary *ergon* or work, a mediating figure that comes forth from God and establishes a link between the world and man, representing the world to God as a high priest or advocate, a personal Mediator. Philo's distinctive term *logos theou* gives *logos* a characteristic unlike Plato's speculative philosophy and brings it closer to the idea "Word of God" in the Christian usage. Still, Philo leaves his readers at the level of an "invisible divine reason, perceptible only to the intellect," which presses its image upon all things. It is determinative, but impersonal.

Going from Philo to the Epistle to the Hebrews makes one acutely aware of a completely different atmosphere. Whereas Philo is philosophical and speculative, in Hebrews suddenly the revelational, God

Himself, is present in the acts of creation. Consistent with other New Testament writers, our author is proclaiming Incarnation, God in the flesh, not Plato's dualism or Philo's "intelligible only to the intellect." Out of the realm of ideas comes God's personal manifestation in Christ—here the Christ of creation, and in a moment, the Christ of humanity.

Our author appears to be pointedly staying clear of Platonic or Philonic terminology in explaining creation. Of the twelve times he uses the word *logos,* in nine he speaks of the gospel of the Old Testament or the apostolic message of Christ, in two he speaks of *logos* as accountability or responsibility, and in the last he describes his epistle as a *logos* (word) of exhortation. Never does he use *logos* as the agent of creation.

We look now at our author's use of *rhēma* to approximate Plato's or Philo's *logos.* Of the four times he uses *rhēma,* in two he means the gospel (6:5) or the revelation at Sinai (12:19), once the sustaining power of the Son (1:3), and once the agent of creating the world (11:3) in that classic definition of faith. It appears that our writer is purposely shying away from the hellenistic term and concepts that might identify the Creating Son with the intermediary powers of creation in Plato or Philo. The relation of our writer to the Hellenistic school indicates probable knowledge and familiarity with Hellenism but certainly not agreement or acceptance. The writer is thoroughly confident of his belief; assurance pervades his argument like a fragrance of ointment that cannot be hidden.

He moves on to show the nature of the relationship of the Son to God, describing Him as radiance, character, and sustaining power.

RADIANT LIGHT

"Who being the brightness of His glory" (v. 3a). The word for "brightness" in the Greek is *apaugasma* and for "glory" is *doxa. Apaugasma* is used only here in the New Testament and in the Old Testament only in the writings of wisdom literature, the Wisdom of Solomon 7:26. This marvelous word, filled with wonder, is a great word for the twentieth century, the first atomic century. Any time we detect radiation, whether light from a distant star or from alpha, gamma, or X-rays, we know there is a radiating source. The radiation that proceeds can be called effulgence or radiance, especially with light. It is not

reflected, but a primary radiation coming straight from the source. If there is radiation, there must be a radiating source; if there is a radiating source, there must be radiation appropriate to the source. The nature of the radiation is determined by the source and the character of the source may be identified by analyzing the radiation.

So it is with Jesus Christ and God. Christ is the primal radiance of God's glory; that is, because of the nature of Jesus Christ we know there must be some radiating source—God's own glory. Nicodemus could see that: "No one can do these signs that You do unless God is with him" (John 3:2).

In our present-day atomic laboratories an atomic reactor must have a shielding to protect the bystanders. Yet to gain access to the atomic mass, a small door may be provided through the shielding through which instruments for experimentation may be inserted. Humorously and accurately the scientists call this the "glory hole." Just so, the character of God *must* radiate; He must express Himself. Jesus Christ is the earthly and human expression of God, God's own character in human form. Moreover, when we analyze Jesus Christ we learn about the radiant source, the glory of God. There is no other being that so radiates the glory of God, and no other one by whom we may completely know the Father. "He who has seen me [recognized my true identity, accurately analyzed me] has seen [understood, comprehended] the Father" (John 14:9).

THE IMAGE OF GOD

Charaktēr in the Greek, translated in verse 3b as "image," means more specifically either the die that makes an impression, or the impression made by a die. A comparison of the word's use by other New Testament writers and by Philo may add helpful perspective on our author's use of the word.

Paul uses the thought, although not the word, on several occasions, with two meanings: (1) that the image of God is man, as stated in Genesis 1:26–27; (2) that the image (*eikōn*) of God is Christ (Col. 1:15). In this last sense the term might be translated the "express image" or "personal likeness," indicating that Christ is peculiarly the revelation of God Himself.

Philo, on the other hand, speaks of the image of God as "the invisible divine reason, perceptible only to the intellect," which laid out the plan of the universe. Philo's reason in turn impresses its image upon all things in the world, but is itself perceived only by the intellect. To the student of Philo this is a very clear example of Plato's dualism.

However, when one goes from Philo to the Epistle to the Hebrews one is quite conscious of a completely different atmosphere. New Testament thinking is in terms of the Incarnate Christ, which is the very opposite of the dualism of Plato. Christ is the personal manifestation of God on earth!

Whether or not this manifestation is also essential congruity with God in the mind of our author is answered by his use of the term *hupostaseōs autou,* "of His very essence." Jesus Christ is the manifestation of the very essence of God. This is quite different from the notion of the divine impression upon the souls of humans. The concept of perfect similarity is the key point here, not that Christ is "just like" God, but that He has the *same essence* as God Himself. Again and again, this concept is a key theme in the New Testament documents.

A small boy was looking at a picture of Jesus, musing long over it in thoughtful silence. Noticing the boy's studious quietness, his father asked, "What are you doing, son?"

"Looking at this picture of Jesus." Then with an approving and decisive nod of his head, the boy added, "Hmm, best picture God ever had taken."

He had caught the meaning our author was attempting to portray—Jesus is the unique likeness of God the Father. Again "If you have seen me, you have seen the Father"; or, to paraphrase, "If you have recognized my true identity, then you know what God is like."

Sustainer of the Universe

Our writer now adds a second phrase. The former phrase, "being in the likeness of God," spoke of His being. This parallel phrase speaks of His activity, *"upholding all things by the word of His power"* (v. 3c).

The thought here is not that of Atlas holding the world on his shoulders, but of that power which holds the internal functioning of the cosmos together. Not only has the Son created the world, but He continues to supply it with the very force without which its elements would disengage in a sudden and catastrophic separation.

That force is *"the word of His power,"* an essential characteristic of the Son that not only creates and sustains, but, as Westcott says, carries all created things forward to the end or purpose of their creation. Thus the Son is gloriously Creator, Sustainer, and Perfecter of all things, reminiscent of Paul's thought in Ephesians 1:10 "that in the dispensation of the fullness of the times He might gather together in one all things in Christ, both which are in heaven and which are on earth."

It is obvious that the author has connected the *hupostasis* (translated "person," v. 3) of God's very essence with the *dunamis* ("power") of the Son. Jewish teachers made this very statement of God, that He not only created but moved all things toward their created design.

HIGH PRIEST OF PERFECTION

At this point our author shifts from emphasis on the being and essential character of the Son to the redeeming work of the Son and its results. This also shifts emphasis from the preincarnate to His incarnate work and character. Certain titles belong to Christ because of his essence; others belong to Him because of His redeeming activity. The phrase *"when He had by Himself purged our sins"* (v. 3d) leaps ahead to introduce the major theological theme of the epistle, namely, the priestly and sacrificial ministry of Jesus our High Priest. Through his choice here of the word *katharismon* ("purging, cleansing"), our author gives an even more categorical sense than he could have achieved with the word *thusia* ("sacrifice"), which he uses frequently in later chapters of his epistle. Sacrifice would be one of the elements of cleansing; cleansing includes the whole of all the parts in dynamic relationship of completed redemption, the hope and purpose of the Day of Atonement.

This theme of completion is carried on in the next word, translated *"[He] sat down."* As we shall see in 10:11 and 12, the priest did not sit down until his task was completed. The very term "sat down" implies a superiority over other priestly cleansings, which will be more fully explained in chapter 10. The magnificence of the Son reaches a climax in this next phrase. Three factors lead to this climax: the Son's being of the same essential character as the Father, His upholding all things by the word of His power, and His having made a perfect cleansing of sin. The climax is this: the Son has *"sat down at the right hand of the Majesty on high."* He is not *any* priest that has finished his daily task at the altar; rather, this priest has a place of executive power over the cosmos, at the very right hand of God! The passage is a striking recall of the claim of Christ in Luke 22:69 so filled with messianic overtones that the council judging Christ asked if He meant He was the Son of God. Also, Matthew 22:44 has Christ quoting Psalm 110:1 regarding the messianic reign: "The Lord said to My Lord, 'Sit at my right hand, till I make Your enemies Your footstool.'" This theme of executive authority that will one day judge the world occurs in the familiar passage where the King judges the nations as a shepherd separates sheep and goats (Matt. 25:32 ff.). It occurs also in His promise to the disciples in Matthew 19:28 that they will sit on the twelve thrones judging Israel as colleagues of their Master, who is seated at the glorious throne of the Son of Man, a messianic term cradling the high hopes of every Jew eagerly anticipating the reign of the Messiah.

SUPERIOR TO THE ANGELS

Having made the foregoing claims, our author now compares Christ to the angels most favorably. His excellence over the angels is shown in that the name He has received is more excellent than theirs. God never said to any angel, *"You are My Son, Today I have begotten You."* Nor has God ever said to any angel, *"I will be to Him a Father, And He shall be to Me a Son."* That the terms *Father* and *Son* are not used in connection with angels shows definitely and conclusively Christ's superior relation to the Father. Moreover, the angelic message that came to Mary regarding her child was, "His name shall be 'Son of God.'" No angel ever received that name.

Because of the Son's superior name and because His very essence is that of God, the angels are to worship Him, says our author (v. 6). That angels should worship the Messianic Son is a rabbinic concept with which the Jews were quite familiar. When the Messianic Son comes He shall be above Abraham, above Moses, and greater than the ministering angels. Again the Hebraic nature of the epistle comes forth in contrast to the Hellenistic.

This passage and those that follow focus on the essential nature and attributes of the Son. The name refers to the begotten rather than the created nature of the Son; that implies essential character as suprahuman. The eternal nature of the Son certainly is superior to that of created beings, even though those beings are angelic (vv. 6–9, 13–14). The Creator is the Son (vv. 10–12), unchanging, enduring; whereas even the heavens and earth will grow old like garments and be changed, the Son will never change. No angel could be thought of in these terms. Only God is unchanging; all other creatures alter their existence, reach an end of their usefulness like a wornout cloak and must be discarded. Only the Son, after the likeness of God, is unchanging and eternal.

In only one passage might we say that the emphasis is upon the work of Christ and not upon His essential nature, and even that is questionable. *"A scepter of righteousness"* (v. 8) might refer to the redemptive and forgiving work of the Son in the atonement, but even the love of righteousness and hate of lawlessness may be considered characteristics of a Holy God, holy and refusing any consorting with sin because of His very nature.

Before our writer finishes comparing Christ with angels, he must make one more statement. Not only is the Son superior in His name; not only is He superior because of His eternal, creative, and unchanging nature; but He is superior in that one day all the Son's enemies will become a stool for His feet. No angel will ever hear the celestial lauding him, *"Angelus victor!"* No, angels will always be the servants of the victorious King and Messiah, bowing before Him, coming and going at His behest, ministering to whomever the Lord sends them. And that Lord is the Son.

EXALTED KING; LORD OF RIGHTEOUSNESS; THE ETERNAL, ULTIMATE CONQUEROR

The Expectation of the Messiah

A number of the passages in this first chapter that are used to support the superiority of the Son are classic messianic expressions of the national and spiritual hopes of Israel. The expectation of the Messiah's coming burned in the heart of every Jew. Certain familiar passages were automatic stimuli conjuring up in the mind of the hearer or the reader images of the coming Messiah and what He would accomplish for Israel.

A look at the history of the messianic concept helps us understand

the nature and intensity of this hope. God's self-disclosure had convinced the Jewish people that He was a personal God, deeply interested in the world He had created and the people He had chosen.
He was the God of the family of Israel, present in pillar of smoke
and fire, speaking face to face with Moses and seeking out for His
friend a man like David.

This personal God was nonetheless sovereign and bound to liberate
the oppressed. Even the military, political, and technological superiority of the Egyptians could not stand against the might of Jehovah
in delivering His oppressed people. A God of justice and righteousness, He swiftly judged all nations that refused to obey His laws.
He was a God who entered into a covenant relation with Israel, making
this people His chosen for the sake of the gentile world. He had
made a promise that a king of the house of David would rule forever
upon a throne of justice and equity. Even though He had allowed
the people of Israel to be taken away into captivity to a foreign
land, He nevertheless would bring back a remnant to live in the
land under the established king of the house of David.

By the time of Jesus, the Jewish people had been in captivity or
exile seven of eight centuries. The Assyrians captured the Northern
Kingdom in 721 B.C. Then the Southern Kingdom fell to the Babylo-
nians in 586 B.C. From that time on, the people were passed off from
one oppressor to another—to the Medes and Persians, then to the
Alexandrians, then to the Syrians, and finally to the Romans. Only
one brief century of quasi-freedom under the Maccabeans eased
the pain of oppression, and then there were only short-term guer-
rilla victories. Even that was swept away by the coup of the Roman
general Pompey as he captured the city of Jerusalem by dishonest
treachery.

The Jews' revelational theology, their sense of chosenness, their
belief in God as a deliverer from oppression, and the longstanding
occupation of their country left them aching and crying out for the
liberating Messiah. Their hope was a mixture of the spiritual, political,
and religious. Life under the Messiah might be divided into distinct
portions, but these would be unified, bound together by the Spirit
and the life of the Lord.

Messianic Psalms

As we consider the Psalms that are quoted from the messianic
hymnody of Israel in the first chapter of Hebrews, let us note their

varying emphasis, now upon God and again upon the messianic king.
Psalm 2 was a classic reference to the hope of a trodden people:

> Why do the nations rage,
> And the people plot a vain thing?
> The kings of the earth set themselves,
> And the rulers take counsel together,
> Against the Lord and against His Anointed, saying,
> "Let us break Their bonds in pieces
> And cast away Their cords from us."
>
> *Ps. 2:1–3*

Then, speaking of the king whom God would set on His holy hill,
the psalm continues:

> "You are My Son,
> Today I have begotten You.
> Ask of Me, and I will give You
> The nations for Your inheritance,
> And the ends of the earth for Your possession.
> You shall break them with a rod of iron;
> You shall dash them in pieces like a potter's vessel."
>
> *Ps. 2:7b–9*

It is not difficult to see how this psalm spoke directly to the messianic hope of Israel seeking an end to the seven centuries of agonizing
bondage. This psalm our author applies to Jesus the Son in verse 5.
Psalm 97 has as its theme God's magnificence and victorious might.
The following quotation includes verses 1–4a and verse 7a:

> The Lord reigns;
> Let the earth rejoice;
> Let the multitude of isles be glad!
> Clouds and darkness surround Him;
> Righteousness and justice are the
> foundation of His throne.
> A fire goes before Him,
> And burns up His enemies round about.
> His lightnings light the world;
>
> . . . .
>
> Let all be put to shame who serve carved images,
> Who boast of idols. . . .

The line appearing in verse 6 of the epistle, however, is taken from the Septuagint, Psalm 97:7, quoted in that version from Deuteronomy 32:43: "Let all the angels of God worship Him."

In this psalm the power of the Lord that will reign over all nations is part of the messianic belief that God Himself will be involved in the vindication of Israel. Zion is to rejoice and the daughters of Jerusalem are to be glad because God preserves the lives of His saints. Was there any doubt that the saints were the people of Israel? Jesus is made the sovereign Lord of this psalm.

Jesus is presented by the author of Hebrews as being this magnificent and victorious Lord. Surrounded by the awesomeness of the cosmos, He is the one to be worshiped even by the angels. He was not created, but is described as the "firstborn," begotten of God as the unique Son of God. Superior to angels—indeed!

Psalm 104, from which our author has quoted in verse 7, erupts in a torrent of praise to the greatness of God, depicting Him as a sovereign ruler, using all creatures as His servants.

> Bless the Lord, O my soul!
>
> O Lord my God, You are very great:
> You are clothed with honor and majesty,
> Who cover Yourself with light as with a garment,
> Who stretch out the heavens like a curtain.
>
> He lays the beams of His upper chambers in the waters,
> Who makes the clouds His chariot,
> Who walks on the wings of the wind,
> Who makes His angels spirits,
> His ministers a flame of fire.
>
> *Ps. 104:1–4*

There is no doubt at all that the reference in this psalm is to God Himself. Yet, this psalm is attributed to the Son-Messiah, who, far superior to the angels, sends them on their way for His purposes.

Psalm 45 lauds the King as the blessed, mighty one, surely a messianic figure. Verses 6 and 7 of the psalm are quoted in Hebrews 1:8–9.

> My heart is overflowing with a good theme;
> I recite my composition concerning the King;

My tongue is the pen of a ready writer.
You are fairer than the sons of men;
Grace is poured upon Your lips;
Therefore God has blessed You forever.

. . . .

And in Your majesty ride prosperously because of truth,
    humility, and righteousness;
And Your right hand shall teach You awesome things.
Your arrows are sharp in the heart of the King's enemies;
The peoples fall under You.

Your throne, O God, is forever and ever;
A scepter of righteousness is the scepter of Your kingdom.
You love righteousness and hate wickedness.
Therefore God, Your God, has anointed You
With the oil of gladness more than Your companions.
                                                Ps. 45:1–2, 4–7

With his quotation of these last two verses, our author swings
back to the emphasis upon the messianic king, applying this psalm
to the throne of Jesus which our writer claims is going to be an
eternal throne of righteousness; the Son will have no peer.

Psalm 102 speaks of the writer's distress and despondency, which
could so easily have been the feeling of the people of Israel in their
suffering through the centuries. With verse 12, the tone suddenly
alters, expressing confidence in the everlasting character of God:

But You, O Lord, shall endure forever,
And the remembrance of Your name to all generations.
You will arise and have mercy on Zion;
For the time to favor her,
Yes, the set time, has come.
                                                Ps. 102:12–13

After further statement of hope in the liberating power of God,
the psalmist continues speaking of the might of God.

Of old You laid the foundation of the earth,
And the heavens are the work of Your hands.
They will perish, but You will endure;
Yes, all of them will grow old like a garment;
Like a cloak You will change them,

And they will be changed.
But You are the same,
And Your years will have no end.

Ps. 102:25–27

Although the psalm is one on the majesty of God, it is connected with the hope of deliverance of the people of God. The messianic hope is inseparably tied to the power and majesty of God. The writer to Hebrews has God addressing these words directly to the Son, attributing to Him creating power and eternal endurance of unchangeable nature. Certainly this attribute is superior to that of the angels. This psalm is again one of messianic overtones of deliverance.

Psalm 110, the final messianic psalm used by our writer, appears in verse 13 of this first chapter of Hebrews. He quotes the first verse, which starts right out with the theme of ultimate victory. Undoubtedly, the messianic mind would take this thought to itself.

The Lord said to my Lord,
"Sit at My right hand,
Till I make Your enemies Your footstool."
The Lord shall send the rod of Your strength out of Zion.
Rule in the midst of Your enemies!

Your people shall be volunteers
In the day of Your power;
In the beauties of holiness,
  from the womb of the morning,
You have the dew of Your youth.
The Lord has sworn
And will not relent,
"You are a priest forever
According to the order of Melchizedek."

Ps. 110:1–4

Nowhere else in the New Testament is there such an array of messianic literature brought to bear as argument for the glorification of Christ. As short quotations from the foregoing were used, they were sure to be recognized immediately by any Jewish reader. Our author was certainly familiar with not only the literature but also the aspiration of the Jewish heart that the literature expresses. The deepest desires of the waiting and expectant hearts were now being fulfilled in Jesus Christ, the Messiah-Son of God. Whether these verses refer to the messianic human, or to the majesty of God Himself, the author of Hebrews applies them equally to Christ as proof of His supreme status before the face of God.

Two important movements have characterized the arguments of this first chapter. First, the comparisons with the angels show that the Messiah-Son is in a superior category above that of the angels. They are simply ministering servants to the sovereign Lord who sends them on their way.

Second, the messianic figure usually identified with the kings of Israel is identified with God Himself. The messianic literature always made the distinction between the acts of God in fulfilling the messianic hope and the Messiah figure Himself. In this epistle both are made one! Passages always accepted as depicting the human messianic king are now interwoven with those depicting deity. The human Messiah and the Son of the Most High are one and the same!

As though with a fanfare of ultimate glory our author concludes this first chapter in which he has heaped up a mountain of description, unsurpassed in any other passage of Scripture regarding the character and credentials of the Messiah-Son. No higher essence could be attributed to any being than that attributed to the Son. He is the very essence of God, the perfect revelation of His character and the true nature of His existence. After speaking in many and various ways, God has now completed His revelation of Himself in a Son: Creator, Eternal, radiant in His glory, whom He has set over all and under all that exists. Every existence that ever opposed Him will one day bow before Him and be as a stool for His victorious feet. Even great angelic powers will be but servants ministering to those upon whom the Son bestows the inheritance of salvation.

The Messiah-Son is God's supreme self-revelation.

When one steps into the arena of New Testament writing, one cannot help being impressed with the apostolic conviction of the absolute and magnificent uniqueness of Jesus Christ. Excitement of revelational discovery leaps from every page. Awesome revelation from a heavenly source is personalized in Jesus of Nazareth. A white-hot ingot, incandescent with the radiant glory of God, shines from every gospel or epistle. The early church was alive—impacted, overwhelmed, and saturated with the Person who had made such a radical change in their lives.

Whenever the church loses this sense of the awe, the wonder, the excitement, and the radical change, it begins to atrophy. To handle heavenly revelation with a dispassionate attitude or cool rationalism is to deny its transforming power. It is distressing that today the church is so seldom excited or overwhelmed with Jesus. One feels in certain ecclesiastical circles that enthusiasm for Christ is beneath the sophisticated disciple, that it is a mark of religious peasantry. Yet as we view the history of the church, we see clearly that a lessened christology means a correspondingly lessened church. When we bleach the banners of apostolic brilliance, fewer desire to march under its colors.

When, on the other hand, the church rediscovers the magnificent Christ and is overwhelmed by His Godly Person and sacrificial atonement, the church comes alive and sweeps great segments of history before it. For this reason, the Epistle to the Hebrews is a crucial document for the church to rediscover. Too long it has been the "forgotten epistle." May the Holy Spirit bring it back to our remembrance and understanding, magnifying Jesus Christ so powerfully that once again we are smitten and enthusiastic beyond control! Let this high view of Christ again lift up the church to its apostolic power. Then preaching will be transformed; individuals will be changed by His redeeming grace; societies will be delivered from oppressors no longer able to contain the liberated disciples; and the body of Christ will be alive with His compassion and ministering love. The Messiah-Son is God's supreme revelation. God has said enough. After Jesus nothing can be added. It is finished!

CHAPTER THREE

The First Exhortation: "Hold Fast Your Confession!"

Hebrews 2:1–4

> 1 Therefore we must give the more earnest heed
> to the things we have heard, lest we drift away.
> 2 For if the word spoken through angels proved
> steadfast, and every transgression and disobedience
> received a just reward,
> 3 how shall we escape if we neglect so great a
> salvation, which at the first began to be spoken by
> the Lord, and was confirmed to us by those who heard
> Him,
> 4 God also bearing witness with both signs and
> wonders, with various miracles, and gifts of the Holy
> Spirit, according to His own will?
>
> *Heb. 2:1–4*

New Testament writers are never satisfied with theology alone. Belief must be followed by life. If at any time the behavior of Christ's disciples appears to be less than they should exhibit, then apostolic writers wasted no time in goading them to a life consistent with the call of Christ.

Our author is no exception. Evidently he has a number of concerns that surface at various times in the course of the epistle. Unlike Paul, who gathers all his exhortation after his theological presentation, our teacher-exhorter interrupts his teaching any time the material brings to his mind some weakness in his readers. At that moment he will subtly or forthrightly launch into a goading exhortation.

The passages of exhortation are 2:1–4, 3:7—4:16, 5:11—6:20, and 10:19—13:17. A common pattern appears in each, although there may be additions or variations. That pattern includes, first, exhortation or command, then a warning, and, finally, a supporting, reasoned explanation.

The themes of the exhortation passages may be described as follows:

2:1–4: "Give the more earnest heed to what we have heard!" or, "Hold fast your confession!"

3:7—4:16: "Trust and obey!" (The danger of the disbelieving heart that leads to disobedience and a hardened heart.)

5:12—6:20: "Go on to maturity!" (A plea against slowness of growth and a warning against the danger of aspostasy.)

10:13–39: "Approach with holy boldness!"

11:1–40: "The character of faith" (The basis for perseverance.)

12:1–29: "Run with perseverance!" (The necessity for discipline to endure persecution and hardship.)

13:1–21: A group of short exhortations on various themes: including brotherly love and hospitality, ministry to prisoners, personal morality, Christian community, respect for leaders, avoidance of the love of money, and being wary of false teaching.

In this first hortatory passage, 2:1–4, our author gives no subtle transition but simply states his exhortation and goes on with the warning and the reasoning: *"Therefore we must give the more earnest heed to the things we have heard. . . ."*

Was the earnestness with which his readers had heard the message of salvation, the quickness and sureness of their response, in question? Probably so. The writer desires more focused attention, an urgency born of a complete conviction that there is nothing more important nor more real than what the Lord has spoken.

The warning comes at the end of the first sentence: *"lest we drift away."* The Greek verb used here has several pictorial or allegorical implications. One, "slipping away," is like evaporation. Give insufficient heed with one's mind to the gospel and it will simply vanish into the air. The process is not dramatic, nor sudden; rather, it is insidious and quiet. The shock comes when one returns to use the faith in a time of need and finds it has evaporated with neglect.

Another meaning, "leaking," is not unlike the first. The implication is not so much one of neglect as of a faulty container. Truth leaks out of a mind that is sloppy in its lack of discipline, or unclear because of insufficient mental activity toward understanding. Good ideas fail to mature and so leak out and are lost forever.

The third meaning used in our NKJV text is far more pictorial.

The word describes the fate of a boat that has slipped its moorings during the night and has disappeared. The owner comes to the dock, fully expecting his boat to be ready for use, and finds nothing. The post or cleat to which it was tied is still there; the area is deserted and quiet; as far as the eye can see there is absolutely no evidence of the boat or what became of it. It simply drifted away in a flowing tide because its mooring lines had been carelessly tied.

All these images speak powerfully to us today. In the first instance, evaporation describes so vividly the insidious loss of faith because of our preoccupation with many stimuli in a society abundant with distractions. Busyness and multiple involvements can readily dissipate the Christian's commitment until under difficult circumstances we turn to our faith and find it too weak to be functional.

Our family has an old station wagon we leave in California as a "safari car" for summer vacations. Weeks and even months go by without its being used. The result is that the battery deteriorates. This last summer, when we were unable to get it started, we towed it in and had the engine repaired. But the first time the mechanic tried to start it with our battery, there was not enough energy to turn the engine. A "jump" got it started and we hoped that with several miles of running the battery would charge. Not so. When a breakdown test was put on the battery, it gave one last gasp and quit. I can remember our mechanic saying, "Well, it just died!" A good battery to start with, it still had a good portion of its warranty remaining. In a sense its power evaporated by disuse. Our disuse of faith due to distraction and conflicting commitments of modern life causes our faith to evaporate and be far less than necessary in times of demand.

The image of leaking can be likened to our soft-minded relativism of the twentieth century. Yielding to the popularity of new moral fads and philosophies of convenience causes imperceptible cracks in our vessels of spiritual clarity. I am all in favor of warm relationships, but much of the result of the human relations movement with its emphasis upon "what feels good" has undercut discipline and tough-ness of mind and will, leaving flaccid Christians who are incapable of standing tall in a high wind. I am appalled at the soft doctrine of many church members and leaders that has winked at human sin, deemphasized the atoning death of Christ, and diminished the importance of the experience of redemption and salvation. The mag-nificent truth of Christ's atoning priesthood so dramatically portrayed by the Epistle to the Hebrews has leaked out of the life of the church, leaving it empty and sterile in contrast to vastly reproductive secular ideologies.

The carelessness portrayed in the image of a boat that has slipped its moorings is so terribly costly. The price for carefulness may at times seem burdensome and the resources scant. But the mature Christian disciple, recognizing the long-range results of letting down, digs deep to find the resources for reaching the objective at hand. Maturity is seeing the future results of present action and doing what is necessary to make it right, whether that means taking time or expending an extra bit of energy.

Too often we are tempted in our impatience to tie quick and easy knots so that we may hurry on impulsively to something else. As the restless tides nudge and urge our craft against its moorings, its ties loosen and it slips away. Later, in the midst of critical need, we seek out the boat of faith but find it is gone. Only a lonely desolation haunts us as we gaze with searching eyes for some sign of spiritual assistance. We paid the cheap price of carelessness. Now we have nothing.

Our author's antidote for such "drifting" or slipping away consists of earnest heed, intense concentration, thoughtful clarification. By such means the roots of an idea get deep into our consciousness and consciences.

The reasoning behind this exhortation is twofold. First, the writer must speak out because he recognizes the consequences of not heeding the message. If the former law spoken by angels was disregarded or disobeyed, a heavy retribution came upon the individual or nation. The salvation that Christ has won is far greater. How then can we hope to escape just judgment if we neglect God's supreme act of redeeming love?

Second, he must speak because of the importance of the message as revealed by the persons chosen to communicate it. In this case the word came first from the Lord Christ Himself; then it was proclaimed and taught by the apostles who heard Him as eyewitnesses. God Himself bore witness with signs and wonders and various miracles, and, finally, it was borne on the witness of the Holy Spirit's gifts. "And you are treating it lightly? A gross absurdity, a mindless irrationality! My friends, hold fast your confession; give earnest heed to what you have heard!"

The thread bonding this section to the one preceding and the one following is the role played by the angels. Again there is the theme of comparison. In the earlier case, angels were the ministering spirits and agents communicating God's message. No one took them lightly; the message they brought rang with the clarion authority of God. Disregard or disobey and judgment will fall! was their warning. Yet the messengers of the gospel are so much more impressive than angels that one must bow in even greater respect and obedience.

As important as angels were as messengers of God's former messages, they were not to continue as the focus of attention in our writer's presentation. He now concludes his first exhortation and returns to the main teaching of the epistle, that of the priesthood of Jesus Christ.

CHAPTER FOUR

A Priest Must Be One with the People

Hebrews 2:5–18

The epistle's first chapter portrayed the Son in magnificent terms of deity, eternity, and righteousness—a Lord occupying an everlasting throne, the unchanging, unchangeable, ultimate victor over all His enemies. Having thus completed the first of three major doctrinal themes in the epistle—the Son-Messiah—our author now addresses in far greater length the well-known theme of the priesthood of Jesus Christ. This theme has two doctrinal sections—the Person of the High Priest (2:5—7:28) and the ministry of the High Priest (8:1—10:18).

In the first long doctrinal section, four necessary qualifications of a Jewish high priest are shown to be perfectly fulfilled by Jesus the heavenly High Priest. (1) A priest must be one with the people: Jesus has shared our humanity in every possible fashion (2:5–18). (2) A priest must be faithful in his ministry: Moses, a priest before Aaron took over that responsibility, was faithful to God as a *servant* in the household, but Jesus Christ was faithful over the whole house of God as a *Son* (3:1–6). (3) Each priest must have an appointment from God: Christ did not exalt Himself but was appointed a High Priest after the order of Melchizedek (5:1–10; 7:1–25). (4) Every high priest offering sacrifices on the Day of Atonement must be thoroughly cleansed of all his sins before offering sacrifices for the sins of the people: our High Priest, who is blameless, unstained, holy, undefiled, separated from sinners, need offer no sacrifices for His own cleansing (7:26–28).

5 For He has not put the world to come, of which we speak, in subjection to angels.

6 But one testified in a certain place, saying:
"What is man that You are mindful of him,
Or the son of man that You take care of him?
7 *You made him a little lower than the angels;*
You crowned him with glory and honor,
And set him over the works of Your hands.
8 *You have put all things in subjection under his*
feet."

For in that He put all in subjection under him, He left nothing that is not put under him. But now we do not yet see all things put under him.

9 But we see Jesus, who was made a little lower than the angels for the suffering of death, crowned with glory and honor, that He, by the grace of God, might taste death for everyone.

10 For it was fitting for Him, for whom are all things and by whom are all things, in bringing many sons to glory, to make the author of their salvation perfect through sufferings.

11 For both He who sanctifies and those who are being sanctified are all of one, for which reason He is not ashamed to call them brethren,

12 saying:
"I will declare Your name to My brethren;
In the midst of the church I will sing praise to
You."
13 And again:
"I will put My trust in Him."
And again:
"Here am I and the children whom God has given
Me."

14 Inasmuch then as the children have partaken of flesh and blood, He Himself likewise shared in the same, that through death He might destroy him who had the power of death, that is, the devil,

15 and release those who through fear of death were all their lifetime subject to bondage.

16 For indeed He does not give aid to angels, but He does give aid to the seed of Abraham.

17 Therefore, in all things He had to be made like His brethren, that He might be a merciful and faithful High Priest in things pertaining to God, to make propitiation for the sins of the people.

18 For in that He Himself has suffered, being
tempted, He is able to aid those who are tempted.

Heb. 2:5–18

After having presented intricate and massive arguments in the first chapter of his epistle to show the Son's superiority to the angels, our author must now shift his emphasis. In order to show that Christ is perfectly qualified to be High Priest to all humanity, he must build an argument proving that the Son is truly one with human nature, that His people may come to Him assured that He shares their circumstances and feelings. He must also show that Jesus must share our humanity in order to be the sacrifice for our sins. In that He is not only priest but also the sacrifice, the reason for His becoming human is both psychological and sacrificial.

Verse 5 makes the transition into this new emphasis in smooth literary style: *"For He has not put the world to come, of which we speak, in subjection to angels."* The word "angels" both looks back to the trumpeting proclamation of chapter 1 that Christ is superior to the angels and ahead to the discussion introduced by the Old Testament quotation (Ps. 8:6–8) that makes up the next verses. A look at the structure of Psalm 8 reveals that these verses, in contrast to its first and last stanzas and their praise of God's majesty, are clearly anthropocentric. The first of the quoted verses echoes our personal cry of finiteness and insignificance when we see ourselves in comparison with the universe, while the next two proclaim the stunning and heady notion of our God-designed human dominion over that universe already so boldly hinted at in verse 5 of the epistle. I say "boldly" because there is a segment of Jewish literature that speaks of angels being in charge over the nations, while God is in charge over Israel. Examples of this concept may be found in Daniel 10:13, 21, and 12:1. In these passages Michael the angel is spoken of as having charge over the kingdoms of Babylonia, Persia, and Greece. However, our author attacks that idea head-on in this transitional verse. God "has *not* put the world to come" in subjection to angels but rather in subjection to mankind. Thus the human race becomes the new focus of attention.

"The world that is to come" is described by Calvin as being "later in time, as renewed by Christ." Calvin further argues that the dominion God gave to His human creatures is truly lost because of our being aliens and exiles by our own defection. Any authority we exercise over the earth is usurped authority. We can rightly attain authority afresh only when we are set free by the redemption of Christ, a second donation by His grace.[1]

A slightly different line of argument is to say that humanity was given the dominion over all the earth, but that dominion can become tragically demonic if exercised out of relationship with Christ. Designed for the blessing of all creatures, fallen humanity's authority has become devastating to both the earth and the human race. The purposes of God in creation have been frustrated; the ultimate goal is now unattainable. One cannot consider such a doctrine of creation without simultaneously considering the doctrine of human potential.

Human potential as God created it is staggering. Nothing has been left outside the control or subjection of humanity. The primal statement that begins with Genesis 1:26 is echoed and enlarged in Psalm 8, which states that not only are things of the earth subject to humanity, but all the works of God's hands come under this potential dominion.

The statement surely implies humanity in general. Yet, can't we particularize the truth and say that some part of God's creation is subjected to every individual, whether great or small? Each of us has authority over 168 hours each week. Each of us has emotions and thoughts that are under our determination; every person has some possessions, no matter how meager, to disburse, whether quarters begged on the street or houses and lands of prodigious worth.

Our design as seen from a New Testament point of view is even more meaningful. John the Evangelist proclaims in his Prologue: "In the beginning was the Word, and Word was with God, and the Word was God. He was in the beginning with God. All things were made through Him, and without Him nothing was made that was made" (1:1–3).

Are you something? At times you or I probably doubt that by the way we feel. We could very easily cry out, to paraphrase the psalmist's words, "O God, who am I that You would even consider me? I can't believe that You would take a personal interest in me! The heavens are so immense, the moon and the stars so awesome, how is it possible that You could care for me? I am a nothing, a nobody, compared with the cosmic immensity!"

At times when I have been flying above an inhabited city, I am amazed at what low altitudes one loses sight of human beings. At 10,000 feet you can't see them! Imagine a few light years' distance. Why, our planet is hardly visible! "And yet, God, You say that You take note of me." I want to cry out, "Absurd, impossible, ridiculous!"

The Greek word translated "You are mindful" or "You take note of," (v. 6) carries the idea of focusing on humanity, on even the individual, with an awesomely powerful telescope. The inconceivable immensity of the universe is not able to hide any one of us from His attention. He picks us out, not only in the mass of humanity, but out of the total cosmos. The greater the apparent impossibility or absurdity, the more overwhelming the good news. "God sees me!"

The second phrase, "You care for him," reminds us of a loving physician making a house call.

When I was a seventeen-year-old, I suffered a gunshot wound in my left hand. While emptying a .22 caliber rifle of its cartridges I was surprised to hear an explosion. Evidently two cartridges had hit one another, detonating one of them in my hand. The force of the explosion was enough to send the disintegrating bullet through three fingers, shattering two of them. Our beloved family physician, Dr. E. Forrest Boyd of Hollywood Presbyterian Hospital, surgically removed as many fragments as he dared. He then sutured the mutilated fingers, warning me blood poisoning might result from the bits of shrapnel he had to leave.

Indeed, blood poisoning set in. Massive doses of sulfanilamide staved off the need to amputate. At a time during World War II when house calls were almost unheard of, he came by the house each day to dress the wound. He cared so much that he personally visited and saved those two fingers. For that I will love him forever! In just such a manner God cares for us with healing attention.

The amazing nature of the Gospel is that what appears ridiculous and impossible is actually the Good News. God does see us! He takes note of our condition; He knows where we are! Everyone of us is on His radar screen with identifying codes to differentiate us from others.

Even more, we are not only recognized by God but have been given a special place in His world, a place of meaningful production. In Colossians 1:15, Paul claims that Christ is not only the image of the invisible God, the firstborn of creation, but also the creator of all things. Then he says: "*All* things were created *by* Him and *for* Him." Each of us is something—and that includes every person walking the face of this earth—created not only *by* Christ but *for* a particular place in His kingdom. Each of us has a holy design, a magnificent purpose, a kingdom goal. The term used in the New Testament for

74

such a goal or purpose is *telos.* That is our end, our design. It is full of potential meaning; it implies some authority to be used for God's glory and the blessing of other people. No one else can take our place; without us, the kingdom is less than complete.

If we become productive according to God's design, we say we have matured, or in the old King James language, "become perfect." That does not mean flawless, but rather the emphasis is upon productivity, functioning in accordance with a design. Thus we are described by the adjective *teleios.* The condition of having reached the purpose or goal is maturity—*teleiotēs,* a noun. And the verb *teleioō* means to mature or grow toward our purpose, to complete or make mature. We shall come to this last word in verse 10.

With the psalmist we can take humble joy in the fact of our created design. It is not something we are responsible for, nor can we take the credit as self-made persons. Rather, we humbly recognize God in Christ as our Creator and yet joyfully because we know ours is a good creation. Our personality and our purpose are beautifully matched. Our gifts of the Spirit within the body of Christ are in perfect harmony with our created identity. We need not fear that God will ask us to do something in the kingdom that will violate our personalities. His creation and calling are coordinated! What a marvelous destiny!

Yet there is not one of us who has attained that high calling. In rebellion we have bolted from His pathways and gone our own self-determined way. In sin both humanity in general and we as individuals have experienced tragic frustration in reaching our *telos.* Creative dominion over the world eludes our shaky grasp; our knowledge of the earth and its ways is used to bring others under our dominion. Technology produces nighmarish weapons that voraciously consume our limited resources and that we dare not use. We walk in fear of one another, imagined or real. The world reels under the weight of our stupidity. We rape the earth, taking what we want without regard for the one from whom we take. With regard only to quick profit, we pollute the skies and streams, denude the hillsides, poison the oceans. In response the earth cries out in futility because its master has gone berserk. "Oh, that humanity would come to its senses." Or, as Paul says in Romans 8:19: "The whole creation is on tiptoe to see the wonderful sight of the sons of God coming into their own" (PHILLIPS).

With characteristic scriptural honesty, our author states an existential truth: *"But now we do not yet see all things put under him"* (v. 8c).

Hupotetagmena, "[not] put under him," is a stark denial of the earlier lines of the passage. God's design was for all things to be put under humanity. Something has gone wrong with the realization of the design. Humanity's dominion has been frustrated. Everything is not in subjection to humanity. That is, not yet.

"But we see Jesus" (v. 9). With these words our writer, whose deep insight and creative expression make him more and more dear to us, draws us on to the next engaging thought. In some way Jesus is the answer to humanity's frustrated dominion. Somehow in Jesus each of us can realize the full meaning of God's creative design. But how? The answer is implied in this verse and the next, which, like an overture, introduce the main themes of the emerging drama—His suffering and sacrifice. Before He can offer the liberating sacrifice, He must suffer with His people as one of them.

The first qualification of a priest of Israel was that he must be one of the people—an Israelite, not a foreigner or alien. According to that principle, Jesus Christ had to be made like His brothers and sisters so that He could walk in the human experience, alongside them, stride for stride, and suffer with them. Thus He *"was made a little lower than the angels"* (v. 9). That was where human beings were—lower than the angels—and that is where He had to be.

In making this reference to Psalm 8:5, our writer uses the Greek Septuagint (LXX) instead of the Hebrew text. The Hebrew text uses a root word meaning "to make less, diminish or decrease from an original condition." It then goes on to use a phrase that translates literally as "a little less than God."

The LXX, however, has a different comparison, "a little less than the angels." We must note that it is not uncommon for our author to use the LXX rather than the Hebrew text in a number of his quotations. Here the difference serves his purpose very well, allowing him to challenge us to some mental gymnastics. Having just proven in chapter 1 that the Son is essentially superior to the angels, he now asks us to regard Him as having been made lower than they. The reason is straightforward; Christ must suffer the human experience, even death, in order to become a merciful and feeling high priest and to taste death for every person by God's gracious design.

This is not mankind's answer to its dilemma; it is God's answer. Neither Greek nor Jew would have God coming into human form and suffering in death to separate the people from their sins. This is the radical truth that was so difficult, if not impossible, for many religious minds of that day to accept. It went against all the religious dogma and philosophical concepts of the times.

Here in verse 9 is the first appearance of the theme of vicarious atonement, that Christ died *for* us, that He *"might taste death for everyone."* The Greek text uses a word that means "to taste." In metaphor this can also mean "to feel, to have the experience of." Jesus Christ had the experience of human death, not just as any other human in the process of identifying with us in all our experience, but on our behalf or in our stead. *Huper* in metaphor can mean "for" or "instead of," which is certainly the meaning here as in other New Testament passages. The theme will be developed later in 9:28 and 10:10. As a result of His death, we are cleansed in our consciences (9:14). Jesus Christ appears in the presence of God for us, on our behalf and in our stead, in human form, and His experience becomes effective for every person on this earth. No human needs to go through this sort of death; God in Christ has already suffered it for us. No wonder the Son has been crowned with glory and honor.

Sensing how difficult this concept must have been for the mind of his day, the author rushes on to proclaim that this is neither philosophically ridiculous nor religiously repugnant. *"It was fitting"* (v. 10) indicates that Christ's identification with us and suffering is something quite logical. The Greek word used here has the connotation of being conspicuously clear or obvious, in this instance both circumstantially and morally. It is circumstantially clear in that there is only one way the Son can become our high priest and that is to become one with us (vv. 11–16). It is morally obvious because sin cannot be winked at by a moral God but must be removed in a very costly manner, that of sacrificial death (vv. 17–18).

However, there is a necessary condition for bringing the many children back to their designed "glory" (*doxa*). It is the preparation or making ready of their author of salvation. As we noted earlier, *teleiōsai*, translated at the end of verse 10 as "to make perfect," has the meaning of fulfilling, accomplishing, bringing to maturity. We could well translate it "to accomplish readiness."

The "glory" to which Christ is to bring "many sons" of God is that of their original design (vv. 2:6–8a)—humanity's complete control of all that God has created. Whatever has kept humans from the realization of that glory must be dealt with by this Son through His suffering and death.

The phrases *"for whom are all things," "by whom are all things,"* and *"in bringing many sons to glory"* in verse 10 are reminiscent of other New Testament passages: Romans 11:36, "For of Him and through Him and to Him are all things, to whom be glory forever"; 1 Corinthians 8:6, ". . . there is only one God, the Father, of whom are all things, and we for Him"; Colossians 1:16b, ". . . all things were created through Him and for Him"; and John 1:3, "All things were made through Him. . . ." There runs through all these passages a strong consistency of apostolic thought that gives a sense of eternal purpose in the divine creation. This glorious purpose is going to be fulfilled in a realized dominion (Ps. 8:6–7), a reconciled relationship (Gen. 3:3), and the recovery of everlasting life (John 3:16, 5:24, 8:35).

For all this God is both initiator and culminator, giving life meaning and fulfillment without which the human heart cannot survive. Viktor Frankl's insight into the deep hunger of the human spirit for meaning and purpose finds its most complete theological basis in these passages of design and deliverance.

Since fulfilling the first high priestly qualification of being identified with us comes *"through sufferings"* (v. 10), there is no escape for the Messiah-Son; He must be our brother in full identification with our feelings and human pain. In verse 12 of our epistle, our author turns to one of the great psalms of suffering, Psalm 22, which opens with the plaintive cry of rejection, "My God, My God, why have You forsaken Me?" In verse 22 of the psalm, the Sufferer recognizes His solidarity with those who suffer, calling them "My brethren" (cf. Heb. 2:11). From their very midst, sharing their experience in solidarity with them, He is becoming their high priest. He knows every facet of their human pilgrimage.

As a baby, Jesus was born to a teenage girl whose heart agonized at the oppression of her people (Luke 1:51–55). He drank the milk of her breasts while her innermost being throbbed with a passion for liberty. As a lad, He walked streets that were occupied by foreign troops. Swaggering or standing spread-legged in haughty arrogance, with weapons slung over their shoulders, they reflected their ruthless authority in their cold looks. As a teenager, Jesus knew the frustration of having parents who did not understand His radical calling. As a young businessman, He understood the difficulty of meeting payroll and dealing with adamant customers who demanded unreasonable service. He periodically heard the belligerent knock of the tax collector on His door demanding exorbitant taxes for a foreign oppressor. As a leader of a new movement, He was pained by the slowness of His disciples to grasp the true meaning of God's kingdom and His servant identity. He felt the rising tide of hostility from the religious establishment and recognized the tightening vise of inexorable political power that was determined to squeeze all the breath out of His new movement. He seethed at the corruption of an illegal trial. He knew the stinging pain of the lash and the thong, the exhaustion of carrying a heavy cross, the cruelty of the soldiers pounding nails through His hands and feet. As He hung on the cross for hours, His bones began to pull from their sockets; His mouth was parched with the loss of blood and relentless heat. He experienced the alienating weight of the world's sin, the yawning chasm growing between Him and His Father. He quietly watched the shades of death pull over His eyes until finally He gasped His last breath and gave over His life to God in a final act of submission. Then His limp and lifeless form was laid in a borrowed tomb.

Yes, in the *midst* of the congregation and all its life He was truly one of us. Never again can we cry out in the midst of discouragement, opposition, or pain, "But God, You who are secure in Your heavenly sanctuary with all Your massive resources, what do You know of our human struggles? What do You know about living down here in the stench of human decay? Amidst all Your power and glory, You have no idea of the powerlessness and helplessness of our human experience!"

Since Jesus Christ, God does know. Something happened in the Godhead when the human experience was added to the Almighty. Although He was a Son, He learned obedience by what He suffered. He has become our merciful and faithful high priest.

"O God, You know?"
"Yes, My child, I know."
"Then You indeed are our high priest; You understand."

NOTE

1. *Calvin's Commentaries, Hebrews* (Grand Rapids: Eerdmans, 1948), pp. 56–58.

CHAPTER FIVE

A Priest Must Be Faithful

Hebrews 3:1-6

1 Therefore, holy brethren, partakers of the
heavenly calling, consider the Apostle and High Priest
of our confession, Christ Jesus,
    2 who was faithful to Him who appointed Him,
as Moses also was faithful in all His house.
    3 For this One has been counted worthy of more
glory than Moses, inasmuch as He who built the house
has more honor than the house.
    4 For every house is built by someone, but He who
built all things is God.
    5 And Moses indeed was faithful in all His house
as a servant, for a testimony of those things which
would be spoken afterward,
    6 but Christ as a Son over His own house, whose
house we are if we hold fast the confidence and the
rejoicing of the hope firm to the end.

Heb. 3:1–6

"Therefore, holy brethren" has a definitely evangelical ring about it.
The phrase "holy brethren" can be worded "children who have been
cleansed and made holy." The cleansing of the conscience by the
sacrifice of Jesus Christ is the unmistakable emphasis here, but alongside, and also important, is that of a holy calling. Justice and good
works have been and will be an emphasis of this epistle as well as
other New Testament documents. *"Partakers* [or associates] *of the heavenly calling"* reminds us of the scepter of a righteousness that is the
scepter of our Lord and of His kingdom. In Hebrews 9:14 our author
will say again that our consciences are cleansed (personal salvation)
to serve the living God (good works). In Ephesians 2:8–10, Paul shares

this same bifocal nature of the gospel. Not only are we saved by grace through faith, which is a work of God and not our personal work, lest any of us should become boastful, but we have been created for good works that God designed beforehand in order that we walk in them. How often have evangelicals memorized Ephesians 2:8 and 9 but left out or totally forgotten 2:10? After all, what is the purpose of our salvation?

When I was a young Christian of college age, I got into an argument with a person who was noted internationally for a strong evangelistic emphasis. This occurred after a breakfast as we were discussing the purpose of salvation. I stated my conviction that it was not only for our relationship with God, but also for the work of Christ's kingdom which included social justice. I was shocked at the negative opposition I received to what I considered a quite biblical thought. Now that the years have gone by, I am even more convinced of the validity of that argument. Indeed, we are sharers or associates in both the evangelical and justice themes of the kingdom.

These phrases of introduction (3:1) are followed by a recurring theme of our author: "Consider Jesus." A livelier translation here might be: "Bring your mind down on this one." That is, concentrate, focus on Jesus who is *"the Apostle and High Priest of our confession."* This is the only place in the New Testament that speaks of Jesus as an *apostle.* A short study of this word may add some interesting insight.

K. H. Rengstorf, in his article on this word in Kittel's *Theological Dictionary of the New Testament,* says its meaning lies in the authority given to a person to speak for the one who sent him. Certainly a number of passages come to mind where Jesus Himself claimed such authority or others said it of Him. Matthew 7:29 describes Him as one who had authority. In Matthew 9:6 Jesus says, "The Son of Man has power on earth to forgive sins." In the passages we call the Great Commission, Jesus states, "All authority has been given to Me in heaven and on earth. Go therefore . . ." (Matt. 28:18–19). "As the Father has sent Me, I also send you" (John 20:21).

But there is another approach to this word that has helped me understand the meaning of *apostle.* If we break away the prefix (*apo*) of the Greek word, we are left with *stolon.* Biologists use this word to describe a type of root that shoots forth from a plant having the capability of putting down a new set of roots. Ever tried to pick out crab grass? Those stolons are quite capable of sending a shoot and establishing a new colony that can itself send out another stolon to establish yet another colony. So spreads the crab grass!

Jesus was sent out by the Father to establish a new "colony of heaven" called the kingdom of God. Christ in turn has given us that same authority to establish new colonies or churches all over the world. What an awesome authority we have obtained from our Apostle Lord!

Tied in with the concept of apostle is an emphasis on faithfulness. I was talking to my son the other day. He is a microbiologist doing a research thesis on genetic change; the field is called recombinant DNA. He spoke of the DNA helix as "expressing itself" faithfully in reproducing the same pattern of protein beads on the genetic string. When we obey Christ in establishing new colonies of "expressions" of His kingdom, we are being faithful to the apostolic task He has given to us.

In this same way, the Jewish high priests had to be faithful to the task God had given them. They were to be on duty during the assigned time. As a sign of their readiness to minister on behalf of the people, they were not to sit down during this time. Only when their duty was finished could they sit down.

In establishing this second prerequisite of a Jewish high priest, our author compares Jesus with Moses: ". . . *Moses also was faithful in all His house"* (v. 2). Appointed by God, Moses was faithful in several ways that give us a marvelous model for our faithfulness.

1. Moses was faithful to speak all the words given him by God (Deut. 18:18–19). There are times when the message from God does not meet with warm acceptance from the people. Today is no different from the time of Moses.

On one occasion during the racial tension of the sixties, I had preached on Colossians 3:11. California at that time was voting on whether or not to repeal a law forbidding the sale or rental of a house to a person of color, racial origin, or creed. Emotions were running high, and people were being judged as good guys or bad guys on the basis of where they stood on this issue. The town was under an agreement that no one of undesirable racial or creedal origin would be sold property. In my sermon I interpreted the biblical passage "there is neither Greek nor Jew, circumcised nor uncircumcised, barbarian, Scythian, slave nor free, but Christ is all and in all" as a basis for Christians to be inclusive in their social relationships.

After the service was over, a tremendous commotion developed outside as I was confronted by a member who asked, "Where did you get that modlygoop?" When I said, "From Jesus Christ," he snorted, "Then I don't agree with Jesus Christ." He had declared his loyalty—to a politically partisan stance, not to Jesus Christ.

I must admit that I cowered until the next time a similar subject came up. Someone who loved me and did not want to see me get caught up in a painful struggle said, "All right, they know where you stand; back off." Yet I felt very strongly the task was not finished. Rather than backing off, I felt constrained to be faithful to the message.

I then decided to teach seventeen messages on the Gospel of Matthew. Here was teaching of our Lord that I felt could be a foundation for making a biblical response to the issues of the day. It took awhile, but one thing I discovered: though being faithful to the message might be unpopular and costly, it yields the good harvest of the kingdom. About seventy people left the congregation during the next few months and joined a very conservative church on the hill. The congregation I was serving took off in one of the most thrilling and practical forms of mission to the larger city that I have ever seen. The several congregations who bound themselves together as "sharers in the holy calling" changed that town! Moses and Christ were both faithful to the message they had received.

2. Moses was faithful to accomplish all things that the Lord commanded him (Exod. 40:16). This second characteristic of faithfulness caused Moses to go to Pharaoh, even though he first argued with God and tried desperately to get out of the assignment. He had been raised with the man to whom he was to go; he knew his ruthless character and the hate that existed between them. He comprehended the awesome military power of the Egyptian army, whose men were disciplined, quick, well-trained, and cunning. Moses' nomads were no match for the military machine of Pharaoh. Moreover, his own personal history caused him tremendous pain. He was born and reared a Jew until he was sent into the court of Pharaoh to be raised as an Egyptian and son of the princess. In this second period of his life he had one of the broadest and deepest educations ever in history. The resplendent Egyptian culture to which he was exposed included mathematics, astronomy, physics, architecture, political science, and military science. Until the age of forty he was trained for some high position in the Egyptian court.

Yet Moses was a man torn by two cultures. He could see the tyranny of his adopted culture over that of his native culture. Every time he saw the torment of his enslaved people his heart was torn within him. Uncontainable tension built up until one day when he saw an Egyptian maltreating a Hebrew, he killed him and buried him in the sand. His agony and confusion were so great that he fled to the desert and there found a shepherd, Jethro, with whom he lived for the next forty years in the wilderness of Sinai.

Is it any wonder that when God called him he had to say honestly that he was not a good talker? He stuttered uncontrollably. The tension of two cultures warring for dominance reflected itself in his halting speech and inner insecurity. Reason after reason rose up within him to ward off the call of God to this onerous task. But in the final moment, his faithfulness showed itself in obedience to the mandate of God.

3. Another characteristic of Moses' faithfulness is revealed in Exodus 14: his obedience in extremity. This Exodus story tells of a people grumbling like spoiled children with discontent. They were tired of the manna; they had cooked it, broiled it, baked it, and eaten it raw, and they were sick of it. They wailed for meat. More than that, they were anxious about the Egyptians thundering across the desert in their chariots and slicing them to pieces. They would rather go back to Egypt as slaves than remain in freedom in lean and unsure circumstances in the wilderness. "Let us alone, and let us serve the Egyptians," they pleaded.

Off in the distance, sure enough, Moses could see the swirling sand clouds generated by driving chariot wheels. Calling for his people to stand firm at the edge of the sea, he promised them the mighty hand of the Lord. With great signs of God's protection, when Moses stretched out his hand the sea parted, allowing them to cross over on dry land. But when the chariots followed, they were swallowed up as the tides came surging back to their normal position. In all this, Moses was obedient to God, encouraging, disciplining, coddling, persuading. It must have been an exhausting role. Numbers 11 shows Moses finally coming to the end of his patience and endurance, crying out to God, that if God is going to treat him thus and if he has found God's favor, "Please kill me here and now . . . !" (Num. 11:15). Even in these outbursts of burnout and fatigue, however, he held his course in steady obedience to God, in the very midst of extremity.

4. Moses displayed still another characteristic of faithfulness: he remained on duty until relieved; he held a given course until told

by God to go another way. He was under God's control. Jesus said, "Blessed are the meek." Paul said a fruit of the Spirit is meekness (Gal. 5:23).

A lot of us have trouble with the idea of meekness. To us it means weakness, playing doormat, Mr. Milquetoast. But the biblical meaning is quite something else. The Greek word for meekness, *praus,* has nothing to do with weakness. Rather it signifies the kind of gentleness in a strong horse who is easily controlled by the rein.

When I was a boy, I loved to spend vacations in Arizona with my mother's folks. They were Mennonite farmers, and among other things, they loved their stock and cared for it with prize-winning results. I talked to an old farmer of those years about his dray horses, the huge Clydesdales, and knew I had touched a tender place in his heart. Seventeen hands high, almost a ton in weight, able to pull awesome loads, Clydesdales had nothing weak about them. They were strong, but oh, so gentle. I saw the farmer work a Clydesdale with a rope to a calf as it was being born. He touched the rein a bit at a time, and that great horse, sensing the need for absolute control, backed slowly, inch by inch as the calf was brought forth.

Later in the day, I saw another demonstration of the same gentleness. A truck had become mired in the irrigation ditch, and the driver wanted to unload the oranges from the truck to make it light enough to pull out. But my grandfather said proudly, "Let my brace of Clydesdales have a chance at it." After the horses had been hitched up to the truck, they went forward slightly to take up the slack on the line, and then with a whistle and shout from my grandfather, they got to work. They moved their feet around a bit to find firm footing, then leaned their mighty weight into the task. Their great rump muscles bulged; their brisket muscles became taut; they breathed deeply as if they knew honor was at stake. Now the rope was hard with tension, and finally the truck began to move, spinning mud from under its wheels as it added its own power. Out came truck, oranges, the whole load, a bit dirtier for the experience. I could not help looking at those great horses, nostrils distended, blowing from the effort, tossing their heads as though in proud victory, whinnying gently as my grandfather expressed his own love and pride. Weak? Never! Gentle and under control, absolutely. Meek, gentle to the rein.

Moses was one of the most powerful men in history. In today's world I am confident he would have been a powerful corporate executive or a master politician. There was nothing weak about him. Still, he was under the control of God—meek, gentle to the rein, the sort of person who inherits the world by doing things God's way.

I have a special love for Psalm 131. As one who very easily and rather quickly abandons the limits God has placed on me and who steps out into excessive ambition, I find special meaning in these words:

> O Lord, my heart is not lifted up,
>   my eyes are not raised too high;
> I do not occupy myself with things
>   too great and too marvelous for me.
> But I have calmed and quieted my soul,
>   like a child quieted at its mother's breast;
>   like a child that is quieted is my soul.
>
> *Ps. 131:1–2*, RSV

There it is—to be faithful to all that God has commanded and no more. I want to trust Him, to acknowledge that He knows how much is best for me and not try to overaccomplish and thus be harried and torn. I am learning, oh, so slowly, that God's plan and direction are best. So why not yield to the gentle touch of His rein, to the still small voice of His Holy Spirit?

Faithfulness is also seen in the willingness to continue obeying an order until a new one is given even if the length of time seems inordinately long or the circumstances appear to indicate taking things into one's own hands.

When I was a student pilot in San Diego, one day was so beautiful I just had to make use of it and go out for some practice landings and take-offs. The prescribed pattern ran parallel to Miramar Naval Air Station's pattern, so their jets on downwind legs were only a quarter mile or so from all of us who had decided it was a good day to fly. (As my daddy would say, "Everybody and his off ox were out that day.") The pattern was full, and the tower was talking fast in a never-ending flow of words. Because of all the aircraft wanting to take off, the controller was sending us quite far downwind to leave some room for departures. "Musketeer 38 Lima, extend your downwind for departures." I looked back ruefully, a bit frustrated with the delay. I flew, and flew and flew. The distant mountains were coming closer. "Surely he's forgotten me," I mused. I decided to take things into my own hands and began to turn toward the airport. Almost immediately the sharp controller picked up my movement and asked rather tersely, "38 Lima, what are your intentions?" That is polite controller talk for "What the —— are you doing?" In not being faithful to the last command, I quickly discovered that taking things into my own hands was a "no-no." He hadn't forgotten; controllers seldom do. God never does. Faithfulness means continuing on the last orders until God gives new ones. Moses did just that.

5. Moses was also faithful under the circumstances of fatigue. Exodus 18 tells a story that could be repeated thousands of times in the lives of pastors. The story here is one of overburden, fatigue, and burnout.

Tension and anxiety ran high in the land of Egypt as God and Pharaoh wrestled. Plague after plague swept down on the Egyptian nation. Angels of death killed the firstborn of Egypt in a night of wailing and breathlessness. Hebrew families worried. Was there enough blood on the doorpost? Would the angel see it and pass over? Or would this house too be sheathed in the black of mourning on the morrow?

Then came the orders to move out! Take only unleavened bread. Do not delay. The exhilarating flight from the land of bondage demanded great energy. Fear consumed the last ounces of vitality from the people and Moses had to give of his own. Drama after drama unfolded—all in the light of God's power, but with tremendous resources consumed. Then in the relative quietness of the desert camp, the routine burden began to weigh heavily on Moses' shoulders. Day after day the decisions had to be made, instructions provided for camp administration, teaching given regarding the ways of God, the judgments rendered between dissenting parties. That is enough to drive any executive into stress and fatigue.

A great old man—Jethro, Moses' father-in-law—came into camp. He was bringing back Zippora and the boys from safekeeping during the period Israel was fighting its first military battles. That first evening, as Moses told his longtime friend all that God had done, Jethro exclaimed, "God is God indeed!"

Then the next day Moses sat to judge the people. Long hours of toilsome routine administering this wayward and volatile horde took their toll. When the sun set and Moses had sent the people to their homes, Jethro noticed his son-in-law shuffling up the path to his tent that overlooked the camp spread out in all directions beneath him. Moses' eyes were sunken with fatigue, like those of our presidents after they have undergone years of demanding responsibility. His hair was wild-looking, as if standing out in response to an electric charge. The lines of his face were filled with a mixture of sweat and the red sand of the desert. He sat down on a rock, his massive shoulders bowed with exhaustion and fatigue, and his voice was hoarse as he thanked Zippora for a cup of pomegranate juice.

"What is this you are doing for the people? Why do the people stand around you from morning until evening?" Jethro asked.

"Because the people come to me to inquire of God. When they have a dispute I decide between a man and his neighbor, and I make them know the statutes of God and His decisions." Jethro then said, "Moses, what you are doing is not good. You and the people with you will wear yourselves out, for the thing is too heavy for you; you cannot perform it alone." The relentless demands of leadership and responsibility were exacting their price. The burden showed in his eyes, his face, the hoarseness of his voice, in moments of scarcely controllable anger.

Such a time was the occasion of his coming down from the mountain with the tablets of stone. He had been gone forty days, that was true, but was that any excuse for the debauchery he found upon his return? Carousing, orgies, idolatry all stared at him blatantly upon his return. Yet, in the midst of the fatigue and exasperation he held his course steady and brought the people back to the gates of repentance to put their trust in God.

Few of us could claim or match the faithfulness of Moses. With a sense of chagrin, the Jews knew Moses had shown incredible faithfulness to God in spite of their own faithless actions. He was the model of faithfulness.

In the light of this background it is all the more stunning that our author claims the Son is more faithful than Moses. And yet he does not compare the Son to Moses in obedience to the proclamation, to the accomplishment of all that God had told Him to do, in extremity, duty, or fatigue. Rather he compares Moses to the Son in matters of essence.

The Son is worthy of more honor than Moses because of who He is. Moses was faithful as a servant; Jesus is faithful as a Son in the house. Of course a son, even an earthly son, has more honor than a servant for he is the heir. The house is described as His, the Lord's, house, by virtue of His being heir to all things. In Numbers

12:7 Moses is described as the free servant in an honorable and trusted position. Moses' position is derived; that of the Son is inherent.

There is yet another dimension to this superiority; Moses is creature, the Son is Creator. Moses is the "house" that was constructed; Jesus Christ is the Builder of the house.

Then our author makes an equation that appears at first as an astounding contradiction. He says that the maker of all things is God. Has he not claimed that the world was made by the Son? Is there confusion in his mind? No, God is the builder of all things; Christ is the builder of all things. Both are one and the same. This is not contradiction but revelation!

House—an interesting concept of the Old and New Testaments beckons our curiosity here. Moses, a house? Is there any relation to the concept of house here and that mentioned in John 8:30–36? I think so. For years this idea puzzled me but now a thrilling meaning is emerging.

The Old Testament meanings of "house" include quite often the idea of a household or family, an intimate grouping of those related by blood or common responsibilities. Thus when Jesus speaks of one who commits sin being a slave to sin and not continuing in the family of God or the participation in the Kingdom of God, He is indicating that sin has broken the ties and destroyed the household experience. Hosea, whose adulterous wife Gomer bore children to other men, named one of them Lo-Ammi. *Lo* in Hebrew is "not"; *am* is Hebrew for "people"; *mi* indicates the possessive "my": thus the meaning of the name, "Not my people." The name not only told a tragic and painful story of the prophet's marital agony, but also indicated Israel's state with God because of her wanderings after other gods, even as Gomer had wandered after other men.

Now, according to our writer, Christ builds a new house of which Moses is a servant. What is this house but a new family, a household of the redeemed, of those twice-born; of the flesh and of the Spirit?

The Greek verb used here has the basic meaning "to prepare or make ready." The term implies all that belongs to the completion of a house or home; the conception of an idea, the dream or plan, the architectural detail, the construction, the furnishing; but, most important, the filling of the house with the living community. What a beautiful understanding of the house that Christ has built.

Here the house is the Kingdom of God. It was a dream in the heart of God from the foundation of the world. God envisioned a household in which He would be the loving Father and every member a caring, loving, productive person. The architectural plan indicated the need for a redeemer, and Christ was appointed to fulfill that role. The family would be made up of those who responded in faith and obedience, those willing to risk the impossible and follow God out of the Egypts of their particular forms of bondage, through tractless wastes of leanness, crossing swollen rivers to take promised lands, all the while believing God provides for what He has commanded. Thus Moses was a part of this house by his own faith and obedience, as a servant, doing all that God had told him to do.

The Builder of the house was the Son, Jesus Christ, who by His own sacrifice had laid the function for the house, the foundation of forgiveness and redemption. No one could come into that house because of his or her own efforts; only the Son could set humanity free from sin to dwell in the house of the Lord forever. God saw it all; God planned it all; God did it all through Jesus Christ.

I am full of a present experience that I must share with you here. We as a family are building a dream house in the mountains of the High Sierra. It all started when my wife Colleen's parents and my parents each sold homes situated on the same lake outside Los Angeles. These homes on either side of the lake were the gathering place of our "clan" for several years. Thanksgivings, Christmases, vacations saw the uncles and aunts, cousins, grandparents, and friends all together in joyous and at times raucous moments of sailing, swimming, eating, game-playing, and growing acquaintances that meant so much to our children.

With the sale of those homes it was all over. A sadness and nostalgia began to eat away at everyone's hearts. One Christmas, when Dan and Tim and Luanda had come home from college, we all gathered around the table musing and laughing about the great times at the lake. Somebody put forth the challenge—"Dad, one day you are going to be the head of the clan! We've got to provide the clan center!"— and the dream was born. It did not take many minutes to flesh out the dream.

The family decision was made to find a lot in the high country where we and the cousins had loved to backpack in previous years. After searching and acting on faith, believe me, we purchased a postage-stamp lot, and years later we began to build. In the meantime, we shared ideas and sketches and suggested functions that should be built into the house. We saw not only a house, but a living space for people. We envisioned the things that would happen there. Our children wanted a place where their children could grow up knowing a heritage of families, so there should be a gallery wall for pictures. Classics of music and literature—there must be a reading and listening room. Crafts—got to have crafts! How about a room under the garage for any kind of handcraft the kids or grownups ("grups" as they were lovingly called) could make—pottery, model airplanes, pop-sculpture, wood-working or carving on the beams of the house (with permission of design, of course!).

Over the years the sketches grew into detailed plans. Then came the backbreaking work of digging the foundation trenches on a very steep slope (no wonder the lot was cheap!). Cousins, uncles, and aunts all helped throw dirt behind barricades to keep it from tumbling right back into the trenches. Some professionals assisted with pouring the foundations and then, the next year, with the first of the framing. I watched teams of relatives putting up walls, experiencing the thrill of perfect fits, plumb walls, and level floors. "Hey, it's got to be right! Look at that!" Now the roof is on and inner space for living is taking on an atmosphere of hospitality and coziness.

The rains of 1983 were vicious, but the sound roof was doing its job. One January evening of that year I stood on the balcony of the "loft room" in the peak of the A-frame, high above the main floor, and imagined I was a future grandchild, ready for bed, peering down through the balustrades of the balcony railing and seeing the great oval, oak table nestled in a large bay looking through the majestic trees to the lake below. Soft amber light of a massive chandelier would cast a warm glow upon the dessert plates scattered about the table and the members of the "clan" chatting amiably and laughing in waves of good humor.

How would that little tyke feel? I became very soft inside as I imagined it—secure, loved, serene, excited about tomorrow, knowing I belonged to "my people." The words of Jeremiah 31:33 came back to me: "I will be their God, and they shall be my people." What happens to our hearts when we experience that witness of the Holy Spirit? An almost agonizing joy finds deep expression, "Abba, Father! My very own beloved Father, I belong!" How closely the human family experience fuses with the spiritual experience. Is this a little of what God dreamed before the foundation of the world, a household of faith? I really do think so.

All those who hold their relationships firm to the end will know the joys and satisfactions of the clan center as long as they live, for the house will pass on from generation to generation. We dreamed it, we designed it, we are building it, we will put a family in it. It is almost an intoxicating vision! Is this but a tiny sample of what God envisions? O God, I want to hold fast the confidence and rejoice in the hope firmly to the end.

CHAPTER SIX

A Second Exhortation: "Trust and Obey!"

Hebrews 3:7—4:16

THE NEED FOR STEADFAST BELIEF

7 Therefore, as the Holy Spirit says:
"Today, if you will hear His voice,

8 *Do not harden your hearts as in the rebellion,*
In the day of trial in the wilderness,

9 *Where your fathers tested Me, proved Me,*
And saw My works forty years.

10 *Therefore I was angry with that generation,*
And said, 'They always go astray in their heart,
And they have not known My ways.'

11 *So I swore in My wrath,*
'They shall not enter My rest.' "

12 Beware, brethren, lest there be in any of you an evil heart of unbelief in departing from the living God;

13 but exhort one another daily, while it is called *"Today,"* lest any of you be hardened through the deceitfulness of sin.

14 For we have become partakers of Christ if we hold the beginning of our confidence steadfast to the end,

15 while it is said:
"Today, if you will hear His voice,
Do not harden your hearts as in the rebellion."

16 For who, having heard, rebelled? Indeed, was it not all who came out of Egypt, led by Moses?

17 Now with whom was He angry forty years? Was it not with those who sinned, whose corpses fell in the wilderness?

18 And to whom did He swear that they would
not enter His rest, but to those who did not obey?
19 So we see that they could not enter in because
of unbelief.

Heb. 3:7–19

Evidently, describing the faithfulness of Moses and of Christ has
brought to the author's mind some disquieting evaluations regarding
those to whom he is writing. They are not exactly paragons of faithfulness, and he has serious concerns. The soft spots he sees in their
discipleship move him to launch an effort to stimulate them to greater
faithfulness in the likeness of their Lord.

His transitional phrase from the teaching section into this hortatory
section is ". . . if we hold fast the confidence and the rejoicing of
the hope firm to the end" (3:6). What now follows indicates the
importance of the "if"; it is not rhetorical but an expression of a
definite question concerning their firmness of faith.

The passage follows the expected pattern: a statement of exhortation, a warning, and supportive reasoning describing the dynamics
of the writer's concern.

The Exhortation

The exhortation proper begins with three commands: *"Do not harden
your hearts as in the rebellion"* (v. 8); *"Beware, brethren, lest there be in any
of you an evil heart of unbelief in departing from the living God"* (v. 12); and
"Exhort one another daily, while it is called 'Today' " (v. 13a).

Psalm 95 becomes the foundation of the exhortations that comprise
the third and fourth chapters of the epistle. The "rebellion" referred
to is that of Numbers 13 and 14 in which the Israelites refuse to
obey God in taking the land He has promised them.

In the Hebrew, two interesting terms are used in verse 8 of this
psalm. The first, *Meribah,* a name given to the place of the disobedience, also means "rebellion" or "strife." The equivalent Greek word,
parapikrasmos, denotes a faithlessness of heart or refusal to obey. The
second word, *Massah,* which means testing or proof, is the name for
the place of trial in the wilderness. We can compare Numbers 20:13
which tells of the people contending with the Lord even after He
has shown Himself holy among them. Exodus 17:7 alludes to the

same questioning spirit in which the people call out, "Is the Lord among us or not?" Deuteronomy 6:16–17 instructs the people in the very familiar passage of teaching: "You shall not tempt the Lord your God as you tempted Him in Massah. You shall diligently keep the commandments of the Lord your God, His testimonies, and His statutes which He has commanded you."

The second command is: *"Beware, brethren lest there be in any of you an evil heart of unbelief in departing from the living God"* (3:12). Calvin refers to this "evil heart of unbelief" as a heart diseased with sin, corruption, and wickedness that leads to unbelief. Only Christ can heal such disease, giving a new heart of faith in the new creation. Without such healing we suffer a terminal disease, here symbolized in the death of the unbelieving Israelites in the wilderness.

The third command is: *"Exhort one another daily, while it is called 'Today,' lest any of you be hardened through the deceitfulness of sin"* (3:13).

A Warning

This last phrase, "while it is called 'Today,' " brings us into the section on warning and leads us to the realization that there is a limited period of time in which the faith response may operate. After that time, even if the action is correct, it is too late. Timely obedience is one of the great dynamics of the Christian discipleship.

The great biblical example our author refers to in this passage is the lack of faith-response of the Israelites and the resulting tragedy. They have received the command to go up and take the land which God has promised to their fathers.

The story is a familiar one. Twelve spies are appointed to reconnoiter the land across the Jordan. God had said to Abram that He would not only give Abram sons as numerous as the stars of the heaven but that He would also provide them a land. The time for the fulfillment of that second part of the covenant had arrived and spies were sent out to determine the location and nature of the cities of the land, their fortifications and defenses, the ability of the people to defend themselves, their character and numbers, and whatever other information would aid the leaders in determining the strategy for conquest. Of the twelve spies, ten came back in near panic. They reported that the cities were fortified with great walls, that the inhabitants were so large that the Israelites appeared as grasshoppers before them. Even the first fruit was so awesome in size that they brought back samples to display to the Israelites. The summary of their report was, "It is impossible for us to take the land!"

Only Caleb and Joshua felt the mission could be a success, though not through the power or prowess of the Israelites, but by the power of God. However, the two faithful men could not prevail; the people went the route of fear, forgetting all that God had done in bringing them out of a humanly impossible situation in Egypt. God interpreted this forgetfulness as rebellion; the refusal to go forth angered Him so intensely that He swore in His wrath that the unbelievers should never enter the land He had promised their fathers, a land He called "My rest."

The warning is clear; without obedience it is impossible to please God or to enter into the promise of His goodness. The timeliness of obedience is one of the great dynamic principles of Christian discipleship.

As the Israelites heard God's judgment, the people repented of their actions, but it was too late. Even after warnings from Moses that they should not attempt to take things into their own hands, they nevertheless embarked upon a military campaign against the Amalekites and Canaanites which ended in disaster.

Untimely obedience is no substitute for timely or immediate obedience. Getting to the right place too late does not fix the situation.

In 1952 my father, my brother, four other young men from the Hollywood Presbyterian Church, and I were to make a trip to Africa to visit various mission locations. Our travel was to be by ship across the Atlantic and then by plane within the continent. Two of our party made a last-minute decision to get in some hunting supplies that meant a cross-town trip in New York rush hour. They miscalculated the time necessary for the return trip. My father, seeing the hour for sailing fast approaching, implored the captain to delay departure for just a few minutes.

"Absolutely not; we sail on the hour," came the firm reply. My father's face was contorted with anxiety as he watched the clock come to within two minutes of the hour. The first blast of the ship's horn made us all jump. Off came the first set of lines. In one more minute we would be underway. Sailors manned the gangway in preparation for its removal.

Suddenly among the steel stanchions of the dock warehouse, a taxi careened to a stop almost at the foot of the gangway. Out jumped the two spry but worried occupants, loaded with gear. They leaped onto the gangway and raced up to the ship. At that moment the second blast shattered the tranquility of the late afternoon. The last lines at the bow and stern fell away, and the ship quivered as her screws bit into the murky waters of the harbor.

What if they had been a moment later? They would have obeyed the instructions as to the location, but not as to time, and so would have been left behind with no recourse. How often have we done the act of obedience too late, compulsively running after little errands and personal desires that caused us to miss the moment of timeliness? While "Today" lasts, that period in which obedience is possible, our author urges his readers and disciples of all ages to respond immediately to the strategies of God.

The Reasoning

What was it that caused the Israelites to disobey? Was it not their hearts of unbelief mentioned above? Notice the threefold movement of this tragedy. First there was the evil, unbelieving heart; faithlessness, forgetting or ignoring the mighty power of God. Second, there was fear, brought on by that lack of faith. Rather than obey God's command, they asked to choose a captain who would lead them back to Egypt. They whined and murmured against Moses for bringing them out into the wilderness. They were willing to go back into slavery in order to have the luscious foods they could grow in the delta of the Nile. Their minds were on their comfort; they feared the rigors of desert life that would toughen them and make them ready for conquest.

Have we not done the same? Whimpering, we have shied away from the leanness of God, the discipline that involves pain at times, the hard work that will yield abilities and toughness needed for the labor to come.

Third, the final result is a hardened heart—a will no longer stimulated by the desires of God, a mind set on selfish comforts, emotions addicted to quick fixes and easy convenience. Let God or anyone else approach the hardened heart with a challenge, and that one will be repulsed in derision. At this point God comes down with the anger of His judgment and says, "You shall never enter my rest, that holy design for those who obey."

How often in modern church history has a mission study group of a local church's ruling board made a report, illustrated with compelling information and statistics, displaying a fine sensitivity to human need with the mind of Christ, showing the ministries that could be effected in Christ's name for the blessing of the community, and the board refused to go along, pleading the limitations of resources?

Even in the face of God's promise—"[I will] supply all your need" (Phil. 4:19); "seek first the kingdom of God . . . and all these things shall be added to you" (Matt. 6:33)—they appear to be deaf or forgetful and belittle such "spirituality" as lacking good business sense. Is it any wonder so many ministries go unaccomplished and churches languish in slow death? It is shocking how many churches in major denominations are shutting down because of hardened hearts. And judgment falls! No rest for the people of God!

Verses 18 and 19 give this order in reverse: *"And to whom did He swear that they would not enter His rest, but to those who did not obey? So we see that they could not enter in because of unbelief."*

Looking ahead to 4:2, we notice that our author uses an interesting word from the culinary arts. "Not being mixed with faith in those who heard it" brings up the image of a cook mixing ingredients together that they might interact in the baking process. In this condition, there is no ferment of faith in the life of the unbeliever; instead moral decay sets in as described in Romans 1:18–32. Paul's threefold steps resemble those of the writer to the Hebrews. First, there is the refusal to honor God or give thanks to Him for all His creation and redemption. Second, there follows intellectual rationalization, the unbeliever "claiming to be wise" yet experiencing a darkened mind. Third comes the judgment of moral decay as defined in three passages. Romans 1:24–25 shows the dishonoring of the body. How tragic to see youth today shooting up their bodies with addicting drugs, scrambling their brains with hallucinogenic drugs. Verses 26 and 27 show the moral decay of perverse sexual life styles of both heterosexual and homosexual who have departed from the designed and goodly order of God. Verses 28 through 31 give a list of evidences of moral decay, some of them socially acceptable, showing a breakdown of the moral and social fabric of a culture that yields to faithlessness and disobedience. The tragic ending is not that of insight and remorse, but of blatant arrogance that applauds and "evangelizes" to gain recruits to a decadent life style. For these there is a refusal on God's part that they should enter His rest.

THE REST OF GOD

1 Therefore, since a promise remains of entering His rest, let us fear lest any of you seem to come short of it.

2 For indeed the gospel was preached to us as well as to them; but the word which they heard did not profit them, not being mixed with faith in those who heard it.

3 For we who have believed do enter that rest, as He has said:

"So I swore in My wrath,
They shall not enter My rest,"

although the works were finished from the foundation of the world.

4 For He has spoken in a certain place of the seventh day in this way: *"And God rested on the seventh day from all His works";*

5 and again in this place: "They shall not enter My rest."

6 Since therefore it remains that some must enter it, and those to whom it was first preached did not enter because of disobedience,

7 again He designates a certain day, saying in David, *"Today,"* after such a long time, as it has been said:

"Today, if you will hear His voice,
Do not harden your hearts."

8 For if Joshua had given them rest, then He would not afterward have spoken of another day.

9 There remains therefore a rest for the people of God.

10 For he who has entered His rest has himself also ceased from his works as God did from His.

11 Let us therefore be diligent to enter that rest, lest anyone fall after the same example of disobedience.

12 For the word of God is living and powerful, and sharper than any two-edged sword, piercing even to the division of soul and spirit, and of joints and marrow, and is a discerner of the thoughts and intents of the heart.

99

13 And there is no creature hidden from His sight,
but all things are naked and open to the eyes of Him
to whom we must give account.

14 Seeing then that we have a great High Priest
who has passed through the heavens, Jesus the Son
of God, let us hold fast our confession.

15 For we do not have a High Priest who cannot
sympathize with our weaknesses, but was in all points
tempted as we are, yet without sin.

16 Let us therefore come boldly to the throne of
grace, that we may obtain mercy and find grace to
help in time of need.

Heb. 4:1–16

The term "rest of God" figures prominently throughout the remainder of the exhortation. Let us look carefully for our author's meaning.

At first glance the land is the rest. The Israelites had been refused entry to the land by an angry God because of their disobedience. However, our author concludes this section of exhortation by saying that if Joshua had given them rest by bringing them into the land, then God would not have afterward spoken of another day. Westcott assists us here, taking the first entrance to mean an ideal fulfillment of the highest destiny of Israel in perfect fellowship with God. Westcott refers us to Leviticus 26:3–14, in which the people are promised that if they walk in God's commandments they will be blest by good rains, abundant yield of their fields, sufficiency in supply of food and wine, and security in which to enjoy their provender. Moreover, they will find God making His abode among them. "I will walk among you and be your God, and you shall be My people" (Lev. 26:12).

But as the people discovered the unsatisfying character of the temporal or material inheritance, a deeper desire, of spiritual nature, was quickened in them. It was to this the prophets spoke as the realization of true blessing matured.[1]

The definition of rest appears multifaceted. First, it is the place of God's design. It was God who took the initiative (and God always takes the initiative) and promised the people a good land flowing with milk and honey. It is a spiritual principle that we are always to be in a responding mode to God's initiative. His design is not a delightful take-it-or-leave-it option, but rather a mandate for acquisition. God's design is the fulfillment of our highest identity and development. It is not negotiable. To respond in faith and obedience is to step into or enter that design and know all the sufficiency and peace implied in terms of "milk and honey," "rain and abundance."

A good parallel to the concept of rest is the previously discussed concept of house. God's good design for His family is matched by His gracious design of rest. Whereas God is designer and builder of the house and the one who places a family in the house by the grace of Jesus Christ, so rest is the abiding in an ultimate design for each of us, an abiding gained by a faith-response to the will of God. This certainly is one aspect of predestination—a performance of those "good works, which God prepared beforehand that we should walk in them" (Eph. 2:10). In the condition of rest, the faithful believer experiences the exhilaration of creativity and productivity; stress and anxiety are minimized; joy lifts the spirit above the waves of normal frustrations and a holy purpose stimulates a vitality that is not overwhelmed by difficulties. Serenity and laughter are the marks of being in the place of rest. The rest of God is not cessation from activity, but a peace within the toil.

The first time I flew into a rain-drenched overcast sky with my flight instructor, and the rain began to pelt the windscreen like an angry drummer, I was far from a state of rest. Wisps of clouds shrouded the wingtips. A pervasive anxiety clutched at my breathing; my legs became taut and my hands gripped the control horns with a sweaty fear. I jerked and overcompensated in reaction to the instruments, and the plane zigzagged through the sky as though a drunken pilot were in control. As fatigue began to build up, my tension rapidly went from bad to worse. Perspiration cascaded down my face and armpits, while my instructor sat there absolutely unperturbed. When I turned my head to look at him, he met my eyes with a twinkle in his, firmly took my right hand off the control horn, and put my lower fingers on my right knee, a position of ease he had taught me in my first lesson. I remembered; my thumb and index finger were enough with which to control the plane. "Relax," he said, softly. "Louie, you are only in a normal warm front; you're flying a stable aircraft with the strongest wings of any single engine model; they were made for carrier landings! Trust them! Sit back; turn your head and eyes a bit. Now, nice, slow, smooth corrections; keep your sweep of the instruments going in our normal pattern. Rest and enjoy it!"

I tried; I concentrated on the relaxation and the slow corrections to the minor variations in altitude and heading. I was amazed first at his relaxed attitude and then at the improvement in mine. True, it was years before I got over the tummy-tightening and the sweaty palms when entering a cloudbank, but that day the rest came when I was still in the clouds, the rain was still pelting the windshield, the flight was continuing, and yet I got my first taste of peace. Peace and rest in the midst of life's continuation are indications of the maturing people of God.

That is part of what rest means; to be at His place, at His time, doing the thing He has planned for us to do, confident in His strength and resources, in the design of the system. This confidence in the foreknowledge and plan of God is a very accurate definition of faith. This faith permits—urges—the believer to move out in obedience. Living this faith-response keeps the spiritual arteries soft and pliable and staves off spiritual arteriosclerosis, the "hardened heart." It is evidenced in life's happy, productive, serene people who know rest.

It is no wonder the writer urges his readers to enter this kind of rest. How many times are hypertension, migraine headaches, a peptic ulcer, arthritis, nervous exhaustion, illness, insomnia, overweight and irascibility evidences of a life not at peace with the will and pace of God? How far could we take the soul-and-spirit, joint-and-marrow language of our writer and put them into modern terms of the psychological, spiritual, psychosomatic, and motivational? There is no way we can fake it, hide the truth about ourselves. It all comes out, sooner or later, and the later does not necessarily have to wait for the last judgment. God holds us accountable to our design and destiny in the plan of Christ. Indeed, we have been created for the praise of His glory.

In verses 6 and 7, our teacher continues with an interesting twist on the theme of faithlessness and disobedience: the historical incident of failing to enter the rest because of disobedience is treated here not just as a historical incident but as a spiritual principle. The principle is this: The "today" for the Israelites in the desert can be repeated any time, anywhere obedience has a time frame in which it must operate. Long after the original incident, David is God's instrument in "designating a certain day." The word "today" is repeated, placing emphasis upon the new time frame in which obedience must take place. Notice the twofold nature of the spiritual principle: (1) the basis of entering the "rest" is obedience to the plan of God, whatever that plan is, and disobedience is the condition under which one is barred from entering; (2) the timing of obedience is a critical factor.

There is a "window" called "today" outside which obedience is not acceptable and the opportunity to satisfy God is lost.

The interpretation of our writer is that Psalm 95 demonstrates a spiritual principle which is then applied to the current situation of the readers of the epistle. The psalm leads off with an invitation to praise (vv. 1–2) based upon God's creative power and possessiveness (vv. 3–5).

The invitation is then restated (vv. 6–7) with a rather sudden change of atmosphere, one of passionate exhortation: "O that today you would hearken to His voice! Harden not your hearts [in this situation] as at Meribah, as on the day at Massah in the wilderness [the past historical situation]."

The principle is this: such hardening and rebellion will bring the same anger that causes God to cut off from His rest anyone who out of disbelief fails to obey. This is the tragic fruit of disobedience born of too small a view of God.

Now, in verses 8 and 9, the teacher returns to the historical situation of Joshua, claiming Joshua did not give the people rest even though chapters 21 and 22 of Joshua indicate that rest had been won. Our writer counters this apparently obvious truth by saying that if Joshua had truly provided the rest, David would not have spoken at a later time of the rest yet to come, of another day or period in which obedience had to be exercised in order to receive the rest. He states the spiritual principle by saying there remains, or there is reserved, rest for the people of God. This last term reminds us of Romans 8:14, that those who "are led by the Spirit of God, these are sons of God." Compare John 8:31–47. Rest is assured for those who have found peace with God through obedience to His will and design. When that design is completed, the saint ceases from labor and discovers the rest.

The theme of rest is changed to that of sabbath in verse 9. In Jewish tradition, the sabbath was a symbol of the day of the Lord, the ultimate rest, and was a symbol of the world to come. Notice that again Hebrews is in line with Jewish thinking.

This theme of obedience and rest is important to us today in our hectic and demanding life styles. God's plan for accomplishing His design is that leaders are to assist other saints in the discovery, development, and deployment of their abilities and gifts of the Spirit. If this is not done, pastoral leaders carry tremendous burdens as did Moses in Exodus 18 and Numbers 11. On Jethro's counsel, however,

Moses altered his leadership style and shared the mountainous responsibilities with his selected elders from all the tribes. They bore the burden with him. These elders were recognized for their strengths of honoring God, of being trustworthy, capable, and above taking bribes. In obeying God's counsel through Jethro, Moses and the people went to their places in peace, a symbol of the rest promised to God's people, who do things His way. When we leaders fail to honor God's created strengths in others, holding all the responsibility to ourselves, we sacrifice the peace and suffer the loss of rest. In that circumstance there is no cessation of labor. Relentless demands grind us down until our physical strength turns to wind-blown powder, our emotions are flighty as a frightened bird, and our spiritual enthusiasm lies as a crumpled cloak damp with the dew of discouragement.

Those who find the rest of God are those who discover the strategy of God, submit to His timing for events, and appropriate the resources God provides, refusing to fall to the temptation of distrusting or judging the capabilities of others. The job gets done; we can put down the tools; we can enjoy the sabbath rest.

In response to the verses above, verses 11–13 prod us to strive, or make haste, lest any of us be caught in the doldrums of faithless disobedience. We are to be eager, diligent, to accomplish God's tasks with enthusiasm so that we may stride confidently into His rest. Our writer makes an interesting turn of thought in verses 12 and 13. He appears to describe the word of God (*logos tou theou*) as being alive, filled with a diagnostic perception that picks up inconsistencies of motivation between things as close as soul and spirit, bone and marrow. No smoothing over with outward actions can hide from God the real purpose or intent of the heart. We may appear to be utterly sincere before other humans but God knows if there is an ulterior motive. God's word is like a two-edged sword, sharp as a scalpel, discerning every twist and turn of the human mind.

The closing verses of this chapter, 14–16, are a transition from exhortation to the continuation of the doctrine of the four necessary qualifications of a Jewish high priest. The phrase "we have" is repeated in theme if not in exact form in 8:1 ("We have such a High Priest"), 10:19 ("having boldness") and 12:1 ("since we are surrounded"). In each case the phrase is transitional.

The summation of the great truth of Christ's sharing our earthly experience is the foundation of our holding fast our confession. The reasoning is simple and touching; our priest is not so lofty or separated that He is incapable of understanding our human situation. Rather He is one who is totally familiar with it, having been tempted at every turn of the road just as we have been. He can laugh and weep with us about life's foibles and pain because He has been through it all, yet without falling before any of it. Because we know that such a Priest and Prince is on the throne of grace disbursing favor far beyond what we deserve, we can approach without fear or cowering, walking erect and receiving whatever resources we need to live life victoriously, overcoming every obstacle.

NOTE

1. Westcott, *The Epistle to the Hebrews,* p. 82.

CHAPTER SEVEN

A Priest Must Be Appointed by God

Hebrews 5:1–10; 7:1–25

THE APPOINTMENT

1 For every priest taken from among men is appointed for men in things pertaining to God, that he may offer both gifts and sacrifices for sins.

2 He can have compassion on those who are ignorant and going astray, since he himself is also beset by weakness.

3 And because of this he is required as for the people, so also for himself, to offer for sins.

4 And no man takes this honor to himself, but he who is called by God, just as Aaron was.

5 So also Christ did not glorify Himself to become High Priest, but it was He who said to Him:

"You are My Son,
Today I have begotten You."

6 As He also says in another place:

"You are a priest forever
According to the order of Melchizedek";

7 who, in the days of His flesh, when He had offered up prayers and supplications, with vehement cries and tears to Him who was able to save Him from death, and was heard because of His godly fear,

8 though He was a Son, yet He learned obedience by the things which He suffered.

9 And having been perfected, He became the author of eternal salvation to all who obey Him,

10 called by God as High Priest *"according to the order of Melchizedek,"*

Heb. 5:1–10

106

In preparing this section of commentary, I struggled for weeks to find a logical order of progression. I felt like Theodore H. Robinson who stated in his commentary that this section of Hebrews is one "where the writer's mind proceeds from one part of his theme almost insensibly into the next and where the main outline of argument is interrupted by frequent digressions." Indeed!

Still, something intuitively led me to believe there was order of some sort. After weeks of translation, reading and rereading, outlining, and musing, the division I previously explained came to light: separate the doctrinal from the hortatory, and the outline flows with amazing and exhilarating order, admittedly, with soft spots.

The first four verses of chapter 5 comprise one of those soft spots, lacking clear outline and movement. The subjects mentioned in them appear to move back and forth between the introduction of new material to be discussed and the review of material already presented. Observing the movement of the elements of review and preview is not unlike keeping our attention on the ball during a tennis match.

As our teacher prepares for his discussion in verses 4–10 of the third qualification required of the Jewish high priest—appointment from God—his first phrase is one of review: *"For every priest taken from among men. . . ."* The qualification refers to chapter 2 in which our exhorter shows the necessity for a priest to be one with the people (2:5–18). The next phrase, *"appointed for men in things pertaining to God,"* announces the theme of required appointment. Discussed only briefly here, this will be expanded upon in our commentary on 6:13–20 and 7:1–25. A new topic for future discussion (7:26–27) is introduced in the words *"that he may offer both gifts and sacrifices for sins."*

Verse 2 takes us back to review again: *"He can have compassion on those who are ignorant and going astray, since he himself is also beset by weakness* (cf. 2:5–18).

Our teacher now reiterates an idea previewed a moment earlier, that of the need for cleansing of the earthly high priest: *"Because of this he is required as for the people, so also for himself, to offer for sins"* (v. 3).

After this introductory passage, the discussion proceeds with the following main points: (1) "God made the appointment" (5:4–10); (2) "God has sworn by an oath" (6:13–20); and (3) "You are a priest forever after the order of Melchizedek" (7:1–25). An exhortation, "Go On to Maturity," intervenes from 5:11 to 6:20.

Our author can now proceed with the theme of this section—appointment, the third requirement of a high priest according to Jewish law. He spends only a short time in this doctrinal portion before interrupting his intricate and difficult teaching for a most emotional and intense exhortation. We have to credit him with no little sensitivity to his readers. The arguments he is using are based upon sophisticated pharisaical rules of interpretation, and he suspects he may lose his readers' attention or interest. Perhaps they were unsophisticated in the process of Jewish interpretation and the *middoth* which guided such processes. Verse 5:11 begins this passionate exhortation, which we will discuss in chapter 9.

The Middoth and Truth

The relation between truth and the arguments to convince another of that truth is as important to us today as it was to the Jewish readers of our teacher. Truth is truth and can stand on its own without outside help. The revelation of God in Jesus Christ, the truth of His High Priesthood and the efficacy of His sacrifice are absolute and depend on no human argument for proof. However, teachers and apologists who attempt to bring someone to an acceptance of that truth try to use arguments or lines of reasoning either familiar or convincing to the hearer. The validity or lack of validity of the argument or reasoning does not affect the essential character of the truth that is being explained. Moreover, the type of argument and the process of reasoning change from one historical season to the next.

The arguments that had validity and weight for the mind of our writer's day were those of the pharisaical *middoth* and the process of oath-making. You and I may not be impressed with the validity of such arguments in our twentieth century, for we have accepted different criteria for validity. But if we are properly to understand our author and what he was attempting to do, then we must place ourselves in the culture of his day. We must step back into the milieu of the Pharisee and the synagogue, and into the religious attitude and mindset of scriptural interpretation popular at that time. A revelational event had made tremendous impact on the early church; they were transformed by the life, death, and resurrection of Jesus Christ. They could no more deny the witness of the Holy Spirit and the manifestations of the Spirit's power than they could deny their human existence. This was Life; this was Truth!

How could they pass on this Truth so that others could experience it also? They did it in the same way you and I would try to influence and convince the folks of our day. We would use the arguments, analogies, and reasonings we felt would explain most clearly and be most convincing. We would use the logic we learned in our college classroom, analogies of aerospace, electronics, law, and human relationships. A thousand years from now folks might read our material and turn up their noses in disdain, but for us these are effective means of communicating our transforming relationship with Jesus Christ.

We will make mention of several *middoth* in the course of this section so you may want to put a finger in the section on *Middoth,* pages 28-29, and also in the Scripture passage with which we began our chapter.

In earlier times, the role of priest was unified with that of king or ruler. Melchizedek (5:6) was not only king of the city of Salem, but also priest in that city to the most high God. But when later he was instructed by God to appoint Aaron and his sons as the priests, the roles of priest and ruler were thereby separated. Now in Jesus Christ the two functions are again united in the one Person of the Son who is Prophet, Priest, and King. This part of the messianic hope, in which a variety of roles would be brought together in the person of the Messiah, is clearly expressed in Psalm 110:2-4.

It is important to note that this reuniting of roles and persons is by God's initiative. The initiative is always with God. We humans may think that we have initiated the quest for God and cast out dramatically on our journey to find "truth" and "God." The truth is that even the desire to strike out in search is a response to something God already created within us, a hunger for Himself. We are always the respondents to Christ's initiative. So in the case of the High Priesthood of Christ, the initiative was God's, first in begetting the Son, and then in appointing Him to the high priesthood.

Our author, having accepted this revelational truth, now brings in the scriptural reference to the Son from Psalm 2:7 which he had used in his first chapter and applies it to Jesus Christ under the *middoth* of inference by similarity. That is, if two passages have the same words or connotations, both passages are subject to the same interpretation. Notice the return to the theme of Sonship of the first chapter.

Now he pulls forth a phrase from Psalm 110:4 (also used in chapter 7), and applies this to Christ: *"You are a priest forever."*

The sacrificial and atoning ministry of Christ was central to His purpose, to "save His people from their sins" (Matt. 1:21). He interpreted His death in these sacrificial terms recorded in Matthew 26:26–28.

> And as they were eating, Jesus took bread, blessed it and broke it, and gave it to the disciples and said, "Take, eat; this is My body." Then He took the cup, and gave thanks, and gave it to them, saying, "Drink from it, all of you. For this is My blood of the new covenant, which is shed for many for the remission of sins.

And in Matthew 20:28, Jesus said to the ten, ". . . the Son of Man did not come to be served, but to serve, and to give His life a ransom for many."

The Apostle Paul reflects the mind of the first-century church when he says of Christ: "For indeed Christ, our Passover, was sacrificed for us" (1 Cor. 5:7). It is the writer to the Hebrews who adds to the concept of Christ being the sacrifice that of His being the Priest as well. To establish Christ's connection to the priestly ministry, while at the same time showing the superiority of Christ's priesthood, he could want no better passage than the one just ahead in verse 6 connecting Christ with Melchizedek. Later on we shall come to the exegesis of this verse.

Now we hit a "soft spot" in our writer's movement as the outline momentarily steps back to review. Notice how important to our author is the humanity of Jesus in being identified with the people.

The Importance of Jesus' Humanity

With the words *"who, in the days of His flesh"* (v. 7), our teacher recalls some of the priestly aspects of Christ's ministry, those of offering up *"prayers and supplications, with vehement cries and tears."* This verse was foreshadowed by 2:17, in which the author states: "In all things He had to be made like His brethren, that He might be a merciful and faithful High Priest in things pertaining to God, to make propitiation for the sins of the people." The phrase *"with vehement cries and tears"* reminds us of the prayers of the high priest in the Holy of Holies on the Day of Atonement, uttering the name of the Most High with a loud voice not only to be heard by the people, but as a lament of tearful supplication for the forgiveness of God. In Jewish culture there are said to be three kinds of supplication, each loftier than the preceding—prayer, crying, and tears. Prayer is made in silence; crying with raised voice; but tears overcome all things. According to a contemporary saying, "There is no door through which tears do not pass." This is just the opposite of the stoicism of the Greek philosophy so prevalent at the time.

Our thoughts turn to Christ's prayer in the Garden of Gethsemane (Matt. 26:36–42, Mark 14:32–42) where His prayers were so intense that His sweat was as drops of blood, or to His weeping over the city of Jerusalem (Luke 19:41), or to His wailing at the tomb of Lazarus (John 11:35).

The phrase *"who was able to save Him from death"* might have one of two interpretations, or both. The first would be a saving from the death of the redemptive act (Matt. 26:36–44, Mark 14:32–42). Since the divine purpose was the sacrificial death of the Paschal Lamb, the second interpretation is more probable, the saving from death coming through resurrection, saving not only the life of the Sacrificed, but every person believing and obeying Him.

"[He] *was heard because of His godly fear"* places emphasis again upon Christ's humanity and His humble supplication and dependence upon God. *Eulabeias,* "godly fear," may also be translated "reverence."

Verse 8 continues the theme of the Son's maturing humanity. *"Though He was a Son, yet He learned obedience"* is not to be understood as unlearning disobedient behavior, but rather as the positive experience of a child learning normally to receive an instruction and then respond in obedience. Thus Christ's human growth walked stride for stride with His divine nature without faltering through refusal. He learned flawlessly what all others had to learn, a state of submissiveness to the will of God.

"And having been perfected" again lays the stress upon the process of maturation, through which all of us must pass. This experience of the human soul cannot be bypassed by any human being, not even Jesus Christ. *"He became the author of eternal salvation"* stresses the cause or source of eternal salvation. *"To all who obey Him"* does away forever with the idea of "cheap grace" of Bonhoeffer. Simple intellectual or spiritual belief that does not impact the style of life of the disciple has no place in our author's mind. The cleansing of the conscience in 9:14 is directly tied to the service of God in obedience to His strategy of building the kingdom. The same thought is so bold in

Paul's letter to the Ephesians: "For we are [God's] workmanship, created in Christ Jesus for good works, which God prepared beforehand that we should walk in them" (Eph. 2:10).

With verse 10 the writer closes this introductory passage with its major theme: *"called by God as High Priest according to the order of Melchizedek."* The Greek verb translated as "called," *prosagoreutheis,* has an interesting structure. The root *agoreuō* is a word of the marketplace or the public assembly. To be called out in public, or designated out of the assembled people, is the thrust of its meaning. Notice the emphasis is not upon the otherworldly nature of Christ, but upon His being part of the congregation. Note the connection to the Old Testament quotations used earlier: "In the midst of the congregation [church] I will sing praise to You" (2:12); "Here am I and the children whom God has given Me." (2:13). Have you observed how frequently the teacher emphasizes Christ's identification with us in our earthly pilgrimage? Yet, not even for a moment is the divine character of the Son in jeopardy of de-emphasis.

At this point in his doctrinal discussion, our writer wants to present a difficult and intricate interpretation of the passage from Genesis 14. As mentioned before, he knows the arguments will be tedious and complicated, so he breaks off into the most emotional of his exhortations, reaching the apex of his intensity as he challenges his readers to maturity. Rather than join him in the exhortation at this point, we will jump to chapter 7 and continue with his explanation regarding the priesthood of Melchizedek.

AFTER THE ORDER OF MELCHIZEDEK

1 For this Melchizedek, king of Salem, priest of the Most High God, who met Abraham returning from the slaughter of the kings and blessed him,

2 to whom also Abraham gave a tenth part of all, first being translated "king of righteousness," and then also king of Salem, meaning "king of peace,"

3 without father, without mother, without genealogy, having neither beginning of days nor end of life, but made like the Son of God, remains a priest continually.

4 Now consider how great this man was, to whom even the patriarch Abraham gave a tenth of the spoils.

5 And indeed those who are of the sons of Levi,
who receive the priesthood, have a commandment to
receive tithes from the people according to the law,
that is, from their brethren, though they have come
from the loins of Abraham;

6 but he whose genealogy is not derived from them
received tithes from Abraham and blessed him who
had the promises.

7 Now beyond all contradiction the lesser is blessed
by the better.

8 Here mortal men receive tithes, but there he
receives them, of whom it is witnessed that he lives.

9 Even Levi, who receives tithes, paid tithes
through Abraham, so to speak,

10 for he was still in the loins of his father when
Melchizedek met him.

Heb. 7:1–10

To establish that the third necessary qualification of the High Priest
has been fulfilled, the writer to the Hebrews shows how Jesus Christ
was appointed by God, not by human progeny. The section 7:1–25
may be outlined as follows: (1) an introduction—historical allusion
to Melchizedek in relation to the patriarch Abraham, introducing
the story and the interpretation of names (7:1–2); (2) a consideration
of the twofold greatness of Melchizedek as seen in his never-ending
life and the process of receiving tithes (7:3–10); (3) the reasons for
a new priesthood and the changing of the law regarding priests (7:11–
19); (4) the immutability of Christ's priesthood by virtue of God's
oath in appointing Him (7:20–22); and (5) the result of an unending
priesthood (7:23–25).

The story goes back to Genesis 14. Abraham's nephew, Lot, was
captured when the kings of the city-states of Sodom, Gomorrah,
Admah, Zeboiim, and Zoar were defeated in attempting to free themselves from serving Chedorlaomer, the king of Elam, and his allies.
The kings of Sodom and Gomorrah fled in the rout that followed,
and Lot was captured. Abraham, hearing of the loss of his nephew
and his family, marched his men overnight and surprised the adver-
sary after dividing his force of 318 men into two forces. The defeated
forces fled, leaving their gods behind, which Abraham and his men
gathered up as booty.

On returning from this battle with the kings, Abraham met Melchizedek, king of another city-state called Salem; he was a priest to the Most High God. Abraham gave him a tithe of all that he had captured. In return, Melchizedek blessed him:

> Blessed be Abram of God Most High,
> Possessor of heaven and earth;
> And blessed be God Most High,
> Who has delivered your enemies into your hand.
>
> *Gen. 14:19–20*

Our writer now interprets two names that appear in verse 1, Melchizedek and Salem. He indicates that Melchizedek means "King of righteousness"—*melek* in Hebrew being the word for "king" and *zedek* the word for "righteousness." *Salem,* the city over which he reigned, is the Hebrew word for "peace." The allusion to Christ is unmistakable. King He is—of the kingdom of God that He came to establish. From Him comes the righteousness of cleansing, the result of His atoning sacrifice which makes pure the conscience of the believer. Even as Christ created and filled a "house" with His redeemed people, so also He creates a "city of God" in which the Father is Reigning Monarch. Later the city of Salem is called "city of peace" (in Hebrew, *yer-salem,* or Jerusalem).

The earliest biblical accounts tell us that kings often served as priests. Moses, who after being designated the leader of Israel, in some sense a king, also acted as priest. With the division of ministries in which Moses ordained Aaron his brother and the tribe of Levi to act as the priests, the separation of functions was so complete that no one other than the appointed priestly families was able to offer sacrifice. But now in Christ we see a return of the concept of priesthood and royalty abiding in the same Person.

Our author goes on to note that there is no mention of the genealogy or death of Melchizedek. Beginning with this fact, he argues in a perfectly proper Jewish mode of interpretation from silence. In doing so he leans again upon the *middoth* of Hillel, arguing from silence that because Melchizedek's genealogy is not mentioned, because nothing is said of his father or mother nor of his birth or death, that he was without beginning of days or end of life. The Greek words here are simple and powerful; *apator, ametor, ageneologetos,* meaning without father, without mother, without genealogy. This is definitely an audience-related device. His readers knew of the *middoth* and would be impressed by such an argument, our author calculates. There can be no doubt that this argument is targeted at the particular religious culture of Pharisaic Judaism. It could have had an impact only upon a Semitic mind of Israel.

The argument is again buttressed (in both 5:6 and 7:17) by the quotation from Psalm 110:4: "You are a priest forever after the order of Melchizedek." The implication is undeniable. If Melchizedek has no known beginning nor ending, then he must live forever. Because a priest remains a priest as long as he lives, it is obvious that Melchizedek's priesthood continues uninterrupted.

In saying (in v. 3) that Melchizedek is made like the Son of God, our author implies that the Son was existent before Melchizedek. Indeed, our writer has introduced this idea in the psalm quotations in verses 8 and 10–12 of the epistle's first chapter:

"Your throne, O God, is forever and ever; . . ."

"You, Lord, in the beginning laid the foundation of the earth,
And the heavens are the work of Your hands;
They will perish, but You remain:
And they will all grow old like a garment;
Like a cloak You will fold them up,
And they will be changed,
But You are the same,
And Your years will not fail."

Therefore, Christ is like Melchizedek in that His priesthood will never end because of His unending life.

With verse 4 the author weaves yet another argument in a familiar Jewish pattern. It is that Abraham gave tithes to Melchizedek, obviously the action of a lesser toward a greater, and in doing so, involved Levi and the priests of Israel for all time. The argument is based upon a biological presumption. According to Jewish belief, the children or generations yet unborn were still within the loins of their forebears. Thus Levi and the sons of Levi gave tithes to Melchizedek, so to speak.

In receiving tithes from the people, a kind of superiority is indicated. The Levites, who were by law to receive tithes from the people, were in a special sense the highly honored tribe. This was not considered a tribute due a conqueror, but the similarity of importance is there. The priests were specially designated by God for holy and unique functions within the life of Israel in offering sacrifices. No one else was allowed to perform this function. The sacrifices were to be provided for by the people by means of tithes brought to the priests. An interesting comparison is implied between the Levites and the Son. Whereas the dependency of Levites is upon the obedient tithe-giving of the Israelites, the Son is dependent upon no human resource. This is one more factor of superiority of the Son over the Levitical priests.

Moses indicates his great veneration for the priest to the most high God by giving tithes from the very choicest of the spoils. "Abraham gave tithes from the top of the heap" could be a literal translation of the Greek phrase in verse 4. Given the biological assumption mentioned above, it is quite obvious that the Levites were offering tithes to Melchizedek while in the loins of Abraham.

So for two reasons, one of eternal existence and the other of receiving tithes given in honor, *the lesser is blessed by the better"* (v. 7), and regarding this there can be no argument.

Now in verse 8 our apologist for the superiority of the Son reiterates his point: *"Here mortal men receive tithes, but there he receives them, of whom it is witnessed that he lives."* In *"he lives"* there is a strong implication of immutability. This thought relates to a discussion on oaths at the end of chapter 6, which we will be discussing in chapter 9 of our commentary. The point is that He who makes the oath is immutable, therefore the oath itself is immutable.

THE NEED FOR A NEW PRIESTHOOD

11 Therefore, if perfection were through the Levitical priesthood (for under it the people received the law), what further need was there that another priest should rise according to the order of Melchizedek, and not be called according to the order of Aaron?

12 For the priesthood being changed, of necessity there is also a change of the law.

13 For He of whom these things are spoken belongs to another tribe, from which no man has officiated at the altar.

14 For it is evident that our Lord arose out of Judah, of which tribe Moses spoke nothing concerning priesthood.

116

15 And it is yet far more evident if, in the likeness of Melchizedek, there arises another priest

16 who has come, not according to the law of a fleshly commandment, but according to the power of an endless life.

17 For He testifies:

"You are a priest forever
According to the order of Melchizedek."

18 For on the one hand there is an annulling of the former commandment because of its weakness and unprofitableness,

19 for the law made nothing perfect; on the other hand, there is the bringing in of a better hope, through which we draw near to God.

Heb. 7:11–19

Several things stand tall in the mind of our author. First is his previously expressed thesis that the purpose of religion is to bring the worshiper back into the presence of a holy God by means of a cleansed conscience, having been made holy or sanctified. This he calls perfection (*teleiōsis*). It is this perfection that the old covenant was not able to accomplish. Year after year, it had failed to bring final and lasting cleansing. Its only ability was to give an unsettling reminder of sin, season by season.

Second is his conviction that, as a result of the victorious resurrection of Jesus Christ from the dead, there is available to the believer the power of a cleansed conscience, the experience of holiness for which the whole sacrificial cultus was apparently designed. However, in Christ a new perception regarding the old covenant emerges with stunning impact; the old covenant was only a teaching tool showing how one day the restoration of the relationships between God and believer would actually take place. This reconciliation would be by the one perfect sacrifice of His Son. The law could not accomplish this because it was basically flawed with weakness.

Third, with the witness of the Holy Spirit and the transformed lives of the apostles, it was ecstatically apparent to our author that the perfecting of the worshiper had taken place and he or she could now cry out, "Abba, my very own beloved Father," to the majestic creator of the cosmos. The intimacy was established as promised by Jeremiah (31:31ff); the power had fallen on all flesh, menservants, and handmaidens (Joel 2).

If all this happened because of the life, death, and resurrection of Jesus Christ, then indeed He must be the new High Priest. All this reflection was in the mind and experience of the early church. This one word, "perfection," implies the above apostolic experience of the people of the Way.

So, Jesus Christ is the new High Priest. That fact is taken as a given in our writer's mind. That being so, then the law has to change. This new Priest was not called according to the order of Aaron, but that of Melchizedek. If the law says that the high priest must be from the tribe of Aaron, but He has come from another source, then the law must change. Notice the affirmed and unmovable assurance of the apostolic writers. So certain were they that Christ was the Son, the High Priest, that they were willing, yes, even demanding that the law be set aside. No wonder they were persecuted! "For the priesthood having been changed"—the Greek verb form tells us it has happened (*metatithemenēs*). It is obvious then that *"of necessity there is also a change of the law"* (v. 12).

The reasoning follows in verses 13 and 14: This man *"belongs to another tribe, from which no man has officiated at the altar. For it is evident that our Lord arose from Judah, of which tribe Moses spoke nothing concerning priesthood."* Christ is High Priest, yet the law says He cannot be. Then the law must change.

Not only has the apostolic experience convinced the believing community of the high priesthood of Jesus, but they have also been convinced by His likeness to Melchizedek. There is the very power of His endless life, both in that He was eternally present with God in creation (Heb. 1:10), and that through the power of the resurrection He lives forever. His years will never end (Heb. 1:12).

Now comes an interesting play on words between *prodēlon* (v. 14) and *katadēlon* (v. 15). *"It is evident"* (*prodēlon* [historically clear]) *"that our Lord arose from Judah."* That is a well-known historical fact. But a perceptive fact is added to the next phrase. *"It is yet far more evident"* (*kai perissoteron eti katadēlon estin*) stresses the strong comparative of *perissoteron* in conjunction with *katadēlon* to yield a sense of evidence based on something even more than the historical. This new evidence is based upon the insight that comes from revelation of the life that is miraculously endless by virtue of His resurrection and essentially endless by virtue of His essence, of the same eternal reality as the Father. The laws of the flesh fade into oblivion in the face of the obvious. Our author quotes Psalm 110:4, where God Himself testifies: "You are a priest forever according to the order of Melchizedek."

What else can we say then? We have on one hand the basis of *"an endless life"* (v. 16). The sense here is the power of an indissoluble life, one that cannot be destroyed, cast down, or annulled. In contrast to this term our author now says that the old law must be annulled (v. 18). It is annulled or set aside because of its weakness, and its uselessness or unprofitableness (*anōpheles*, derived from *ophelos*, which means "advantage" or "benefit"). The old law was devoid of either, and thus had to be replaced or set aside. Our author's statement is bold and final: *"the law made nothing perfect"* (v. 19). It brought no worshiper into that restored relationship with God similar to a child's exclaiming joyfully and confidently to its father, "Daddy!"

Moreover, not only has something been annulled and set aside, but in thrilling actuality, the new has come. A new hope has been introduced, a much better hope by which we may draw near to God, satisfying that deep hunger of every life that has been created for an intimate and personal relationship with God. The purpose of religion has been fulfilled; the conscience of the believer has been perfected in a sanctification of holiness that utterly removes all fear of coming into the presence of a holy God.

This greater hope becomes the vehicle by which we "draw near" to God. The sense of the verb used here (*eggizō*) is to bring to or approach as in the intimacy of a relative or family member. This meaning is clearly reminiscent of the promise made in the prophecy of Jeremiah that God will be our God and we will be His people; that we will not have to give theological explanation about God because each one of us will know Him intimately, as a child knows a parent.

THE GREATNESS OF THE NEW PRIEST

20 And inasmuch as He was not made priest without an oath

21 (for they have become priests without an oath, but He with an oath by Him who said to Him:

"The LORD has sworn
And will not relent,
'You are a priest forever
According to the order of Melchizedek' "),

22 by so much more Jesus has become a surety of a better covenant.

23 And there were many priests, because they were
prevented by death from continuing.

24 But He, because He continues forever, has an
unchangeable priesthood.

25 Therefore He is also able to save to the uttermost
those who come to God through Him, since He ever
lives to make intercession for them.

Heb. 7:20–25

Our discipling mentor now pounds another stake deep into the
ground of his Jewish readers to hold their tent of insight firm against
the winds of persecution and doubt. This new stake is an argument
based on their cultural acceptance of oaths.

"Think Hebrew, think Semitic!" We must, if we are to understand
this section of our author's argument to show Christ a superior priest.
His thrust is that Christ is superior because God swore by an oath
in appointing Him high priest whereas no other priest had an appointment secured by an oath. It is obvious that the writer considers this
argument to be a weighty one. An understanding and respect for
oath-making is taken for granted by our writer. He argues upon that
foundation in complete expectation of his reader's being persuaded
by such argument.

Some historical background on oaths will help here to bring our
minds into the milieu of the Semitic culture. Before there were written
contracts, courts, or executive authorities to enforce them, oaths were
the binding social force. Oaths, or *nedarim,* are described to a considerable extent in the Mishnah under the section *Nedarim,* which builds
upon biblical principles gleaned from various incidences of oath-
making. Once taken, oaths were binding and unchangeable. Note the
example of Isaac refusing to withdraw his oath to Jacob even though
"the deceiver" had gained his blessing by subterfuge (Gen. 27). Oaths
were taken very seriously, especially when "sworn by God" or by
some other lasting object. God, of course, was the unchangeable,
the immutable. Therefore anything that did not change could become
the object or surety of an oath. If the surety does not change, then
it will be there to bear witness in the future.

Enter now the legalistic mind. Great intricacies were developed
in the process of oath-taking. Technicalities became the tools of the
knowledgeable and educated. The old human desire to cheat or get
something on a false basis was as rampant then as now. So if you

could convince some poor wretch, unsophisticated in the finer points
of oath-taking, that your oath was valid and trustworthy, when in
actuality it was invalid because of the inferiority of that by which
you swore, then he was the loser; it was his tough luck for being
so naive as to be taken in. The *Nedarim* section of the Mishnah shows
the intricacies of the process. No wonder Christ said in reference to
oath-making, "Let your 'Yes' be 'Yes,' and your 'No,' 'No.' For whatever is more than these is from the evil one" (Matt. 5:37). Our Lord
refers to the human desire to deceive. Yet, for the common man an
oath was the end of an argument, the seal of an agreement. The
greater the object by which one swore, the more lasting the oath.

Moreover, to break an oath implied a curse: "Be it so to me and
more also if. . . ." To attach oneself to some great object by means
of an oath and then not to keep the oath was a kind of blasphemy
against the object by which the oath was sworn. Such a curse was
not taken lightly. Did not the Scriptures give abundant examples
of those who were cursed because of their failure to carry out an
oath?

With this background in mind we can now begin our study of
this section. Jesus is not made Priest without an oath, and this is a
significant factor in His superiority. Other priests did not have such
an oath by which to secure their priesthood. In addition, God swore
by Himself, the Great Unchangeable. If God did not change, then
His oath could never change; He will not change His mind. His oath
is that the Son is appointed High Priest, in the likeness of Melchizedek.

"By so much more" (v. 22) yields a sense of the importance of the
argument. Jesus has become *"a surety,"* which may be interpreted here
as one who puts up bail for a prisoner, a guarantee that something
will be delivered or produced or that someone will appear. Jesus is
that surety of *"a better covenant,"* a new covenant that surpasses the
old one that proved weak and unprofitable to those who depended
upon it for the restored communion with God.

Now our teacher repeats a previous theme verse. Not only is the
Son a guarantee of the new covenant by reason of the oath, but
again, by the fact of His unending life. Many other priests who came
before Him were prevented from continuing as priests because they
died. This Priest, however, *"continues forever"*; therefore His priesthood
is *"unchangeable"* (v. 24), unalterable, permanent, or perpetual.

Here our author concludes his discussion of this third necessary quality of the high priest—appointment—with an engaging thought. Formerly, a priest may have built up some effectiveness with a given worshiper because of his knowledge of the intimate needs or information, but when he died, the warm and understanding ministry was brought to an end. No more would that familiar face and sensitive voice be there to hear the cry or comfort the stunned psyche. The worshiper would have to go through the history-sharing all over again with a new priest, perhaps never being able to reproduce that intimacy and quick understanding born of years of close sharing. Is not this the dynamic we experience in the resignation or death of someone who has been in a long-time pastorate?

Not so with Christ. He is able to save with the deepest sensitivity and understanding those who come to God by Him, because He lives forever to make intercession. *"He is also able to save to the uttermost"* has a marvelously rich meaning—He is quite able to save in an absolute, perfect, and consummated manner. His knowledge of each of us through the years is so complete that there is not a facet of our personalities or relationships that will not come under His sensitive understanding and therapeutic and liberating salvation. Complete, all-encompassing new life will be the result of this High Priest's ministry to us, both because of His great power and His unending life. In His fathomless knowledge and perceiving sensitivity, He makes intercession for us to our everlasting joy. Oh, the greatness of the New Priest!

CHAPTER EIGHT

A Priest Must Be Pure

Hebrews 7:26–28

26 For such a High Priest was fitting for us, who is holy, harmless, undefiled, separate from sinners, and has become higher than the heavens;

27 who does not need daily, as those high priests, to offer up sacrifices, first for His own sins and then for the people's, for this He did once for all when He offered up Himself.

28 For the law appoints as high priests men who have weakness, but the word of the oath, which came after the law, appoints the Son who has been perfected forever.

Heb. 7:26–28

Our exhorter brings us now to the fourth and final qualification of the high priest—purity. Before the high priest could offer sacrifices for the sins of the people, he was required to offer sacrifices for his own sins and those of his household. However, once again our teacher shows the superiority of Christ in stating that this High Priest has no need for offering a sacrifice for Himself, because He is sinless. *"For such a High Priest was fitting for us."* The Greek word for "fitting" may be translated "conspicuously proper" or "obviously suitable." In the characteristic style of our author, the word at once looks backward and forward. In looking backward we are reminded of 2:10: "It was fitting for Him . . . to make the author of their salvation perfect through sufferings." Here in verse 26 of chapter 7, *"such a High Priest was fitting for us,"* that is, for us who have believed and been made holy, not for humanity in general.

Three terms are used to describe this High Priest. This first is *hosios, "holy."* Another word that could also be translated "holy" might have been used here: *hagios. Hagios* has the sense of that which has been cleansed of impurity and made ready for some special use of God. In the process it is cleansed, sanctified, set aside for a sacred use. Thus we sinners are *hagioi,* those cleansed and set apart for a holy use of God. *Hosios,* on the other hand, describes the primary moral quality of a person or thing, that which of itself is pure without cleansing. Such a person is one who does perfectly that prescribed by God, who is utterly pure in His eyes and yields to no temptation. The one who yields to no temptation is the one who knows its full power. To withstand temptation to the point of victory is to experience its last full measure of intensity. In such a battle, temptation has utterly expended itself, exhausted its power, without success. Those who give in to temptation do so prior to its full expression and so never know its full power. Christ was tempted not only in all things, but with the full power of the Tempter; He alone knew the full intensity of temptation.

The second term is *akakos,* translated *"harmless."* It comes from *kakos* meaning "bad, ugly, mean, base, or cruel." Christ was just the opposite. He was unknowing of ill or evil intentions, therefore guileless. He was innocent of false motivation, simple in truthfulness, not filled with duplicity. In His relations to others, He was undamaging, healing, and beneficent. He was so filled with love that His reaction to injury was love—automatic, natural, spontaneous; "Father, forgive them; they do not know what they are doing." His every act uplifted, improved, ennobled. Were He to have walked down the endless line of humanity and looked searchingly into every eye, imploring each to answer His question, "Have I in any way injured you?," the heartfelt response would come back in every instance, "In no way, Friend and Master; You have blessed me in every facet, every moment of my life!"

The third term, *amiantos,* translated *"undefiled,"* also means pure, without any moral blemish that would keep Him from God. The earthly high priest had to be without blemish, but the blemishes proscribed were physical; he could not be lame, blind, mutilated in his face, or have a limb too long; he was not to have an injured foot or hand; he could not be a hunchback or dwarf, nor could he have a defect in sight, an itching disease, scabs, crushed testicles, or any other physical abnormality. However, no mention was made of the moral or spiritual requirements for priesthood.

The next phrase, *"separate from sinners,"* should not be construed as denying the humanity of Jesus but rather putting Him in a category by Himself as One uniquely without blemish. If one were to sort out all of humanity into the completely whole and without blemish over against those imperfect and blemished, Jesus would stand alone. His humanity was the only example of that which God had designed it to be: undistorted.

"And has become higher than the heavens" most probably refers to His escalation in ascension, His being forever part of the Godhead in His resurrected form, at the right hand of power.

In verse 27 our teacher now turns to the process by which the earthly priests were cleansed for their ritual duties. The *Mishnah* describes this process in the section *Yoma.* The high priest is taken from his house to the Counselors' Chamber. A stand-in is prepared for, if for any reason the high priest cannot perform the ritual; even a spare wife is selected in case of the death of his wife so that he may have a "household" for which to confess sins. For seven days he must receive and toss the blood of the Daily Whole Offering, burn the incense, trim the lamps, and offer the sacrifice. He may do so on other days only if he is minded to do so.

Then representative elders of the Court read the prescribed portions regarding the ritual, refreshing his mind on the things to be done. On the eve of the Day of Atonement they deliver him to the elders of the priest who adjure him that he is a delegate of the Court and should change nothing they have read to him. He then reads from the Scriptures if he is able, or they read to him, and if he is a teacher he exposits upon them.

On the Day of Atonement he immerses himself five times, and he sanctifies his hands and feet ten times. He then receives the blood of the Daily Whole Sacrifice, tosses the blood, and goes inside to burn the morning incense and trim the lamps. He then immerses himself again and dons the white garments made of fine linen.

At this moment the bullock he has chosen and purchased with his own money is brought to him. He places both hands upon it and makes confession for the sins of his household and for himself, saying:

> O God, I have committed iniquity, transgressed, and sinned before thee, I and my house. O God, forgive the iniquities and transgressions and sins which I committed and transgressed and sinned before thee, I and

my house, as it is written in the Law of thy servant Moses, "For on this day shall atonement be made for you to cleanse you; from all your sins shall ye be clean before the Lord."

Yoma 3:8

He then slaughtered the bullock and received its blood in a basin, offered the incense within the Holy of Holies, and finally offered the blood of the bullock at the altar for his sins and the sins of his household. Every year, century after century, this sacrifice was offered.

In the case of Jesus Christ, however, He offered no sacrifice for Himself; He was sinless and without blemish. He offered but one sacrifice and that was for the people of the world, once and for all time. With this thought, the author begins his short transition into the subject of chapters 10, 11, and 12, that of the Ministry of the Priest.

He closes out this section with a brief summary statement of verse 28, which we have covered above. Now it is time to go back and consider the exhortation passage, "Go On to Maturity!" (5:11—6:20).

CHAPTER NINE

A Third Exhortation: "Go On to Maturity!"

Hebrews 5:11—6:20

Spiritual Immaturity

11 of whom we have much to say, and hard to explain, since you have become dull of hearing.

12 For though by this time you ought to be teachers, you need someone to teach you again the first principles of the oracles of God; and you have come to need milk and not solid food.

13 For everyone who partakes only of milk is unskilled in the word of righteousness, for he is a babe.

14 But solid food belongs to those who are of full age, that is, those who by reason of use have their senses exercised to discern both good and evil.

Heb. 5:11–14

Our exhorter wastes no time getting into this next section. The transition is sudden, lacking the "dance" he sometimes goes through in making his transition out of doctrine into exhortation or back again, a "dance" that often leaves the reader in confusion as far as an outline is concerned. His attitude is one of tough love. He states the spiritual immaturity of his readers straightforwardly. "[*About this difficult doctrine of Melchizedek*] *we have much to say, and* [*it is*] *hard to explain, since you have become dull of hearing.*" A more literal translation might even have a touch of humor in it, "You have become dull in the ears." The Greek adjective here, *nōthros,* meaning "sluggish," "torpid," "having lost momentum," "dead in the water," "apathetic," or "dormant," carries strong implications.

The reason for the torpor of those for whom the letter is meant—

is it not their spiritual immaturity? Our exhorter is making a crescendo to the emotional peak of the epistle. His statements are almost shocking, and meant to be. They had been Christians for some time now; ordinary growth would have them capable of teaching others the faith, but here they are, hesitatingly mumbling through their ABCs. He sees no excuse for this whatsoever. *"For . . . by this time you ought to be teachers"* (v. 12). Reproduction for the sake of the Kingdom; that's the name of the game! And yet here they are needing to go over basic principles; they are like children who can't get off the bottle or the breast. Pablum is too much for them; solid food causes them to choke. With cutting clarity he states the diagnosis: everyone who is limited to milk is *"unskilled"* (*apeiros*, from *peirazō*, which means "to test or prove") *"in the word of righteousness,"* that is, the teaching regarding God's imputed righteousness. They lacked experience which belongs to endeavor, understanding which belongs to practice and familiarity. In short, such a person is a baby (*nēpios*, "suckling child"). Solid food is for the mature (*teleiōn*), those who have arrived at a functional level of competence, who have attained to operational ability according to their potential and design (*telos*).

It is this thought frame that tells us a great deal of the apostolic mindset. The Apostle John declared that everyone is made by Jesus Christ. Nothing, no person, exists that was not created by Him (John 1:1–3). Moreover, according to the Apostle Paul this Christ was the Image of the Invisible God who created all things and gave a purpose to every item of creation, including each individual (Col. 1:15–16). This purpose (*telos*) gives a dynamic reason for life; when realized, a sense of deep satisfaction. But the reason or purpose is not for the individual's joy alone; it is for the kingdom of God and the praise of Christ (Eph. 1:12). The condition of maturity (*teleiotēs*) is described by the adjective "mature" (*teleios*). So why all the emotion from our author? He sees his readers failing to arrive at that maturity which is so necessary for the proper functioning of the kingdom. They treat carelessly the holiness of God's sovereign purpose. Endeavor, practice, sweat, agony of perseverance, and experience through involvement are the components that make for maturity, and he sees little or none of these. They are yet where they began—at the starting gate, still in their blocks at the starting line while others are well into the race; babies needing to be suckled by a wet-nurse.

Such a condition is unacceptable to him; he is stirred, agitated, angry, and concerned. He must encounter them with a loving honesty to stimulate them to go on to maturity.

A Passionate Exhortation

1 Therefore, leaving the discussion of the
elementary principles of Christ, let us go on to
perfection, not laying again the foundation of
repentance from dead works and of faith toward God,
2 of the doctrine of baptisms, of laying on of hands,
of resurrection of the dead, and of eternal judgment.
3 And this we will do if God permits.

Heb. 6:1–3

The exhortation is clear: go on to maturity! Our author is saying,
"Leave the elementals; go on to maturity; and this you can do if
God permits." Here are three aspects of the early church's understanding of the Christian life and discipleship that may be summarized
even more briefly: "Come," "Get ready," "Go."

The first phase of the Christian life begins with an invitation from
Jesus Christ, "Come to Me, all you who labor and are heavy laden,
and I will give you rest" (Matt. 11:28). Numerous times He beckons,
"Come, follow Me." He takes the initiative and knocks upon the
doors of our hearts promising that if we open the door He will enter
and eat with us in a covenant relationship. When we respond, a
new birth takes place, a birth of our spirit from the Holy Spirit,
and we become newborn babes. This invitation comes to us in the
preaching or proclamation of the word (*kerygma*). It is to this phase
that the writer to the Hebrews alludes when he says, "We must
give the more earnest heed to the things we have heard. . . . spoken
by the Lord, and . . . confirmed to us by those who heard Him"
(2:1, 3).

The metaphors include those of new birth (John 3:1–11), of
Christ entering our lives as a house and dwelling there in covenant
eating (Rev. 3:20), or His dwelling with us, actually pitching
His tent in our lives (John 14:23). In this phase we are newborn
babes.

The second phase of the Christian life is that of teaching (*didachē*),
or nurture (*paideia,* training of a child, educating), in order to stimulate
growth. In this vein our exhorter chides his readers for still being
in infancy, which requires breast-feeding, as it were—milk. Our author is not the only one to use this terminology. Paul speaks of milk
in a passage very much like this one where he is on the backs of
the Corinthian Christians to go on to maturity. "And I, brethren,

could not speak to you as to spiritual people but as to carnal, as to babes in Christ. I fed you with milk and not with solid food; for until now you were not able to receive it, and even now you are still not able" (1 Cor. 3:1–2). Peter mentions the milk of nurture; "As newborn babes, desire the pure milk of the word, that you may grow thereby, if indeed you have tasted that the Lord is gracious" (1 Pet. 2:2–3).

This basic milk in the mind of our author includes elementary principles, that is, teaching basic doctrine: the foundation of repentance from dead works, faith toward God, the doctrine of baptisms, of laying on of hands, of resurrection of the dead, and of eternal judgment. Evidently, these were foundational elements of the faith taught by the catechists of the early church to the new converts; this was the milk.

Solid food and strong meat belonged to later stages of growth, but the purpose of this nurture was to stimulate a maturity characterized by fruit-bearing or functional production according to design. Matthew records the teachings of Christ regarding soils that support a growth resulting in harvest of thirty, sixty, or a hundredfold (Matt. 13:4–8, 13). Paul speaks of Christ's creating all things for Himself, His giving every human being a holy purpose in life. To this end, Paul warns and teaches every person in order to bring each one to maturity in Christ (Col. 1:28). This is the sense of our teacher who desires maturity (*teleiotēta*) in his readers, not this repetitious babbling of infants. The goal of the Christian life is fruit-bearing, which is an honoring and glorification of the Father (John 15:7–8), expressed in ministering to the world for which He so deeply cares. Maturity in the New Testament sense is never simply a matter of personal attributes, but developed attitudes and abilities accomplishing the mandate Christ gave to His church.

The third phase of the Christian life is that of ministry or mission, the "Go" of the apostolic mandate (*diakonia*). The first instance of this mandate is the inaugural sermon of Jesus in the synagogue of His hometown, Nazareth. Reading from the lection of the day, Isaiah 61, He said,

"The Spirit of the Lord is upon Me,
Because He has anointed Me to preach the gospel to the poor.
He has sent Me to heal the brokenhearted,
To preach deliverance to the captives

And recovery of sight to the blind,
To set at liberty those who are oppressed,
To preach the acceptable year of the Lord."

Luke 4:18–19

In Matthew 10 He sends out the twelve with authority to cast out demons; to heal the sick and those with emotional softness who are so easily bruised by life; to preach the imminence of the kingdom of God, the cleansing of lepers, the raising of the dead.

Later in that same Gospel, He sets the criteria by which the nations and the members of the kingdom will be judged; by feeding the hungry, giving water to the thirsty, welcoming the stranger, clothing the naked, visiting the sick and the imprisoned (Matt. 25:31–46).

In the closing verses of his Gospel, Matthew records Jesus as instructing His disciples to go into all the world and preach to all creatures, baptizing them and teaching them in all the things He had commanded (Matt. 28:16–20).

Luke reports Christ's promise that after the Holy Spirit came upon them, the disciples would receive power and become His witnesses in Jerusalem, in all Judea and Samaria and to the ends of the earth (Acts 1:6–8).

We might summarize this apostolic mandate as one to the spiritual, intellectual, physical, social, economic, political, and human needs of all humanity—a whole gospel to the whole person in the whole world. There is no evidence whatsoever that the Gospel was divided into a dichotomy of soul-saving or social action. Both were part of one great plan to touch every human need with the power of the gospel of Jesus Christ. The fulfillment of the mandate was the evidence of maturity (*teleiotēs*) to these early Christian teachers and exhorters.

This was no philosophical concept for speculative discussion, but a compelling urgency born of the heart of a God whose passion and concern ran deep and periodically erupted in great acts of liberation and ministry. Moses felt that compassion and activity when he discovered something about this God who was speaking to him from the burning bush. He was a God who saw their suffering, heard their cry, and intimately knew their pain. These three sensory verbs revealed the sensitivity of God to human conditions. Then Moses discovered something else of God; He notified Moses that He had come down to deliver His people from the hand of the Egyptians, but moreover, ordered Moses to be part of that campaign of liberation. Moses, appalled at the command, stammered and stuttered his resistance, citing his stuttering and his knowledge of the kind of reaction he would receive from the pharaoh. God, however, was adamant in His determination, and He promised to Moses the resources necessary for the mission.

It is this same God who sends forth the apostles in the power of the Spirit to accomplish the purpose of His will. This purpose was and is the *telos* of every Christian. Each of us is provided with some gift of the Spirit for our participation in the mission to the world. There is no room for either languid lolling nor individualism that denies the Body (the church) and its interdependent functions. The world is out there, hurting, blind, ignorant, oppressed, imprisoned, sick, alienated, in spiritual darkness, and without God or hope. Our author exhorts, "Get on with it; grow to your ministry potential; touch that world with the redeeming love of Jesus Christ in every facet of its agonizing need!"

Yes, Jesus Christ calls us to Himself in a cleansing forgiveness made possible by His single and sufficient sacrifice; yes, we look into His eyes and see there the acceptance and love that utterly convince us that we are forgiven and children of the living God. But then, even as we are looking into His eyes, they leave ours and look beyond us to a world in such desperate need that we see the tears of concern and a stern determination that in turn fills our eyes with the same resolve. The next time His eyes meet ours, they are compelling in their invitation that we should follow Him out into the streets and nations of the earth to proclaim, enlighten, touch, heal, liberate, and be part of that seething throng that God intensely wishes to touch—through His church. Our consciences are "cleansed to serve the living God" (Heb. 9:14). Let us remember: "We are [God's] workmanship, created in Christ Jesus for good works, which God prepared beforehand that we should walk in them" (Eph. 2:10). This is the maturity our writer longs to see in the lives of his readers. Nothing less will satisfy.

"And this we will do if God permits" (v. 3). If God permits? His whole being pulsates with a passion that His church may rise to the imperial design. For that accomplishment He has cleansed the church and provided it, as He provided Moses, with every resource required for the operation. For that purpose of His will, through our teacher, He now goads His people to their readiness and maturity.

132

A Warning Concerning Apostasy

4 For it is impossible for those who were once enlightened, and have tasted the heavenly gift, and have become partakers of the Holy Spirit,

5 and have tasted the good word of God and the powers of the age to come,

6 if they fall away, to renew them again to repentance. . . .

Heb. 6:4–6a

A simplified restatement of this warning might be: "It is impossible to restore again to repentance believers who fall away." With this passage we enter into the controversy that has surrounded the epistle from early days. Novatian, a Roman presybter, although quite orthodox in his views of Christology and the Trinity, nevertheless was a rigorist in matters pertaining to those who had defected the faith during the persecution of Decius (A.D. 249–50). Decius was the first Roman emperor to persecute Christians in a systematic manner, requiring that all show evidence of having sacrificed to the emperor. Many submitted, although others escaped either by means of bribery or through flight. After Decius's death (251), a great debate developed between Cyprian and Novatius regarding the lapsed or apostate— whether or not they could be included in the life of the church, or should suffer lifelong excommunication. Novatian was consecrated rival bishop of Rome and pled this epistle as reason for not offering concession to the lapsed. For this reason the Western church took a dim view of accepting this epistle into the canon.

We must remember that this epistle was written during a period of growing persecution (12:4) that had not yet come to its full force; our author appears to be a preludal figure for the rigorism of later periods.

In addition to controversy concerning the treatment of the lapsed, controversy exists also with regard to the eternal security of believers. Dispute about this passage may possibly have caused this epistle to be a "forgotten epistle" among reformed scholars. Strong differences of opinion swirl around the first phrase of this section: *'It is impossible. . . .'* Some would take the Greek word *adunaton* to mean "rare" or "difficult," but not Chrysostom. He claims the renewing of a lapsed believer is not a matter of its being fitting or proper (*prepei*), nor agreeable, fit, or profitable (*sumpherei*), nor allowable or possible (*exesti*), but rather *"impossible,"* (*adunaton*), without capacity or ability. Interestingly, Calvin appears to agree with the possibility of this "perfidy so heinous." He says, "Satan stealthily creeps upon us, and by degrees allures us by clandestine arts so that when we go astray we know not that we are going astray. Thus gradually we slide, until at length we rush headlong into ruin."[1] After convincing the reader that such falling away is possible, he then states this is so only for reprobates but not for the elect.

Let us turn to the various terms used in this section. What is the description given by our author of those falling away?

They were *"once enlightened"* (*apax phōtisthentas*). *Apax* in the New Testament often has the sense of uniqueness and finality, "once for all." The term "enlightened" is common in the New Testament and almost always means a radical transference out of the condition of darkness into the light of the gospel, into fellowship or relationship with Jesus Christ (see Col. 1:13; 1 Thess. 5:4; 1 Pet. 2:9; 1 John 1:6). It is difficult to separate this term from the experience of salvation.

They *"have tasted the heavenly gift."* Does this mean tasting only in part, as one tastes a morsel of food, but without committing oneself to truly imbibe? Our author's use of this word elsewhere may give us a clue. In 2:9, where he speaks of Christ's tasting death for every one, he certainly meant not simply a morsel but eating in the fullest sense. Calvin describes tasting in these words: ". . . the things which Christ confers on us above nature and the world, and are yet tasted by faith."[2]

They *"have become partakers of the Holy Spirit."* *Metoxous,* translated "partakers," means a sharing, or partnership. To partake in the Holy Spirit was the verifying experience of inclusion in the company of Christ.

They *"have tasted the good word of God"*—in Calvin's words, "the sweet testimony of God's love," in contrast to the "law's severity and condemnation."[3]

They have tasted *"the powers of the age to come,"* which again Calvin describes as being "admitted by faith as it were into the Kingdom of Heaven so that we see in spirit the blessed immortality which is hid from our senses."

We might add to these a portion of 10:26, they "have received the knowledge of the truth." The Greek word used in 10:26 for "knowledge," *epignosis,* is most often used in the New Testament to mean that intimate knowledge promised in Jeremiah 31 or experienced by Christians as the knowledge of God, Jesus Christ, or of truth that comes from the revelation of Him (Eph. 1:17). Moreover, 10:29 describes such a person as having been sanctified by the blood of the covenant. It is extremely difficult to deny that our author is speaking of those who have become Christians in the apostolic sense.

If such persons *"fall away"* (6:6) it is impossible to restore them again to repentance. The term employed for "fall away" should most probably be interpreted as the most radical sort of falling away because of the radical judgment that results; such persons cannot be renewed again (*palin anakainizein*) to repentance (*eis metanoian*). *Anakainizō* and *anakainoō* ("to renew or cause to be renewed"), when intensified with *palin* ("again"), emphasize the former repentance that cannot be repeated. The redundance is purposeful. *Metanoia* ("repentance; change of mind, or alteration in decision-making") must certainly be that first and life-changing confession of Jesus Christ as Savior and Lord.

If one has experienced all that has described the believer in the above phrases and then turns his back on such a Savior, how under any circumstances can he crawl back? Is this a psychological impossibility or a spiritual impossibility?

DRAMATIC REASONING

6 . . . they crucify again for themselves the Son
of God, and put Him to an open shame.
7 For the earth which drinks in the rain that often
comes upon it, and bears herbs useful for those by
whom it is cultivated, receives blessing from God;
8 but if it bears thorns and briars, it is rejected
and near to being cursed, whose end is to be burned.
Heb. 6:6b-8

The reasons for our author's deliberate stand are no less dramatic than his description of the lapsed believer.

He turns to simple but devastating indictment as the rationale for denying the possibility of renewing such to repentance. First, *"they crucify again for themselves the Son of God."* Having tasted the sweet salvation of God and the witness of the Holy Spirit, they now rail on Christ and nail Him to the cross again, with their own hands. They show the same ridicule and despising hatred of that first hostile crowd who shouted, "Crucify Him!" They mock and jeer at the One who had given them forgiveness; they brutally lash at Him with whips and cruelly offer Him vinegar when His throat is parched with the thirst of dying. Could such a one be reinstated to repentance? Impossible!

Second, they *"put Him to an open shame."* The Greek word used here means to put to open ridicule or to make a mockery or example of someone. Here it signifies those who have turned with derision on one who has sacrificed all for their benefit. This would be comparable to the treatment of a poor mother, who, determined to give her son the best opportunity in life, works her aging body to its limits of fatigue; she skimps and sacrifices herself and every resource unstintingly to put him through school and watches him march into the very best segments of society. This same son, now a striking success, openly ridicules her before his fashionable associates, sneering at her rough hands, laughing at her uncultured speech, or blatantly mimicking her uncouth manners.

When those former believers treat the unparalleled love of Jesus with raucous laughter of disdain and regard His fathomless forgiveness as a circus sideshow of ridiculous naïveté and absurdity—could such ones be reinstated to repentance? Impossible!

Our author presents the image of earth that brings forth a good harvest as a result of the rain falling upon it. It is blessed by the love of its master. But if such a land, having received of the nurturing care and toilsome labor brings forth thorns and thistles, the farmer must burn it over to kill the seed lest another harvest like this one be repeated in a coming season.

UNEXPECTED ENCOURAGEMENT

9 But, beloved, we are confident of better things concerning you, yes, things that accompany salvation, though we speak in this manner.

10 For God is not unjust to forget your work and labor of love which you have shown toward His name, in that you have ministered to the saints and do minister.

11 And we desire that each one of you show the
same diligence to the full assurance of hope until the
end,

12 that you do not become sluggish, but imitate
those who through faith and patience inherit the
promises.

Heb. 6:9–12

Here our exhorter makes a sudden change in tactics. The previous
passage has been tough, an alarming warning, a shock that has undoubtedly raised both the anxiety and ire of his readers. Now he
shifts emphasis into a soothing, encouraging, and hope-filled statement of confidence.

The first word sets the tone: *"we are confident"* (*pepeismetha*, which
may well have as its root *peisma*, a ship's cable to the anchor), as
we shall see in just a few verses (6:19). The writer holds to a firm
conviction, strong as a cable, that better things accompany salvation.
He is almost self-conscious of the tough manner in which he has
spoken for he calls attention to it: *"though we speak in this manner."*

I have noticed in my own teaching that when I come to this section,
or to any warning of a severe nature, the listeners make haste to
embrace the daggers of rejection, expressing their readiness to believe
they have lost their salvation by some past deed. I find myself rushing
up reinforcements to assure them that better things do indeed await
them. The human personality is prone to self-deprecation or doubt,
always willing to believe the worst about itself. Such is the price
of Satan's despicable work among us; he is well named "Accuser."

In our determination as disciplers, let us not make the mistake of
many parents or coaches who do nothing but belittle their charges,
thinking that by so doing they increase the determination toward
better effort. Without positive encouragement and the affirmation
of their potential, people begin to think of themselves as incapable
or stupid, labeling themselves "Dummy!" Worse yet is thinking that
someone has given up on you; that is rejection supreme! Coaches
lose both affection and motivation that way.

Our author wants no part of that kind of stimulation. He is ready
with his affirmation—*"beloved"* (*agapētoi*). He continues to add other
statements of ego-fortification, mentioning that their God is not so
unjust as to forget their *"work and labor of love"* ("labor of" is left out
in most texts) which they have *"shown toward His name."* Moreover,
they have ministered to the saints in the past and continue to minister

at the time of the writing. All these terms and phrases escort us into a chamber of a family, a place of community and belonging. They have been sedulous, avid, diligent, of untiring spirit ministering to other members of the family. These labors have been in the name of the Lord and to the saints with whom they share the experience of the Holy Spirit.

One is reminded of Christ's statement that those who feed the hungry, clothe the naked, and give water to the thirsty are actually ministering to Him (Matt. 25:39–40). Paul's statement in 2 Corinthians 9:12 also comes to mind, in which he says they both minister to the saints and thanksgiving is given to God. The emphasis is that of the outflow of salvation, not its cause. God has granted His salvation by sheer grace, and the works flow forth as a result, out of the grateful heart that recognizes the full purpose of salvation. Take heart; God will not forget your good works; they will not escape His notice.

Now notice a personality characteristic of our writer; he cannot state all this affirmation just for itself; rather, it becomes a platform for his persistent purpose—to goad his readers on toward a mature faith. Works are fine and good, but his concern in this section is the clarity of their faith.

Thus in verse 11 he leaps upon the platform of their good works and urges that just as they have done these good works, they might show or prove the same diligence in pursuing their faith. The exhorter expresses the depth of his own longing for their spiritual progress by the use of the verb *epithumeō, "desire."* The word means not just a wish, but a driving passion. When used elsewhere in the New Testament, it stands either for the passion of the flesh in the debased or for the constraint of Christ. It can be the craving for meat in the wilderness (Num. 11:34) or the passions of the flesh (Gal. 5:17; Matt. 5:28). It can express the desire to be a bishop or elder (1 Tim. 3:1) or Christ's desire to eat the Passover (Luke 22:15).

Why do those who discipled the early believers feel such passionate desire? Their intense concern is for the disciples to come to a full assurance of hope that will see them all the way to the end without a moment of faltering. The *"full assurance of hope"* has the connotation of bringing hope to its full measure or complete satisfaction. Is hope the source of this satisfaction or is satisfaction described as hope? Either can be the case, most probably. We will discuss this further in verses 19 and 20. For now, notice two things. First, this assurance of hope is as a catalyst that sets the believer's heart immovably on Christ. In a day of threatened intensity of persecution, it was very important that every believer hold rank and not break in retreat. To fail to hold would be disastrous to the morale of the whole body. The catalyst set the solution so that it could no longer be altered.

When my two older boys, Dan and Tim, were in high school, they had a business making surfboards in La Jolla, California, where one of the favorite sports was surfing. Dan would design the boards to the custom specifications for speed, weight of the surfer, and the type of surfing desired. Then would come the sizing with the power plane, the sanding, and final shaping. Truly, the finished blank looked like a magnificent piece of sculpture. Then Tim did the glassing, in which fiberglass was secured to the board by a resin that was the consistency of thick cream. He would mix a very exact proportion of catalyst depending on temperature and the speed with which he wanted it to "go off." With the fiberglass all cut and prefit and the mixture ready, the hasty process of glassing would proceed without *any* interruption. They would work quickly, with amazing dexterity, to have all the edges smoothed out by the time the catalyst hardened the mixture. My study was just above the garage where this was going on and every once in awhile I would hear frantic shouts for assistance and expeditious manipulation: "Hurry, it's going off!" Once it was hardened, there was nothing they could do to change its configuration. It was *set!*

This is how our author looks upon full assurance. It is that catalyst that sets forever firm in the heart of the believer the eternal hope that will hold firm to the end. No amount of tugging or pressure from the persecutors would be able to alter the direction and commitment of the heart possessing full assurance.

This assurance would hold firm *"until the end"* (*achri telous*). *Achri* has the sense of "as far as" or "utterly, without pause, without faltering or cessation." *Telous* means not just the end interim of time, but of completion, having fulfilled a purpose or design.

The second thing to notice is the relation between diligence and hope. Diligence flags when hope deteriorates. When the light at the end of the tunnel goes out, a numbing darkness moves in upon the human spirit, chilling and enervating it, dissipating its energy. Motivation leaks quickly from the heart and a listless resignation spreads its wet blanket over the hot coals of our desires. What things destroy hope? Fatigue? Yes, it distorts the perception, making molehills look like mountains. Loss of success, absence of results? Yes, these cause us to lack confidence in the effectiveness of our belief or labors. Doubt of ultimate victory? Certainly. If we don't win after all our effort, what's the use? Under these conditions, diligence stumbles and falls exhausted beside the road, forsaking its goal, apostate. Is this why our teacher is so passionate in his desires that the believers come to a full assurance of hope and understand what victory Christ has won and will win? I believe it.

In verse 12 we see him continuing his reasoning. Hope must continue so *"that you do not become sluggish"* (*nōthroi*). Here compare sluggishness with zeal, earnestness. Hope gives zeal; lack of it produces torpor and loss of motivation. He desires that they be followers (*mimētai*, "mimics") of those whose faith and patience inherit the promises. The word translated "faith" is *makrothumia* (*makro*, "large"; *thumia*, "emotions" or "passions"). It could be translated "large emotions," signifying wells of endurance that will not dry up, no matter how much is drawn from them. The Christian with this patience will have refreshing water to sustain continual effectiveness even in the face of unrelenting pressures. Those with such patience and faith are those who receive or *"inherit the promises."*

This last phrase is a transitional one. It leads into the theme of promises as the immovable foundation upon which confidence is built.

THE IMMUTABLE PROMISE OF GOD

13 For when God made a promise to Abraham, because He could swear by no one greater, He swore by Himself,

14 saying, *"Surely blessing I will bless you, and multiplying I will multiply you."*

15 And so, after he had patiently endured, he obtained the promise.

16 For men indeed swear by the greater, and an oath for confirmation is for them an end of all dispute.

17 Thus God, determining to show more abundantly to the heirs of promise the immutability of His counsel, confirmed it by an oath,

18 that by two immutable things, in which it is impossible for God to lie, we might have strong consolation, who have fled for refuge to lay hold of the hope set before us.

19 This hope we have as an anchor of the soul,
both sure and steadfast, and which enters the Presence
behind the veil,
20 where the forerunner has entered for us, even
Jesus, having become High Priest forever according to
the order of Melchizedek.

Heb. 6:13–20

This section continues the exposition on hope, a most important and critical element if Christians are to stay loyal to Christ their Lord in a day of increasing persecution. The winds of diabolical temptation are increasing in their force, tending to blow Christians off their course and against the rocky shores of apostasy where they will be dashed to pieces and destroyed. What can hold them on course? Is it not an unwavering hope, a confidence in the Person of the Priest and His perfect sacrifice that opens to them a way into the presence of God at all times?

How to deepen and confirm this hope is the challenge on our author's mind. His response is this section on the promise of God which God then also secures with an oath.

When God made a promise to Abraham, that was enough in itself. God does not make idle promises and what He makes He keeps. Remember the threefold nature of that covenant: (1) that God would give Abraham offspring as numerous as the stars or the sands of the sea; (2) that God would provide those offspring with a land of their own, a good land flowing with milk and honey; and (3) that God would bless all the nations of the earth through these offspring (Gen. 12:1–3). After Abraham has been willing to offer his miracle son as a sacrifice to God, showing his complete and utter trust of Him (Gen. 22:15–18), God adds to His promise and oath in order to secure it even more firmly in the mind of Abraham and those who come after. It cannot change, regardless of the circumstances that swarm about God's people.

Let us review now the previous discussion of 7:20–22 in which we perused the cultural setting of oaths (see pp. 120–21). The basis of an oath's validity was the unchangeableness of the things by which one swore. If one were to swear by some unchangeable object, then it would be blaspheming that object if the oath were not carried through.

Here God not only promises to bless and multiply Abraham, but

141

He also swears to accomplish it. Thus there is a double certainty. It is impossible for God to lie under any circumstances and certainly under this double guarantee. The promise is secure.

The fulfillment of the promise, however, is not immediate. So long a time elapsed that Abraham and Sarah became concerned enough to take things into their own hands. Sarah suggested Abraham have a child by her handmaid, which would be born on her knees as a symbol that the child would be the heir of their house. It was not until Abraham was one hundred years old that the promise was fulfilled, a decade and a half after it was first given.

I am sure this gap between promise and fulfillment was in our teacher's mind as he exhorted his readers. If things appear slow with God, that does not mean He has forgotten, nor that He will not perform. Even as Abraham waited patiently and was rewarded for his faith, so too, believers of this time must wait patiently and not lose heart. The Greek word translated *"patiently"* (*makrothumēsas*) in verse 15 emphasizes the untiring emotion of Abraham in waiting for the promise. He then *"obtained the promise."* Verse 16 summarizes the thesis: If an oath among men confirms a word and ends all strife, how much more should the oath of God end all unbelief or doubt? Who is greater than God? By what greater object can anyone swear? None whatever! God is to be trusted!

Verses 17 and 18 express the results of this oath-making. God, determining to show even more than sufficiently *"to the heirs of promise the immutability of His counsel, confirmed it by an oath."* The powerful result is that we have a *"strong consolation."* The word *paraklēsis* ("consolation") has the meaning of calling (*kaleō*) alongside (*para*) as though shouting encouragement or instruction in the midst of confusion, thus legal counsel. This mobile exhortation becomes even more important when the recipient is in dire straits and in flight. His readers evidently are experiencing a refugee flight from some condition, or soon will be. What can we trust? Whom can we believe? What is there to hold onto in the midst of this violent storm that tosses our ship and threatens its very integrity? But our encourager sends calls across to his own listeners and hails them with the good news that there is such a hold in the tempest. It is the hope that has already been set before them, which they grasp with firmness and trust to hold them against the tides of the storm.

Using a sailing metaphor, he describes this hope in verses 19 and 20. The hope is an *"anchor"* (*ankura*) *"of the soul, both sure"* (*asphalē*, also "steadfast, secure, safe, sound, unyielding") *"and steadfast"* (*bebaian,* "reliable, established, guaranteed"). These are characteristics that sailors long for in an anchor holding them against a storm.

While serving in Korea in the occupation forces after the Second World War, I was stationed on a repair ship in the harbor of Inchon. At times the tides there ran at thirteen knots. We were anchored in a bay a few hundred yards off shore with only a few fathoms of water. The bottom was muddy and not at all firm, so the anchor had a tendency to shift in high tides and high winds. One night, in the midst of a storm, the ship pulled its anchor sufficiently to put us in jeopardy of grounding. We started our two V-12 diesels and began resetting our anchor. In the process we bent one of our screws so that the last twelve inches of each blade were almost at right angles to the remainder of the screw. That plagued us all the way home to the United States, giving the ship a vibration above that normal for LSTs. We did not enjoy a sure and steadfast anchor. Not so the readers of this epistle: their anchor was Jesus Christ, who had entered into the very sanctuary of God's presence and there secured amidst the solid rock. Nothing can move that anchor, for it is fastened to the very heart of God that is immovable in its sacrificing and redeeming love, the motivation of His heart from the very foundations of the world. Nothing is able to alter that determination that was willing to give His only begotten Son as the perfect sacrifice for our sins.

Verse 20 names Jesus as the forerunner of our hope. The term used here is one that describes the scouts who precede the troops. Scouts went ahead of the early settlers of our nation to look for safe passes, watering holes, and dangerous situations. The term could apply also to persons who work their way through a mine field in a battle zone and then lead others through to safety.

For us who believe, Jesus is our Scout, our Leader, who has run first this race and can take us through it safely and surely. He has become a merciful and sensitive High Priest after the order of Melchizedek, having more than fulfilled all the necessary qualifications of a high priest.

1. He was one of the people, thoroughly identified with us in our humanity.

2. He was faithful to God in the fulfillment of His task.

3. He was appointed by God with an oath for the task of High Priest.

4. He was perfectly pure, needing no sacrifice for His own cleansing.

He is our High Priest, ready now to offer the sacrifice once and for all, a "perfect and sufficient sacrifice for the sins of the whole world." He will offer it according to a new covenant that completely displaces and satisfies the old. He will offer it in a temple not made with hands, eternal in the heavens. And the sacrifice He offers will be that of His own body, according to the will of God.

We now move to the Ministry of the High Priest.

NOTES

1. *Calvin's Commentaries, Hebrews,* p. 136.
2. Ibid., p. 137.
3. Ibid.

CHAPTER TEN

The Superiority of Christ's Ministry

Hebrews 8:1–13

We have come to the third and final main section of doctrine—the Ministry of the High Priest. This ministry has three main ritual elements: the priest himself; the sanctuary in which he served and its equipment; and the sacrifices he offered. Our teacher begins this section with a brief, five-verse introduction, mentioning those things he will discuss in the finale of his doctrinal sections. In verse 1 he reviews the preceding section with one simple statement: *"We have such a High Priest."* In verses 2 and 5 he introduces the theme of the sanctuary. As is so characteristic of his style, he makes a comparison of the earthly and the heavenly sanctuaries, which he will further develop in 9:1–10. In verses 3 and 4 he introduces the theme of sacrifices, comparing the continual sacrifices of the earthly priests with the single sacrifice of the Great High Priest, which he will discuss in 9:11–14.

After this brief introduction he lays the foundation of the covenant basis of the ministry by quoting Jeremiah 31:31–34 (in verses 8–12). He then goes on to argue the superiority of Christ's ministry by comparing the two covenants first in ritual (9:14) and then in ratification (9:15—10:14). The section ends with a finale of affirmation regarding the completed ministry of the High Priest, Jesus Christ (10:15–18).

THE RITUAL ELEMENTS

1 Now this is the main point of the things we are saying: We have such a High Priest, who is seated at the right hand of the throne of the Majesty in the heavens,

2 a Minister of the sanctuary and of the true
tabernacle which the Lord set up, and not man.

3 For every high priest is appointed to offer both
gifts and sacrifices. Therefore it is necessary that this
One also have something to offer.

4 For if He were on earth, He would not be a priest,
since there are priests who offer the gifts according
to the law;

5 who serve the copy and shadow of the heavenly
things, as Moses was divinely instructed when he was
about to make the tabernacle. For He said, *"See that
you make all things according to the pattern shown
you on the mountain."*

Heb. 8:1–5

The clarity of our author's statement in verse 1 is striking. No
one could mistake his key point: that *"we have such a High Priest."*
Kephalaion, "main point," comes from a root word meaning "head,"
thus indicating the importance of the idea so described. Several other
times in the epistle he uses the verb "we have" as almost a transition
from one section to another. The thought of what we have stimulates
confidence: "We have a great High Priest who has passed through
the heavens" (4:14). "[We have] boldness to enter the Holiest
by the blood of Jesus" (10:19). "[We have] a High Priest over the
house of God" (10:21). Both of the latter statements are introductory to his exhortation, "Let us draw near with a true heart in
full assurance of faith" (10:22). The Greek construction is similar to that of 12:1: "Therefore we also, since we are surrounded
by so great a cloud of witnesses, let us lay aside . . . and let us
run."

The statement of verse 1 demonstrates once again our author's
pattern of using retrospect or review as a means of transition. *"We
have such a High Priest"* reaches back to the section just concluded but
serves also as a launching pad for the next section. However, our
author adds a thought he has not explicitly stated before, that this
High Priest is presently *"seated at the right hand of the throne of the Majesty
in the heavens."* It is not a surprising thought, for he has already shown
that the Son-Messiah has been given a throne which is forever and
forever; a scepter of righteousness is the scepter of His kingdom (1:8).
The phrase *"in the heavens"* looks ahead to what he will say in comparing the earthly and the heavenly rituals and ratifications.

Now he broaches the subject of the ministry of the Priest by using the word *"Minister"* (*leitourgos*), meaning one who serves the king or public, usually on one's own expenses. In religious terms, it signifies a minister of worship. A second introductory thought is offered: that this Priest will minister in the sanctuary; the term used here, *tōn hagiōn* ("holiest") refers to the Holy of Holies, the inner sanctuary. He compares this sanctuary very briefly with the earthly, saying it is a *"true tabernacle"* which the Lord has set up, not man.

Skipping two verses to verse 5 to complete the comparison, he describes it as a *"copy"* (*hupodeigma*, a pattern or artist's illustration of that which is to be constructed) and a *"shadow"* (*skia*, "reflection, image, model"). Moses was shown this pattern or image on the mountain and was instructed to reproduce it in the tabernacle with faithfulness and fidelity. Our author will pursue this argument later (9:9–14). Some argue that the term "copy" is evidence of the influence of Hellenistic Platonism on our writer. I do not think the admitted similarity is to be taken seriously, especially in the light of our discussion earlier on our writer's relationship with the Hellenistic school. This argument is unsupported and the use of the word must be seen as coincidence.

Verses 3 and 4 contain yet another preview of what is coming: the theme of priests offering gifts and sacrifices. It is true, this One must have a sacrifice to offer. However, His gift is not according to the law by which the earthly priests offered their sacrifices. His is utterly unique; His sacrifice is His own life and body.

Following this brief introduction, our author now settles down to the next main topic, that of covenants.

THE COVENANT BASIS

6 But now He has obtained a more excellent
ministry, inasmuch as He is also Mediator of a better
covenant, which was established on better promises.

7 For if that first covenant had been faultless, then
no place would have been sought for a second.

8 Because finding fault with them, He says:
"Behold, the days are coming," says the LORD, *"when
I will make a new covenant with the house of Israel
and with the house of Judah—*

9 *"not according to the covenant that I made with
their fathers in the day when I took them by the hand
to lead them out of the land of Egypt; because they
did not continue in My covenant, and I disregarded
them," says the* LORD.

10 *"For this is the covenant that I will make with
the house of Israel: After those days," says the* LORD,
*"I will put My laws in their mind and write them
on their hearts; and I will be their God, and they shall
be My people.*

11 *"None of them shall teach his neighbor, and none
his brother, saying, 'Know the* LORD,' *for all shall know
Me, from the least to the greatest of them.*

12 *"For I will be merciful to their unrighteousness,
and their sins and their lawless deeds I will remember
no more."*

13 In that He says, *"A new covenant,"* He has
made the first obsolete. Now what is becoming obsolete
and growing old is ready to vanish away.

Heb. 8:6–13

In verse 6, Christ's ministry is termed *"more excellent."* The Greek
word, *diaphorōteras*, means not simply better, but superior to that which
is of itself excellent. And upon what is this even more excellent
ministry founded? Upon better promises. The verb used here is a
strongly legal or administrative term referring to law that has been
established or enacted.

And what are those better promises? Our author answers with a
long quotation from Jeremiah 31:31–34, in which the new covenant
is prophesied. Why was there need for a second or new covenant?
Because there was fault in the first covenant. The fault was twofold:
first, the old covenant could not take away the sins of the people
and bring them into the designed relationship with God; second,
the Israelites had broken the first covenant by their rebellion mentioned above (3:5—4:20). That covenant was suspended by God until
a faithless generation died off; now there was need for another that
had not only a plan but also a power to forgive the penalty incurred
by that generation and every generation thereafter.

What must this covenant look like? Jeremiah gives three distinct
characteristics of this new covenant, characteristics that meet the
deepest desires designed into the heart of all humanity by the very

creative act of God. Having created humanity for Himself, He fulfills that designed relationship through this new covenant.

First, this covenant will be written upon their minds and upon their hearts. Much is being said today about the need to internalize lessons or experiences that are critical to mental health. To internalize in this sense means to "cathect," a term used in psychology meaning to get up in one's psyche certain basic perceptions critical to health. For instance, a healthy child must internalize or cathect a sensitive and loyal love from its parents, a love that is willing to sacrifice whatever is necessary and possible to provide for basic human needs. Once a child is convinced of that love, a sense of security fills that young life, preparing it for the difficult tasks of the future. No child without that security is about to risk the difficult or unsure and so turns away from challenges carrying no guarantees of success. That sort scarcely leaves home in the morning!

Second, this new covenant will establish an intimacy between God and the believer. In this intimacy, God promises to be our God and we will be His people. This means family, in the deepest sense of the term. Such an intimacy is expressed in the expression, "Abba," which almost explodes with exuberance. Abba might well be translated "Daddy, my own beloved Daddy!"

When our children were small, it was our custom after dinner to have a rough-and-tumble time with them, which might be bucking-bronco, wrestling, hand balancing, or "airplane." (The latter meant gathering all the pillows in the house and stacking them on the "big bed" and being tossed onto the pile from several feet away). Then would come the quiet reading time, followed by prayers and goodnight kisses and affirmations. On the way, our daughter, Luanda, would often want one last moment of excitement; without warning she would shout, "Daddy!" I knew what that meant. I had to drop anything in my hands and turn to meet a squealing missile. From a few feet away she would leap and I would catch her; she would wrap her legs around me and put her hands around my neck and off to bed I would carry her.

One Thanksgiving after she was grown, I went to National Airport to meet her. I watched her coming toward the security check point; then she saw me. She cleared the barrier, tossed her two pieces of hand luggage to the side, and shouted one word: "Daddy." And here she came! I caught her and we wheeled around in sheer joy of one another's presence. I suppose some wondered what sort of "daddy"

I was but that didn't matter. That one word said so much: "Oh, it's so good to see you again; like old times, isn't it; we understand each other, don't we? We're friends and we're going to have a great time!" I deeply and joyously believe she cathected and internalized a father's love. Perhaps that is one of the reasons she is so strong in facing life. God knows His children and disciples will never be able to stand up to the demands of correcting oppression and seeking justice without that internalized love; that we never risk life itself for the sake of the kingdom without that witness of the Holy Spirit.

Verse 11 states that so complete is this assurance that one will not have to say to a fellow citizen or a sister or brother, "Let me tell you about God." Each of these children will know God, intimately. Two contrasting Greek words are used for "know" in this verse. The first is a form of *ginōskō*, from which we get our word "know." In the phrase "all shall know me," a form of *horaō* is the word translated "know." Although both words have somewhat the same meaning, when they are used in contrast, we must interpret *horaō* as conveying a deeper perception or intimacy. A similar intimacy is meant in Hosea 2:20 when God says, "I will betroth you to Me . . . and you shall *know* the Lord" (italics added). In this case the word is *epiginōskō*, a very intense and personal form of knowing, describing the sexual relationship between husband and wife. It is God's own Spirit that witnesses to us and convinces us of this intimacy. When compared with the prophecy of Joel—that the Spirit will come upon all flesh—it is seen that the intimacy is indeed a mark of the kingdom in which God's people *know* Him (Joel 2:28–29). To our teacher, such intimacy is the very purpose of religion, to bring God and the people into a full personal relationship again.

Third, this new covenant will be marked by a complete forgiveness of God that no longer even remembers our sins: *"I will be merciful to their unrighteousness, and their sins and their lawless deeds I will remember no more"* (v. 12). One of the most fulfilling experiences of the human heart is to be embraced with such tenderness and strength by someone we have hurt that it is as though nothing had ever stood between us. Even though one may be able to reach back in the memory bank and say, "Yes, I remember when you did this or that, but I have forgotten it," nothing remains in the emotions. Such a forgetting allows the future to unfold without the restraints of the past. Emotions and creativity are free to express themselves; the refreshing streams of intimacy and love flow unhindered. This forgetting makes all things new. Scarlet sins are made whiter than snow; those that are red like crimson will become like washed wool (Isa. 1:18). No promise to the human heart is more satisfying and liberating. This promise of such complete reconciliation is the meaning of covenant faith.

No better foundation could be laid for the relationship between God and His children than this one. Christ has mediated this new covenant, which is better than the first because it is based on internalized and intimate knowledge and a forgiving so complete that no memory of misdeed remains in the mind of God.

The chapter ends with a summary statement: *"In that He says, 'A new covenant,' He has made the first obsolete. Now what is becoming obsolete and growing old is ready to vanish away"* (v. 13). The first covenant could not produce this reconciliation; it could show the manner in which sins would one day be forgiven, but it could not produce that perfecting atonement. Telling again and again what could happen but without causing it to happen only increased the frustration and disappointment of the worshipers. That was its great fault—impotency, nonperformance. Now that another covenant has accomplished what the first said was needed, what further remains for the first? The new has made the first obsolete; the first is growing old.

I am partner in an aircraft that is used for Christian ministry. It has been equipped with what was at the time of installation the latest and most sophisticated equipment, able to navigate the plane by computer and automatic pilot right down to the runway. By computer it could place phantom navigational homing devices where none actually exist, a great help in finding little airports with no electronic facilities. Now, five years later, two or three completely new generations of electronic gear have emerged. These new systems make so many more functions available to us, we wonder how we can get along without them. Soon we will update our plane's equipment and be thrilled about its new capabilities. We know that the old is not only growing older, requiring more maintenance and repair, but that something far better waits for us. Obsolescence will one day make museum pieces of our present equipment. It is ready to pass away. The new has come. Why be satisfied with second best when our lives depend on it?

If our author was concerned about his readers relapsing into Judaism, one of the greatest deterrents would be the realization that the platform upon which they might step could soon sink. If the old has been used for teaching, then when the actual comes, the need for the teaching vehicle is removed. If God commanded the old for the purpose of bringing the Jewish people to the place of instruction, then once they are inside, the guide or tutor (*paidagōgos;* see Gal. 3:24–25) steps aside and permits the teacher to carry off the lesson; the guide vanishes from the scene. The first covenant has done its work; it is now ready to step aside, for the Teacher has arrived.

CHAPTER ELEVEN

The Superiority of the New Covenant

Hebrews 9:1–28

Having established the covenant basis for ministry, our author now shows the superiority of the new covenant in both ritual and ratification. He will discuss first the older covenant's ritual as to sanctuary and sacrifice, and then the new covenant's in sanctuary and the ministry of Christ in securing the eternal redemption. In summary he will show the limitation of the old as a cleansing of flesh only for liturgical purposes, whereas the new cleanses the conscience of the worshipers.

The chapter also includes a comparison of the ratifications to the covenants preceded by a discussion of the need for the death of the one who made a will or testament to activate it. The first was ratified only by the blood of animals.

THE EARTHLY SANCTUARY

1 Then indeed, even the first covenant had ordinances of divine service and the earthly sanctuary.

2 For a tabernacle was prepared: the first part, in which was the lampstand, the table, and the showbread, which is called the sanctuary;

3 and behind the second veil, the part of the tabernacle which is called the Holiest of All,

4 which had the golden altar of incense and the ark of the covenant overlaid on all sides with gold, in which were the golden pot that had the manna, Aaron's rod that budded, and the tablets of the covenant;

5 and above it were the cherubim of glory
overshadowing the mercy seat. Of these things we
cannot now speak in detail.

Heb. 9:1–5

It is important to our writer to speak of the furniture of the sanctuary. The reason will become apparent in the next section when he gives his interpretation of the meaning of the physical layout. Let us look briefly at the plan.

Picture the sanctuary laid out on an east to west orientation. The sanctuary, called the tent in some translations, was situated within the Court of the Priests. It was divided into two parts by a veil. This might be a single curtain for the desert tabernacle, as described by Josephus, or a double veil, as described by the *Mishnah*. In the latter instance, the outer veil was looped up on the south side and the inner veil was looped up on the north side. The ark is mentioned first as a chest about four feet long and two and a half feet high and wide, covered with gold and fitted with a gold ring at each corner, through which two poles gilded with gold could be inserted for carrying on the shoulders of priests. In it were three articles: a golden urn containing manna, Aaron's rod that had budded as a sign of God's power, and the two tablets of stone containing the Ten Commandments. Our author puts the altar of incense in this Holy of Holies ("the Holiest of All," v. 3), as does the *Mishnah*. Here also was the mercy seat, a symbol of God's forgiving nature, covered by two cherubim, facing one another, with their wings covering the mercy seat.

In the outer sanctuary was the table of presence in which each week one loaf representing each tribe of Israel was displayed to signify Israel's constant communion with God through the things which He supplied and which were to be used in His service. Across the room from it was the lampstand with its center shaft supporting one lamp and three arms branching out on the left and right, each holding a lamp, making a total of seven. Outside the tabernacle of the two sanctuaries stood the altar of burnt offerings and the laver in which the priests washed their hands and feet before entering into the sanctuary.

Our author does not discuss these arrangements in detail. What was the meaning of all this to him? Notice the symbolism. No one could enter the Court of the Priests but the priest on duty for the

The Plan of the Tabernacle
As Described in Hebrews 9:2–5

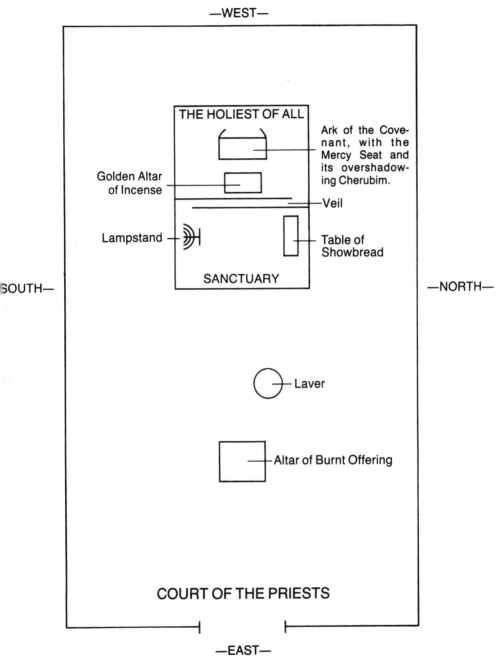

—WEST—

THE HOLIEST OF ALL

Ark of the Covenant, with the Mercy Seat and its overshadowing Cherubim.

Golden Altar of Incense

Veil

Lampstand

Table of Showbread

SANCTUARY

—SOUTH—

—NORTH—

Laver

Altar of Burnt Offering

COURT OF THE PRIESTS

—EAST—

people. He could not enter the sanctuary without washing and then only to offer the daily sacrifices. In the inner sanctuary were very significant articles, all of which represented God's presence and power in some way. The mercy seat represented His forgiving nature, but it also symbolized that no one could enter His presence without His mercy. The ark of the covenant contained symbols of His holy order for a moral universe and for relations between Him and His people and among His people. The rod of Aaron showed His liberating presence when the children of Israel were being enslaved in Egypt. The manna in the urn represented His sustaining presence in the wilderness where He provided the basic necessities of life for His people. The altar of incense in the Holy of Holies symbolized His majesty and absolute holiness. All of these representations of His presence were denied the people as a whole because of their sins.

The meaning: sin alienates us humans from God. To deny or break His moral laws is to experience distance from God; a holy God will not have sin in His presence without destroying it. The veil, more than any other object in the tabernacle, symbolized the separation between God and His human creatures; as long as it hung intact, the separation existed. As long as a single priest alone could enter that holiest of sanctuaries and then only with a blood sacrifice, it was quite apparent that the reconciliation of God and human beings had not yet taken place. Every item in the temple pointed to this truth.

"Isn't that a bit hard on God's part?" you might ask.

Let me ask another question in response. Is it the narrowness of God or is it the structure of reality? If somebody steals from you, what happens to the relationship between you and that person? If your spouse has an affair with another person, what does that do to your relationship? If someone falsely accuses you before others, lying, defaming your character, and bringing about your professional demise, what happens to that relationship? If someone denies you the justice and liberty assured you in this land, because of your race or ethnic background, so that your children go hungry and velvet-covered doors slam in your face with every attempt you make to find a job, what does that do to the relationship? Aren't anger, alienation, and hostility the usual results? If you were the one on the receiving end of any of these injustices, would you share the emotions just mentioned? Yes, you say? That's part of the structure of reality, isn't it?

God, in His honesty, was making that very point in the design of the tabernacle and temple. But more important, He was indicating a way in which the situation could be reconciled. The temple and its furnishings were the first step of portraying the results of sin.

The Earthly Ministry

6 Now when these things had been thus prepared, the priests always went into the first part of the tabernacle, performing the services.

7 But into the second part the high priest went alone once a year, not without blood, which he offered for himself and for the people's sins committed in ignorance;

8 the Holy Spirit indicating this, that the way into the Holiest of All was not yet made manifest while the first tabernacle was still standing.

9 It was symbolic for the present time in which both gifts and sacrifices are offered which cannot make him who performed the service perfect in regard to the conscience—

10 concerned only with foods and drinks, various washings, and fleshly ordinances imposed until the time of reformation.

Heb. 9:6–10

Having discussed the physical surroundings in which the ritual was to take place, our teacher now describes the ministry of the earthly priests. With all the above in place, the priest on duty went continually into the first part of the tabernacle in order to accomplish the ministry (the Greek phrase indicates there were no formal limits of time, a period without definite duration or end). Our teacher here refers to the repetitious nature of the sacrificial process which he will interpret momentarily. In saying *"the first part,"* he means the outer sanctuary used for the daily sacrifices.

Into the second part, the inner sanctuary, the high priest goes alone, and that but once a year, and *"not without blood, which he offered for himself and for the people's sins committed in ignorance."* His representative act on behalf of the people is symbolized by the breastplate he wore with a large precious stone for each of the twelve tribes. It was vicarious liturgy.

Returning to the diagram of the temple, let us note the route of the high priest. According to *Mishnah Yoma* 5:1, he moves south to the opening in the outer veil between the two curtains. Then he turns north, having in his left hand a ladle of incense as large as his two hands, and in his right, a pot of coals. He enters the space between the two curtains, which was less than two feet wide, and when he reaches the north end, turns to his left so that the curtain is on his left until he comes to the ark, which we would take to mean in front of or even with the ark where the altar of incense was. There he deposits the pot of coals and heaps the incense upon the coals, which suddenly fills the sanctuary with smoke. He then retreats by the way he has come, saying a short prayer so as not to cause anxiety in the people who might fear he has been struck down by the holy God. (I can imagine he retreated as quickly as possible, after a short prayer indeed, because of the stifling density of the smoke.)

He then takes the blood that is being stirred by an attending priest so it will not congeal and enters a second time into the Holy of Holies and stands where he has stood before, sprinkling the area. He then returns to the outer sanctuary and places the basin of blood upon the golden stand.

Attendants then bring him the he-goat which he has slaughtered, and they receive its blood in another basin. A third time he enters the Holy of Holies, sprinkling the mercy seat and the area in front of the mercy seat. (Note that the *Mishnah's* order of goat and bull is inverted from that of Leviticus 16.) He pours the blood of the bull into the bowl of the he-goat and then sprinkles the altar outside the tent as an atonement for it. The blood of his offering, according to the Mishnah, is mixed with the blood of the peoples' offering, indicating his complete identification with them.

The second goat is then brought to him. Laying his hands upon it, he confesses the sins of the people as though transferring the guilt of them to the goat. Notice again the vicarious nature of the sacrifice. The goat is then taken into the wilderness and released in a lonely place, a symbol that God separates us from our sins by a vast distance so that we do not see them again.

Yet the people did see their sins again, year after year. The process had to be repeated regularly. It was obvious there was nothing permanent about the sacrifice. Our author's spiritual insight loses no time identifying the real problem. It is, after all, quite obvious that the way is not yet open into the presence of God as long as that first tabernacle stands isolated and cut off from every person's access to the Holy Father of us all. The words of a well-known Advent hymn come to mind here, expressing the longing desire for this restored relationship. Israel agonized for the release from sin as a hart longs for the water brook.

> Come, Thou long-expected Jesus,
> Born to set Thy people free;
> From our fears and sins release us;
> Let us find our rest in Thee.
>
> Israel's strength and Consolation,
> Hope of all the earth Thou art;
> Dear Desire of every nation,
> Joy of every longing heart.
>
> *Charles Wesley, 1744*

One day in the mountains of California I was working on a high road doing some masonry. My work was quiet and my movements small. Not far from me trickled a small stream, gently flowing from a sandy bank with scarcely a sound. Its water was intoxicatingly sweet; it had slaked our rabid thirst many times in the heat of the day. Suddenly I heard a sound of hooves beating down the rocky slope with staccato impact. I looked up, hardly moving, to see a doe thundering down the mountainside, zigzagging, leaping, obviously in panic. Was a mountain lion after her? They were in the area. She stopped and then I saw her panting as though her sides would rupture. Her tongue hung from her mouth; her almond eyes were wide with fear. Motionless, she stood looking back over her shoulder; her body trembled with fear and exertion. She bounded a few more times, coming to rest so close by me I could see her heaving chest. Then she heard the sound of trickling water. After several minutes, she gave one last look over her shoulder to make sure her pursuer had relinquished the chase, then walked to the stream and drank almost insatiably. "As the deer pants for the water brooks, so pants my soul for You, O God" (Ps. 42:1).

The panting hearts of the nations, longing for the intimate relationship with God for which they had all been created, could never be satisfied by endless liturgy that taught the same lessons over and over again. In many different cultures and religions the panting thirst was an agonizing experience. Was there no answer? Verse 8 states that the Holy Spirit had been making plain that the true answer had not yet been unveiled.

My New Testament professor at San Francisco Theological Seminary, Dr. John Wick Bowman, had been a street preacher in India for seventeen years before becoming a professor. He had heard the story of Sadha Sunda Singh, one of the famous holy men of India who had found Christ. Singh said something to this effect: "I know God alone could forgive sin, but I did not know how until I heard of Jesus." He too had longed for that intimacy of which Jeremiah spoke in his new covenant.

Presbyterians have a useful phrase when making an enabling motion in which all the circumstances are not clear at the time the motion is made—"if the way be clear." At the time of the earthly priests, the way was not yet clear; it had not yet appeared or been made manifest.

Liturgy was there in all its propriety, exactness, and holy ordinances, but the conscience of the worshiper was untouched. The aching thirst for forgiveness was untouched; fear and near panic still gripped the sensitive spiritual psyche; no water could be found to slake this thirst; the Enemy was still in hot pursuit. The best the liturgy could do was to cleanse ceremonially the foods and drinks with various washings. Religious paraphernalia were readied for the annual atonement, but nothing happened to cause the hearts of the people to rejoice. Israel pined for redemption, that day in which crimson sins would become white as wool, and iniquity red as blood would be as driven snow. Would God ever remove their sins as far as east is from west, or even as far as the goat Azazel was taken into the wilderness? When that time came, surely there would be reformation (*diorthōseōs,* "making straight").

The earthly ministry was limited—severely!

THE HEAVENLY MINISTRY

11 But Christ came as a High Priest of the good things to come, with the greater and more perfect tabernacle not made with hands, that is, not of this creation.

12 Not with the blood of goats and calves, but with His own blood He entered the Most Holy Place once for all, having obtained eternal redemption.

13 For if the blood of bulls and goats and the ashes of a heifer, sprinkling the unclean, sanctifies for the purifying of the flesh,

14 how much more shall the blood of Christ, who through the eternal Spirit offered Himself without spot to God, purge your conscience from dead works to serve the living God?

15 And for this reason He is the Mediator of the new covenant, by means of death, for the redemption of the transgressions under the first covenant, that those who are called may receive the promise of the eternal inheritance.

Heb. 9:11–15

The author of the epistle now gathers up considerations of both sanctuary and ceremony of the earthly cultus and puts them in stunning comparison with the ministry of Jesus Christ. He reaches back to the establishment of Christ's high priesthood with an interesting new term. Rather than using the simple verb "come," he speaks of Christ having "come alongside," *paragenomenos.* Just a moment ago we spoke of the exhaustion of one who has expended life's energies on longing for an undefiled relationship with God. He or she is like a runner who, having used every ounce of energy, staggers at the end of the race, or tragically, even before. Often at a track event one sees a runner come alongside an athlete who is stumbling as though to fall, put his arm over his shoulder and grasp him with his other arm, sustaining his weight until his time of recovery has set in. Jesus, Savior, that is what You have done for us! Exhausted, weary, stumbling through life, we have experienced Your coming alongside as our merciful and effective High Priest and putting Your strong arms around us, Your perfect atonement under our shaking feet that we might stand firm before God without fear. The progressive sense of the verb used here is highly stimulating. As the fellow athlete comes alongside his stumbling teammate, he not only says, "It's okay; I've got you," but, "Your potential is awesome; the best is yet to come!"

The sanctuary in which Christ has offered His atoning sacrifice is not one *"made with hands"* but *"greater"* and *"more perfect . . . not of this creation."* The sanctuary of Christ's atoning ministry is a heavenly one, in the very presence of God. He offers Himself before the eternal mercy seat. No incense is necessary to symbolize God's majestic presence, for God's presence is overwhelmingly full. There is no need for an ark to remind heaven of God's mighty acts symbolized in manna, rod, and tablets, for there is endless praise of His mighty acts from the throats of those who were His eternal messengers on earth. And when Christ suffers upon the cross, the earthly veil is miraculously and suddenly torn by powerful forces so that any heart that has a mind to believe might be forever assured that now absolutely no barrier exists between God and His people.

How many times had the blood of bulls and goats, the ashes of a sacrificial heifer been thrown against the altar and all the accouterments of the sanctuary without any change in the lives of the worshipers? Yet these things had been ordered and had had some effectiveness for the readying of the ceremony. Our writer asks, if there was that modicum of effectiveness, how much greater will be the atoning effect of One who offered this sacrifice through the eternal Spirit? He did not bring the blood of any bull or goat, but *"with His own blood He entered the Most Holy Place once for all"* (v. 12). The author emphasizes the singularity of this offering in contrast to the continual offering of the earthly priests. ONCE, never before, never again, ONCE, at the completion of the age Christ offered His own blood in an act of eternal and sensitive love. That is how much He and the One who sent Him loved us. No price was too much, so He paid the maximum; never could there be any doubt or question about the sufficiency of the payment.

The result is the complete cleansing of the conscience of the worshiper. This is not just an objective cleansing recorded on the books of heaven for the purposes of ingress or admission. The cleansing is subjective as well; it is a conscious experience of the conscience, a happening of which the recipient is fully and joyfully aware. If Israel's shouting and dancing was quite a show on the Day of Atonement, how much more is the joy of the new Israel's rejoicing for a cleansing and salvation that is complete and eternal? Even as the Holy Spirit indicates that the way is not open in the first covenant, He indicates that the way *is* open in the new covenant. The Spirit communicates with our spirits that we are the children of God (Rom. 8:15–16). Removing all fear, He causes us to erupt in exclamations of confidence, "God, my very own beloved Father!"

Our author does not leave us in the individualistic experience of joy, however. Immediately he reminds us of the purpose of our cleansing: the good works that God has planned beforehand for us. Justice must go hand in hand with the justification; social concern must march stride for stride with salvation. Having received grace by faith, now we must do works of faith. Having been cleansed, we are to be about the tasks of the kingdom (Eph. 2:8–10).

The typewriter I am presently using is one that I have had for nearly twenty-five years, an old SCM electric. I love it, but it is in need of a good cleaning and some repair. On these cold mornings in Washington where we have just had a record cold wave, some of the keys double or triple strike; the margin stop does not hold as it should, so I must return the carriage by hand. After it is cleansed and repaired, what will I do with it—put it upon the mantle for display? No, I'll joyfully take it to the special typing table beside my large desk with the bookshelves above containing all my reference works. It will be part of a work area specially designed for sermon preparation and writing. This area is separated by the width of the study from another area specially designed for finances and flying materials. The typewriter has a very special task that no other piece of equipment can fulfill. My purpose for having it cleaned is that it can be used productively.

God has a work area specially designed for you, and once He has cleansed your conscience by the blood of Christ and witnessed to you that the way is open to Him at all times of day or night, then He desires to prepare you for your unique task in the kingdom. Nobody can take that place; each of us has his or her own place that will require every ounce of our energy and more. Cleansed to serve— that is the name of the game!

During this section, our exhorter, like a great composer, has been introducing a new theme to his symphony. It is mounting in crescendo to the doctrinal climax of his epistle, which will have its finale in the first eighteen verses of the tenth chapter. There not only the atonement for the sins of all humanity will be raised as a banner to His name, but He will be crowned with the messianic title of Ultimate Victor over all His enemies, who will become stools for His feet.

In verse 15 of chapter 9, yet another theme is introduced as a transition to the next section. This is the theme of the ratification of a covenant or testament by the death of the one who made it. He calls Christ the Mediator and the means of ratification, death.

The purpose is the redemption of the transgressions (*paraboseōs*, from a verb meaning "to step aside," therefore "to violate or transgress"). Any transgressors *"who are called"* (*hoi keklēmenoi,* from *kaleō,* the source of our word "call") may receive the promise of the eternal inheritance. In receiving they become heirs of all that God desires for His children. His plan that each and all should know the internalized and intimate promise, should experience the complete forgiveness and forgetting of their sins, is now expressed in terms of heirs and their inheritance, which is eternal in character. It will last forever. The promise is as good as the Maker, and He never faults on any of His promises.

The word for inheritance has an interesting background. *Klēronomos* has as its root *klēros,* which means appointed by lot. *Nomos* (law) would indicate the rules. Early on, inheritance was often determined by lot, and according to the rules of lot-drawing, one became an inheritor of this or that piece of property or other object.

As any inheritance is gained only upon the death of one who placed it in his will, so it is with this eternal inheritance. Death is necessary before this inheritance becomes available to those to whom it has been promised. It is Christ who has promised the inheritance, and it is Christ who must die. With this thought our teacher makes his transition to a section on testaments and death, comparing the two covenants now as to ratification.

RATIFICATION BY BLOOD

16 For where there is a testament, there must also of necessity be the death of the testator.

17 For a testament is in force after men are dead, since it has no power at all while the testator lives.

18 Therefore not even the first covenant was dedicated without blood.

19 For when Moses had spoken every precept to all the people according to the law, he took the blood of calves and goats, with water, scarlet wool, and hyssop, and sprinkled both the book itself and all the people,

20 saying, *"This is the blood of the covenant which God has commanded you."*

21 Then likewise he sprinkled with blood both the tabernacle and all the vessels of the ministry.

22 And according to the law almost all things are purged with blood, and without shedding of blood there is no remission.

Heb. 9:16–22

Since chapter 8 our author has been using the term *covenant.* Here he adds a dimension that was not apparent before, that of the covenant's being a will or testament. No implication of the necessity of the death of the covenantor was made in speaking of God's making a covenant with the people through Jeremiah, but the issue becomes very important to him now when speaking of the new covenant made in Christ.

His thesis is simple enough: before a testament is activated, there must also be the death of the one who made the testament. The word used here has the very meaning "to dispose of, make a will." It is obvious that a will is in force only after the maker dies.

I have made a will. Several tithes of the residual estate will go to the Lord's work, being designated for training young people for church vocations and for missions, with Christian colleges receiving a good part of the will. It is important to Colleen and me that our Christian colleges receive ongoing support in a day when expenses and increasing complexity and sophistication of training put heavy demands on these institutions. Our children have received such quality and personalized instruction in a milieu of relevant faith that we want to see that opportunity given to others. In fact, I have spoken to our attorney informing him that we want to increase the portion going to the Lord's work. That will is properly drawn up; I have spoken to my two lawyer sons about its execution should both Colleen and I go suddenly in a flaming commercial air or automobile accident (not in a private aircraft, of course). It is all set forth. But as long as we live it will not go into effect. It has value only upon our death.

By the way, do you have a will? Is your last opportunity to make a witness for Christ and to exercise your stewardship for the glory of His kingdom written, signed, and properly placed? I understand it is shocking how many Christians die intestate, letting the disposition of their estates be determined by the secular state. I won't mind if you lay this book down right now and see to this Christian duty and opportunity. What a marvelous privilege! The other day I heard someone repeat the superstition that if someone makes out the will, he or she will die. Nonsense! Is not Christ greater than superstition?

Even the first covenant was ratified by death. True, it was not the death of the One who made it, but was there, even in that early ratification, an implication of the necessity of Christ's death? Referring back to Exodus 24:1–8, our author draws attention to the fact that Moses, after he had come down from the mountain, ratified the giving of the law with the blood of animals.

He built an altar at the foot of the mountain, and also erected twelve pillars. Using young men from the various tribes as assistants, he offered burnt offerings and peace offerings of oxen to the Lord. Half the blood he put in basins and the other half he threw against the altar. Then, having read the book to the people and having received their response of promise to obey all that God had said, he sprinkled them, saying, "Behold the blood of the covenant which the Lord has made with you in accordance with all these words."

Only then did they see God in one of the most powerful of all human experiences. Moses, Aaron, Nadab, and Abihu with the seventy elders saw the God of Israel; they beheld God, and they ate and drank (Exod. 24:11). Did our author have in mind that after the blood sprinkling of the people, they had a moment of fellowship with God? That accessibility was to be lost in another moment of time, for God was to call Moses within the day to come up on the mountain where He gave him the pattern of the tabernacle with its symbolism of alienation and atonement. After all these things were built and created as God had planned and communicated them, Moses who had been the faithful leader of the people and obedient servant of the Lord, was himself unable to go into the presence of God in the tabernacle. For Moses particularly, who had known the intimacy of His presence, the exclusion must have been very painful. It was not a matter of obedience or personal qualification or past experience; it was a matter of blood sacrifice before one could be in the presence of God. Without shedding of blood there is no remission (*aphesis,* a carrying away, putting away).

I was talking some time ago with a church leader. We were discussing his aversion to "evangelicals." I pressed him on the issue until the core of it seemed to be the emphasis upon the blood of Christ. Quite derisively, he used the term "slaughterhouse religion." Finally he said, "I don't believe in blood sacrifice; we don't do it anymore."

I have thought about that through the years, and wish I had thought it through by that time so I could have had a response. "We don't do it anymore." Don't we? In this twentieth century we have killed more people in our various wars than in the preceding eight centuries. During World War II we saw the waves on Tarawa washing over the bodies of forty thousand young Americans. I walked through the city of Dresden, where, in one night of fire bombing, three hundred thousand lost their lives. I have a dear friend of Russian background whose family fled the Caucasus before twenty million fell to the "social surgery" of the Communists. Hundreds of thousands more died in a searing explosion in Hiroshima and Nagasaki; millions more have died in Cambodia and Vietnam. The sin of humanity's inhumanity is costing us more human lives than we are willing to admit. We have even stopped reporting or counting, where the results do not directly affect "American interests." Sin is costly and still demands the blood sacrifice. What do we mean, "We don't do it anymore"? Either we proclaim the One perfect sacrifice and the blood that was shed to cleanse humanity of its mindless stupidity as well as its ignorance or we shall continue to pay for our sins by our own blood sacrifices that can never take away sin, but only reproduce them in uncontrollable numbers. Oh, that we had the eyes to see and the intelligence to accept God's great act of redeeming love in the sacrifice of the Great High Priest!

The Greatness of Christ's Sacrifice

23 Therefore it was necessary that the copies of the things in the heavens should be purified with these, but the heavenly things themselves with better sacrifices than these.

24 For Christ has not entered the holy places made with hands, which are copies of the true, but into heaven itself, now to appear in the presence of God for us;

25 not that He should offer Himself often, as the high priest enters into the holy place every year with blood of another—

26 He then would have had to suffer often since the foundation of the world; but now, once at the end of the ages, He has appeared to put away sin by the sacrifice of Himself.

27 And as it is appointed for men to die once, but after this the judgment,

28 so Christ was offered once to bear the sins of
many. To those who eagerly wait for Him He will
appear a second time, apart from sin, for salvation.

Heb. 9:23-28

In a style we have already noted, our author backtracks in a kind
of repetition or "softness of outline" to teach further on points already
introduced and discussed to some extent, but evidently not sufficiently
for him. Verse 23 is an expansion on verses 8:5 and 9:6-7. His point
in this verse, however, is a direct comparison of the two ratifications.
The requirements for cleansing the earthly copies are of one level.
The requirements for cleansing the heavenly realities are of a higher
level. The implication of the heavenly sanctuary needing cleansing
(which is implied) is interesting, but our author does not indulge
our interests. As before, he uses the word *kreittosin*, *"better,"* as the
agent of comparison. In the case of *"copies,"* in verse 24 he is not
content to use the same word as in 8:5 and 9:23 (*hupodeigmata*) but
chooses a word containing the prefix *anti* to accentuate the idea of
comparison (*antitupos*). In speaking of the cleansing, he reaches back
to the word he used in 9:14 and 9:22, *katharizō*, which he will use
yet again in 10:2. This word is used often in the Gospels referring
to Christ's healings, especially of lepers. It is used in the ethical sense
in Acts 15:9 speaking of God purifying gentile hearts just as He
did Jewish. Here in Hebrews 9:23 it is used in the ceremonial sense.

Verse 24 expands on 9:11, speaking of *"the holy places"* (*hagia*) as
being not *"made with hands."* The same phrase is used in both instances.
(Verse 9:11 reinforces the idea by adding, "that is, not of this creation.") His ministry is in the presence of God where He *"appear[s]
in the presence of God for us."* The word used for "appears" carries the
sense of "Here I am," and in Christ's case, "to do Thy will." The
word leads us forward to the thought that will be expressed in 10:7,
"Behold, I have come . . . to do Your will, O God." In essence,
Christ is saying, "I come to represent as High Priest the children
You have given me; I am one of them, knowing their human experience, their temptation, their fatigue, their pain, and their suffering.
They are mine, O Father and I am theirs. Accept now this sacrifice
which I make in their behalf." The phrase *"for us"* is distinctly vicarious, meaning "on our behalf" or "in our stead."

Two similar prepositions are used by our author to express "on
our behalf" or "in our stead." They are *huper* and *peri*. For a moment

let us analyze their uses. Passages in which the terms identify His vicarious suffering for us are 2:9 and 5:3. Passages in which the terms refer to His representing us are 5:1 and 6:20. The third meaning, used by far most often, is that of sacrifice or redemption and is found in 7:27; 9:7; 10:13; 5:3; 10:6, 8, 18, 26; and 13:11. The emphasis is upon "a saving deed which men are not able to accomplish for themselves" as expressed by Vincent Taylor in one of his three books on the atonement, *Atonement in New Testament Teaching*.[1] Christ's act is of great benefit for us who have sinned and was an act in our place. Whatever happened, happened for us.

Now in verses 25–28 our teacher emphasizes the single sacrifice of Christ in comparison to the continual sacrifice. The first covenant had the priests offering continually, without ceasing, the same sacrifices every day at the altar outside the tent. When one would offer the sin offering, the same identifying procedure would take place; the worshiper would place his hands upon the head of a sacrificial animal and then slay the animal before the door of the tent of meeting, after which the priest would take the blood, sprinkle some of it before the veil in the first sanctuary, put some on the horns of the altar, and then pour the remainder at the base of the altar before the tent of meeting (Lev. 4:1—5:13).

In the case of the yearly offering of Yom Kippur (The Day of Atonement), it was the high priest who would make the sacrifice as described above. Day after day, year after year, continually, without interruption or ceasing, this liturgy went on. Now if Christ were to offer according to the first covenant, He would have to have offered the sacrifice from the foundation of the world, for He was a priest forever like Melchizedek. It is interesting to note that our author appears a bit inconsistent here. To become our High Priest, which He had not been before, He had to share our human experience and learn obedience and temptation. We should not spend time on this point, however.

Instead, Christ now—and here the writer emphasizes the difference in period by saying *"now, once at the end of the ages"*—*"has appeared to put away sin by the sacrifice of Himself"* (v. 26). "Now" is emphasized by the use of *nuni*, a strengthened form of *nun*, the usual word for "now." The Greek for "end" has the sense of consummation or completion. The verb translated "put away" has the sense of sending away, carrying off, or divorcing, signifying the separation of the sinner from the sin. (Compare Isa. 1:18, Ps. 103:12).

Referring to Galatians 4:4 gives us some idea of what our author might have had in mind in this verse. "The fullness of time," reached when God sent forth His Son yields the same sense of completeness as *"at the end of the ages,"* in contrast to the unfinished. At the time of Christ, every basic type of religion had been tried. Since then we have only introduced new combinations of former basic portions. Every effort of humans had proved futile in attempting to bring about reconciliation with God on their own effort. At the point in time when there was no more to be tried and yet frustration reigned, Christ appeared to make known another way—the way of His own sacrifice as the answer to the dilemma of human sin and its guilt. The great desire of nations was satisfied; after all else had been tried and failed, Christ appeared and showed the answer. Legalism, asceticism, agnosticism, secret knowledge, sacrifices, liturgies, good works, ancestral worship, escape from the physical world, hedonism, reincarnations, and nihilism had all failed to answer our human problem of separation from God. At the end of the age, after we had attempted through all these religious routes, God showed us the way in the sacrifice of His Son. Until we had tried it all, we were not ready for His way.

Paul expressed that agonizing frustration in Romans 7, from the standpoint of ceremonial law. We had to experience the futility before we were ready for Christ's appearing.

While ministering at the Bel Air Church, I was preparing for church one Sunday morning. Luanda, our daughter, who was then two years old, was sitting on the living room floor attempting to put on her shoes and socks. Her efforts were obviously doomed to failure; she was holding the toe of the sock in one hand, the top in the other, not understanding at all the hole in the top of the sock. Seeing that she needed help, I said, "Andy, let Daddy help you."

"No," she retorted curtly, "Andy do it."

Ah, but daddies know better, so I picked her up and took her to her bedroom where I proceeded to do the necessary. I got no thanks; only a pouting lower lip and cranky little hip swing to her petticoat. A few moments later I returned and found her again on the living room floor—that's right, with her shoes and socks off and trying the whole process again.

Daddies learn. I figured she would have to be convinced of her need, so I let her try for quite sometime, honestly wondering if perception would come soon enough. I called off the minutes left before departure time hoping to add a little catalyst to the reaction. It worked. I heard a pathetic whimper behind me and turned to see a teary-eyed, frustrated darling choking back the tears but with contrite voice asking, "Daddy, put on Andy's ga-ga's, please."

"Of course I will, Andy; Daddy would love to."

A second time I carried her into the bedroom, sat her in exactly the same location and performed the same process. This time I got a kiss and saw her skip out to the car delighting in her new shoes. She had come to the "end of her age" of self-trust.

In an almost backhanded manner, we are stunned by the implications of this next verse, *"It is appointed for men to die once, but after this the judgment."* No returns, no reincarnations, no escape; after death, the great evaluation ending in judgment. This happens *"once"* (*hapax*) in any person's life. So Christ once (*hapax*) was offered to bear the sins of many. Notice the passive mode of the verb, "was offered," contrasted to "He offered Himself." Both are true. By the plan of God He was offered by hateful men; by His own voluntary action He offered Himself. Note also the word "bear." The Greek *anapherō*, literally "to carry up," surely meant in our writer's mind a priest's carrying up the sacrifice to the altar in the process of offering it for the sins of many—all humanity.

Although our teacher has never brought before us the theme of the second coming of Christ, he mentions it here as a topic taken for granted by the early church. Saints of God eagerly wait for that moment, especially in times of trial and persecution, to know their last full measure of salvation—completed, glorified.

NOTE

1. Vincent Taylor, *Atonement in New Testament Teaching,* 2nd ed. (London: Epworth Press, 1945).

CHAPTER TWELVE

Christ's Perfect Sacrifice

Hebrews 10:1–18

A SINGLE SACRIFICE

1 For the law, having a shadow of the good things to come, and not the very image of the things, can never with these same sacrifices, which they offer continually year by year, make those who approach perfect.

2 For then would they not have ceased to be offered? For the worshipers, once purged, would have had no more consciousness of sins.

3 But in those sacrifices there is a reminder of sins every year.

4 For it is not possible that the blood of bulls and goats could take away sins.

5 Therefore, when He came into the world, He said:

"Sacrifice and offering You did not desire,
But a body You have prepared for Me.

6 *In burnt offerings and sacrifices for sin*
You had no pleasure.

7 *Then I said, 'Behold, I have come—*
In the volume of the book it is written of Me—
To do Your will, O God.' "

8 Previously saying, *"Sacrifice and offering, burnt offerings, and offerings for sin You did not desire, nor had pleasure in them"* (which are offered according to the law),

9 then He said, *"Behold, I have come to do Your will, O God."* He takes away the first that He may establish the second.

10 By that will we have been sanctified through
the offering of the body of Jesus Christ once for all.
Heb. 10:1–10

Our teacher and exhorter now comes to the final section of his teaching: the single sacrifice of Christ as having fulfilled all the necessary requirements of atonement for all humanity and for all time. This one perfect sacrifice made unnecessary any further sacrifice of bulls and goats. The closing verses of chapter 9 have already introduced this theme, but our author now gives them their finished form. His use of the same term, "shadow," which he used in 8:5, but without its companion word "copy," and of the word "law" instead of "first covenant," emphasizes that these are not *"the very image of the things."* The law, along with the sacrifices which are offered year by year, cannot make perfect those who approach. If such were the case, then surely they would have ceased to be offered; that would indeed have been overkill for the cause of atonement. If one has no consciousness of sin, what need, what motivation is there for offering further sacrifices? There is none. The fact that they continued indicated the impotence of the sacrifices; their only power was that of reminder (*anamnēsis,* "bringing again to mind") of sins. In such a reminder there is little comfort.

And when one stops to reason, sins against a moral God can in no way be atoned for by amoral animals. True, in their death there is a statement regarding the costliness of sin; sins demanded the very sustenance of life, the wealth of the nation, tomorrow's food. On the other hand, they cannot take away arrogant disregard or flaunting of God's will, much less sins ignorantly committed.

What then is the necessary sacrifice sufficient for atonement? It is a body which God has prepared for Christ. The body which walked this earth, the body that shared flesh and blood with the children in perfect identification, the body stainless and sinless because of the Person whose body it was, is now ready for the sacrifice. The teaching liturgies of peace offerings (Lev. 3:1–17) and thank offerings (Lev. 7:11–34), sin offerings of acts of ignorance (Lev. 4:1–35), burnt offerings (Lev. 1:1–17, 6:8–13) and the Day of Atonement (Lev. 16), although ordered by God, were not designed to satisfy the massive requirements of carrying away sins. They were strictly preparatory guides toward the real thing. In that sense God took no pleasure in them. They were like model airplanes when society needed jets; no designer of mass transit systems is satisfied with models.

Behind all this there was a plan, a will; it was recorded in the book of God's self-revelation. Isaiah 53 reveals something of the plan; Someone is going to bear our griefs and carry our sorrows. Even though He is not the type we might have chosen, yet He is to be wounded on our behalf and for our transgressions. When judgment should have been upon us, He bore our sins; when punishment should have been meted out, it was He who took it. His meekness was deceiving; His silence disarming. And yet it was the will of the Lord to bruise him. After He has been made an offering for sin, He shall see His offspring, those born again to new life, accounted righteous before the God of flawless morality. He bore the sins of many.

Who is interested in half-scale models of the space shuttle when the completed shuttle is doing its work in the skies? They have become museum pieces of the past, no longer the focus of interest or excited pleasure. They have been replaced.

It is by that body of Jesus Christ offered once and for all people in all time (*ephapax*) that we have been sanctified (*hēgiasmenoi*, "having been made holy, pure") according to the will of God. This concept of the plan and will of God for the suffering of the Anointed is so very characteristic of apostolic thought. Luke, Peter, and John all refer to it (Acts 2:23, 3:18, 4:27–28; 1 Pet. 1:20; John 17:4–5, 12). This death was no martyrdom; it was the grand fulfillment of an eternal plan. God took the risk at creation of giving His creature free will. He knew right well what the outcome would be, and He prepared for that from the first acts of creation. God was not surprised by Calvary; we might have been—and disappointed, too—but not God. The body, the death, the atonement were His plan all along, and we simply played into it.

That great sacrifice was made but once, and it was sufficient.

A COMPLETE, SUFFICIENT SACRIFICE

11 And every priest stands ministering daily and offering repeatedly the same sacrifices, which can never take away sins.

12 But this Man, after He had offered one sacrifice for sins forever, sat down at the right hand of God,

13 from that time waiting till His enemies are made His footstool.

14 For by one offering He has perfected forever
those who are being sanctified.

15 And the Holy Spirit also witnesses to us; for after
He had said before,

16 *"This is the covenant that I will make with them
after those days, says the* LORD: *I will put My laws
into their hearts, and in their minds I will write them,"*

17 then He adds: *"And their sins and their lawless
deeds I will remember no more."*

18 Now where there is remission of these, there is
no longer an offering for sin.

Heb. 10:11-18

Like a track runner, our author now turns the last corner of his
teaching and heads for the great home stretch of his doctrine with
the greatest theme of the Christian faith—the atonement of Jesus
Christ through the one perfect single sacrifice. Still making comparisons, he directs our minds to the priest of the first covenant standing
all day, as long as he is on duty; every day one of them is attending
to the responsibility of each position around the tabernacle. Here
comes a man who sinned unconsciously; he discovered it but no
one else knew. He is bringing his bull for which he has spent a
tremendous part of his meager resources, but he is a faithful man.
A priest approaches him and the ceremony begins. The man lifts
his eyes to heaven, places his hands upon the head of the unsuspecting
beast and confesses his sins. He then takes the ceremonial sword
and thrusts it into the place indicated by the priest; quickly a basin
catches the blood until the bull slumps to his knees in weakness.
The priest then takes the basin to the outer sanctuary and with his
finger sprinkles a bit of blood before the veil as though to say, "O
God, forgive this my penitent brother; hold not his sin before Thy
face. Be merciful to him, a sinner." He then sprinkles some blood
on the four corners of the altar and pours out the remaining.

In another place a second priest receives a peace offering of cakes;
in yet another place, a person brings a thanks offering; here comes
a woman—evidently poor, for she has only two turtle doves—a newborn baby in her arms, to offer the sacrifice of cleansing after her
postnatal discharge has ended. The court of the temple was a busy
place of liturgy; some came with obviously sincere and humble hearts;
others swaggered their way through crowds and the process with a
kind of haughty disdain and arrogance, nevertheless fulfilling the

law. Some wore the garments of Pharisees, some of peasants; some were businessmen and others, housewives. All Israel was there, every day, month after month, year after year. The dust never seemed to settle in the area of the tabernacle. It had been going on like this for centuries and probably would continue. But was there not a better hope? Joel, Isaiah, Jeremiah—what did you mean? David, where is the joy?

Then the word swept through Israel: "Christ is risen!" Some saw; some believed; thousands were transformed. Now as they walked by the temple they wanted to shout, "There is no need for any other sacrifice; the One Great Sacrifice has been offered!" Is that why they spent so much of their time around the temple (Acts 2:46–47)? Among themselves they said that Christ was now seated at the right hand of God. He no longer had to stand in the position of a priest on duty. His work was done; it was finished. Those words of Christ on the cross rang through the very core of their souls like massive bells pealing the good news of a war's end or the coronation of a new king. This Man had offered One Perfect Sacrifice whose efficacy was not just for this one sin, but every sin of every age, before and to come; for every person, then, now, or ever.

In addition to this Good News, He is the Messiah, victorious and seated on the right hand of God, that place of executive power and authority, waiting for that final victory when all His enemies shall be made the stool for His feet. Then He would share His eternal dominion with every one of His disciples, giving them authority to reign with Him through the ages with no end.

His one offering accomplished it all. He *"has perfected"* (*teteleiōken*) *"[now and] forever those who are being sanctified"* (*hagiazomenous*) (v. 14). Notice the verb forms. The perfect tense of *teleiō* indicates that something has happened that has continuing effect, and he emphasizes this point with the present tense of the verb *hagiazō*. Something has happened and something continues to happen. Growth—there it is again, going on to maturity.

All this is objective fact, but with a very important subjective component. The Holy Spirit witnesses to us that the covenant promised us by God has been fulfilled. The Spirit's witness which Christ promised, a teaching Spirit, convinces us that God is our loving Father. We cathect that, get it into our deepest psyche. The wells of assurance overflow with the coursing streams of artesian joy and we shout, "Abba, my very own beloved Father; Daddy!" When Satan again

approaches us with past sins and holds them up to our faces in taunt-
ing ridicule or condemning recall, the Spirit says quietly and firmly,
"The Father says He has forgiven that and has forgotten it; tell him
to peddle his wares of accusation somewhere else. You are forgiven
and free, My child."

"Now cast your eye across the temple courtyard to the endless
activity of sacrificial liturgy. What does it mean to you now? Yes,
every sin is forgiven by that One Sacrifice; those of the past? Yes,
even those. Present failures—the one this morning? Yes, He forgave
that in the Name of Christ. Tomorrow's sins which make you tremble
now. Fear not, He will forgive that too, in the name of Christ. The
account book, my child? Here, look at your pages; what do you see?
Yes, go ahead, turn all the pages; they are perfectly clean, aren't
they? Do you want to go back to the dust, the daily bustle, the
slaughtering?" Of course not. There is no longer any need. Where
there is a perfect payment and removal of sins, there need be no
further sacrifice. It is all finished. And one day the annals of history
will show that this very temple courtyard of sacrifice and liturgy
will be no more. Mark my words—because the One Great Sacrifice
has been offered, this will pass away. When He said from the cross,
"It is finished," He meant just that.

I hesitate to break into this atmosphere of apostolic expression,
its pristine vitality and unsophisticated theology, with the tools of
systematic theology. They so often have forged the sharp implements
of theological warfare that have been used in the hate-filled lists
by the knights of opposing points of view. And yet there is something
about us humans, God-given I imagine, that desires to search out
even the depths of God and understand Him more. So we gather
data, probe, categorize, summarize, and systematize in hopes of grasp-
ing clearer answers to pass on to the next generation. Perhaps we
can try to do this without the hardening of theological weapons to
exclude or slay our opponents.

Interestingly, systematic theologians did not turn their efforts to
the atonement until the scholastics of the twelfth century did so.
Athanasius and Augustine of the early fathers gave some preliminary
considerations to the doctrine, discussing among other themes the
necessity for the atonement. This appears to be the focus of interest
in the doctrine in the early stages, followed by discussions regarding
the nature of the atonement.

The necessity was argued from three points of view. The first, expressed by Irenaeus in the second century and later by Anselm in the eleventh, was that of *absolute* necessity. In *Cur Deus Homo?* Anselm portrayed the main thoughts; the necessity for atonement was grounded in the justice of God and in His moral perfection. Therefore, any transgressor must be inflicted with punishment. The only way to satisfy God's justice was through atonement and satisfaction. The confessional standards of the reformed churches by and large held this position. Scriptural passages used to support this point of view were Exodus 34:7, Numbers 14:18, Nahum 1:3, and Romans 3:25–26.

Things at stake were the immutability of God's divine law, God's own veracity ("let God be true but every man a liar," Rom. 3:4), the need for assuaging of guilt which requires either personal or vicarious sacrifice, and the fact that God's immense sacrifice implies the necessity.

The opposite argument was held by the nominalists who said there was no absolute necessity but only the *arbitrary* will of God who said it had to be, so it had to be. Therefore the suffering of Christ did not have infinite value, but only enough to be equivalent to the satisfaction due, which God was pleased to accept. God might have had other ways to accomplish atonement or He could even have waived Christ's death, redeeming humanity by some other method. However, it was His will to do it this way. In modern theology, Schleiermacher and Pitschl followed this reasoning, breaking with the judicial concept of atonement, and emphasized more a mystical or moral sense of the atonement.

Between these viewpoints was that of the relative or hypothetical view of Aquinas and a number of the reformers, including Luther, Zwingli, and Calvin, who all avoided the absolute necessity. Instead, they held to the sovereign free will of God and His divine decree in setting forth the manner of the atonement.

With this very brief attention to the historical theology, let us turn back to the epistle to gain clues from our writer as to the necessity for the atonement. We come first to 2:9, in which our teacher claims that Jesus was made a little lower than the angels for the purpose of suffering death so that He might taste death for everyone. Purpose is certainly clear here, but is necessity?

Hebrews 2:10 states, "it was fitting"; again, does this imply necessity? A plan is evident, but could one posit the arbitrary will of God?

Three terms are used in later chapters by the author to indicate necessity: *opheilō, anagkē,* and *dei.* Verse 5:3 states that the priest ought, *opheilei,* "as for the people, so also for himself," to have something to offer. Necessity is certainly implied, whether absolute or arbitrary. In the matter of a will or testament the death of the testator was necessary; this appears absolute from the legal point of argument. Moreover, "without shedding of blood there is no remission [of sins]" (9:22), and "therefore it was necessary," *anagkē,* for the heavenly things to be purified with better sacrifices than the earthly (9:23). In 9:26, necessity is stated for the death of Christ often "He would have had [*edei*] to suffer often," as if He had to offer regularly as did other priests. Once or many times, the necessity is stated.

In chapter 10 a fresh dimension of necessity appears; it is that of the will of God or His design. 10:5 and 6 claim God has no pleasure or satisfaction in sacrifices or burnt offerings of the first covenant, but has prepared a body for His servant, Jesus, which, it is implied, is the satisfaction God seeks. This reminds us of Isaiah 53:6 and 10 where it states that the will of the Lord was to bruise the Servant for the sake of Israel.

One might ask, "Was it necessary for God to will it or could there have been another way?" We can only conjecture, but there is at least one major clue as to the answer. When Jesus asked the Father, with intensity so great that His sweat took the form of drops of blood, if there were another way and none was forthcoming, one would say there was no other way. That certainly seems to imply absolute necessity rather than arbitrary will.

Now let us turn to another aspect of necessity—and this introduces a new theme to our discussion—that of satanic powers. In 2:14-15, our teacher says that Jesus shares in our partaking of flesh and blood, "that through death He might destroy him who had the power of death, that is, the devil, and release those who through fear of death were all their lifetime subject to bondage." This brings to our mind other New Testament passages on satanic bondage. Jesus, in speaking with a group of Jewish disciples, or the greater core, said that anyone committing sin became a slave of sin and that only the Son could set him free. Paul states in Romans 6:16 that those who obey sin become slaves to sin, which leads to death. Again, in Colossians 2:15 Paul says that Christ has disarmed, or stripped off the weapons, of the principalities and powers. Luke, in recounting the sermon of Peter in Acts 9 in the household of Cornelius, describes the devil as being a mutinous captain who has seized control and holds people in a slaveship's prison hold.

All these allusions conjure up a totally new image, that of defeating an enemy and releasing his captives. In the process he was disarmed, rendered inoperative, stripped of his ill-gotten authority, and his captives freed. This aspect of atonement is not just judicial or moral, it is involved with liberation and destruction of an evil power. What did that contest entail? What cost was there to that battle? Evidently it was the cost of the life of Jesus, not that He paid anybody, Satan or God, but that that was what was needed to defeat Satan. Jesus took Satan's powerful weapon, that of death, into His own body and carried it to the grave. In doing so, He stripped Satan of his weapon and left him disarmed and ineffective, no longer a threat or cause of concern to those who accepted the fact of his demise. He may swagger and threaten all he wishes, but all a believer needs to do is to say, "Let me see your sheath," and Satan will be gone, for his sheath is empty. He has no power over those with the Word. However, Satan was not about to lay down his sword by the simple command of God; it had to be wrested from his powerful grasp by the body of Jesus.

Let us consider yet another facet. In the plan of the tabernacle or temple, we saw several things: First, the inner sanctuary represented the presence of God. No one could enter that sanctuary without the proper sacrifice. Second, the veil that separated God from the populace was no idle symbolism, but must have said something about the ontology, the being, of things. Thirdly, no one could enter the inner sanctuary without a sacrifice of blood, a symbol not only of the wealth of a nation and its food, but also of life which the blood carried. Necessity was inherent in both the sanctuary and the sacrifice.

It would do the greatest violence to his writing to say that our author did not consider death for atonement to be a necessity, whether by the absolute nature of things or by the arbitrary will of God. To my mind the weight of evidence falls strongly to absolute necessity if these symbols say anything about the nature of the being and alienation.

As to the nature of the atonement, there appears to be both an effect upon God and an effect upon the worshiper. God is propitiated, or satisfied with the atonement of Christ according to His will. The loving nature of God is only implied in such statements as "in bringing many sons to glory" (2:10) and in promising them a God-people,

Father-child relationship through Jeremiah (8:8–12) that contained a forgiveness so thorough it included His forgetting the iniquity. The impression is not that of an angry God, although certainly a just one.

The effect upon the worshiper, however, is of greater importance, or at least is emphasized by our author. As a result of this atonement, their consciences are cleansed and they are perfected, made mature and whole in some way. Not least of the effects on them is the confidence they now have through the covenant of forgiveness and intimacy that has been fulfilled by the One who made the covenant. The worshiper is made holy, sanctified, and is free to come into the presence of God with holy boldness in the witness and assurance of the Holy Spirit of God Himself. Consciousness of sin is gone; fear and terror of meeting God has been replaced by child's confidence in the face of a loving and accepting father.

Indulge me, please, in one final thought that is stimulated by the phrase "that He . . . might taste death for everyone" (2:9). An analogy in medical terms may give some insight into the nature of the atonement and resurrection. A disease for which there is no known cure sweeps through a population. To get it is to die. Then one in the community contracts the disease and is expected to die like all the rest. However, this one, after a severe bout with the disease, recovers and is well; the disease can no longer affect him. Now what can be made from his blood? A vaccine! In a sense he has tasted that disease for everyone; his victory now becomes the victory of every person who will receive the vaccine. Christ has won the victory over the dreaded disease of sin; He tasted it, even in death, but by the power of God was raised again. Now His victory over the disease becomes the victory of every person who partakes in His victory as symbolized in the bread and the wine of the Supper.

Whether by absolute necessity or the arbitrary will of God, Christ had to suffer for our sakes and in our stead. The sacrifice was vicarious, on our behalf, in our stead. He was the Paschal Lamb slain from the foundation of the world, the One Perfect Sacrifice, which cleanses the conscience of the believer to enter into an intimate relationship with Almighty God.

Our author finishes this last section of doctrine with a quotation (vv. 16–17) which evidently is of great importance to him, from Jeremiah 31; he has used it also in chapter 8. He emphasizes two aspects of that covenant as his summary: the internal character of the covenant and the forgiveness and forgetting of God. The new covenant has been established perfectly, as a sign that God's promise has been fulfilled. Sins have been forgiven and forgotten through one Perfect Single Sacrifice. The final word to be spoken in the light of these facts is this: where the covenant has been fulfilled, where sins have been remitted, which was the teaching purpose of the first covenant, there is no longer any need for any further offering of sin. The Apostle-Son-Messiah who has become the Priest after the order of Melchizedek has offered Himself as the Perfect Sacrifice remitting all the sins of humanity forever.

Indeed, "It is finished!"

CHAPTER THIRTEEN

An Exhortation to Holy Boldness

Hebrews 10:19–39

We come now to the last section of exhortation and teaching extending from 10:19 to 13:25. It may be subdivided as follows: 10:19–39, "Approach with Boldness," an exhortation; chapter 14, "The Character of Faith," an exhortative teaching for developing perseverance; chapter 15, "Run with Perseverance," an exhortation; and chapter 16, a group of "Community Exhortations."

The familiar pattern of exhortation, warning, and reason persists in the section we are about to study, as it will continue to do throughout the remainder of the epistle.

A TRIPARTITE INVITATION

19 Therefore, brethren, having boldness to enter the Holiest by the blood of Jesus,

20 by a new and living way which He consecrated for us, through the veil, that is, His flesh,

21 and having a High Priest over the house of God,

22 let us draw near with a true heart in full assurance of faith, having our hearts sprinkled from an evil conscience and our bodies washed with pure water.

23 Let us hold fast the confession of our hope without wavering, for He who promised is faithful.

24 And let us consider one another in order to stir up love and good works,

25 not forsaking the assembling of ourselves together, as is the manner of some, but exhorting one

another, and so much the more as you see the Day
approaching.

Heb. 10:19–25

"Approach with holy boldness!" The basis of the exhortation is all that
has just preceded plus the previous doctrinal section regarding the
qualifications of the high priest. Now our teacher lays two foundation
stones as bases for his encouragement; we have the boldness and
we have the High Priest.

The boldness (*parrēsian*) indicates a freedom of speech, permission
to approach an authority without fear, with plainness and openness,
therefore boldness without anxiety or cowering. Notice the contrast
in this word to the fear mentioned in 12:18–19 when the law was
given to Moses on the mount in the aura of terror and trembling.
Again compare it to the fear of the people regarding the Holy of
Holies as the abiding place of God among the people (9:7–8). What
has caused the radical transformation of attitude? It is a result of
Christ's cleansing of our consciences so that no vestige of guilt remains
to cause us to cower before an all holy God. The witness of the
Holy Spirit so fills us with the assurance of the love of our Father
God that there remains no residue of fear. Instead we are filled with
a joyful freedom and confidence to come into the presence of God
as a child running to a father she trusts completely and with whom
she has shared a warm and tender relationship. Only under the conditions of forgiveness and cleansing dare we have such confidence and
boldness to enter the Holy Place without being destroyed by the
holiness of God. Our exhorter is saying—we have that boldness!

He goes on to declare the basis of this boldness. It is the blood
of Jesus, an obvious allusion to the blood of the sacrificial offering
referred to in chapter 9, where it was stated that nothing could be
cleansed without the shedding and sprinkling of blood. By this
method things used in the Holy Place were made ceremonially clean
for the liturgy. Now we also are made clean to be in the presence
of God in holy liturgy of worship.

In order for us to enter, Christ has consecrated or provided a *"way."*
The Greek word is one which suggests a means of entrance, a place
of entering or an entrance. Compare 2 Peter 1:11, "For so an entrance
will be supplied to you abundantly into the everlasting kingdom of
our Lord and Savior Jesus Christ." This way (v. 20) is a *"new and
living way"* (*prosphaton kai zōsan*). These two terms appear to be in direct

contrast to one another. *Prosphaton* has as one of its meanings "freshly slain." No sacrifice could be brought that had died somewhere else of causes other than the sacrificial slaughter; it had to be freshly slain. Jesus is that freshly slain sacrifice. Obviously we are dealing in the realm of death. Now our teacher uses the contrasting word *zōsan*, "living." Yes, Jesus has been slain, the one perfect sacrifice, but He has also been raised from the dead by the power of God. He is both slain and living! Once dead and buried, now alive and risen (7:27; 9:12, 26, 28; 10:10). He was slain in the sacrificial environment of the cross, but is alive in the power of the resurrection. By that death a way has now been opened and consecrated; at the time of His death the veil of the temple was torn from the top to the bottom (Matt. 27:51). There no longer exists an impediment to entering the presence of God if one goes through Jesus Christ. His flesh, slain and risen, becomes the way or entrance into the Holy of Holies.

It appears that the phrase "through His flesh" is in apposition to the curtain (*katapetasmatos*, "that which is spread out"), but the context of the epistle and Gospels would lead us to say that Christ's flesh was not to be an instrument of hiding God or separating us from God, but rather a means of revealing God and of our entrance into His presence. Upon the basis of Christ's slain and risen flesh, we have boldness to enter the Holiest.

Second, we have a basis in holding fast our confession in the fact of having a High Priest who is over the house of God. This basis was mentioned previously in 2:5—7:28 which established the four necessary qualities of a high priest and showed how Christ fulfilled them all. We have such a High Priest! For discussion on the concept of "house" see the section on 3:2–6.

On the basis of these two foundation stones our teacher now exhorts us to three actions: (1) let us draw near; (2) let us hold fast our confession; and (3) let us consider one another so as to stir up love and good works.

"Let us draw near." In 10:22 our author desires us to make use of the open way and to come close to the presence of God. After all, that is the true purpose of religion, to reestablish the relationship between God and us humans. Now he says, "Use the way!" "Draw near!" And do it with a heart that is *"true"* (*alēthinēs*, "candid, transparent"), with no guile or sham. Moreover, let it be a heart that is in *"full assurance of faith"* (*plērophoria*, from *plēroō*, "to fill full, satiate, or glut")—glutted with faith, filled until it can hold no more as in the

words of Richard Blanchard in his hymn "Fill My Cup, Lord," "Fill me 'til I want no more." Faith must always have an object or it is sheer sentimentality. In this case the object of faith is described in the next phrase, *"having our hearts sprinkled from an evil conscience and our bodies washed with pure water."* Our hearts have been sprinkled as with sacrificial blood that purified liturgical components. No longer are we bothered by an evil conscience. Our consciences have been cleansed of an evil motivation, of any guilt or memory of wrongdoing. God has forgiven us and forgotten the misdoing according to His new covenant (8:12, from Jer. 31:34). That covenant has been fulfilled and the Holy Spirit bears witness to us that that is the fact.

In addition, just as the priests and the sacrificial animals had to be washed with pure water, so we have assurance that our bodies have been washed with pure water. The reference might well be to the water of baptism.

"Let us hold fast the confession." Verse 23, our writer's second exhortation to hold fast our confession, is reminiscent of 2:1 ("give earnest heed") or 3:6b and following ("hold fast" our confidence and pride in our hope). The Greek verb translated "hold fast" has the sense of holding firm, securing or tightening down our confession of hope. This we must do without wavering (*aklinē,* from *klinō,* "to lean, to slope, or to be off balance"). We must not go off balance or become unlevel as does a faulty foundation. We must not bend or yield to winds of pressure that blow upon us from a seductive yet hostile world.

There is reason to hold firm even though the circumstances of life appear to be laughing at us, even though things have become difficult and at the moment we feel there is little reason for keeping on. The One who made the promise is faithful and will not let us down. He does not count time in the short segments by which we count; therefore, we should not let momentary discouragement cause us to turn away. Tragically, Christian history has too many instances in which pressures of persecution caused the church to turn away and be wiped out as in China or North Africa during the Muslim conquest. Only now in the last decades is there a modest growth of the church of China. This growth is evidence of the very characteristic our exhorter wished to see in the lives of his people, that of holding fast to their confession. The very thing our author warned against has happened in Christian history. Hang on; God is on His way with resources for endurance. Things might even become more difficult (see 12:3–4); in the very process of enduring, discipline and strength will grow as rich fruit in your life and the tragedies of today will become the triumphs of tomorrow (Rom. 8:26–39). God can take even the burned-out cinders of devastation and make building blocks of them. God is faithful but He is not indulgent.

"Let us consider one another." Verses 24 and 25 give us the third and final exhortation in this passage. *Katanoōmen allēlous,* "consider one another," might well be translated "observe well or understand one another in a reciprocal relationship." The emphasis is not upon unilateral observation but upon getting to know one another in the intimacy of a community of faith. This combination of words leads us to a powerful truth in line with much of what we have learned in this day and age from the human relations movement. As we understand one another in a reciprocal relationship, there results a creative interchange that leads to provocative stimulation of both love and good works. The *koinōnia* (a sense of community resulting from having something in common) created by knowing one another deeply or perceiving intimately creates and releases attitudes of love and stimulates the actions of good works done together. "Creativity rises out of relationships" is a powerful adage. When a person is known for all he or she is, with all the wrinkles and foibles, and yet is loved, trust is engendered and creative risking becomes a possibility. We can say, "So what if I fail at a good attempt? I will be loved. I am confident of that. He or she knows me and still loves me; I can attempt my idea." This then makes possible one of the goals of the Christian life—good works; it should be a natural result of the cleansed conscience (9:14), one of the fruits of salvation (Eph. 2:10, James 2:14–18). As Paul discovered in the lives of the Corinthian Christians, such good works do not always come naturally or automatically. Our exhorter encourages his readers to both love and good works.

Next he says they should not abandon (*egkataliepontes,* "forsake, leave behind, or desert") their gathering together, their worship. How many times have we seen people who for the sake of the relational groups have left the worship of the church? Or, from the other side, people who, being involved in works of social justice and the rough and tumble of social confrontation, have considered worship with the other saints a bit too mild? Whether from the sentiment of "warm-fuzzies" or judgmentalism rising out of radical mentality, some have left off worship; it has become their life style, or as verse 25 puts it, it *"is the manner of some."* Notice again our author will not permit us to separate our works from our worship. In this he is in concurrence with Isaiah, who will not let us separate worship and justice (Isa. 1:12–17).

Why is there such importance placed on tying the two together? Worship is the event in which we become radioactive for God. When we are not in the collective worship with God's people, we have missed an exposure to God, and having missed it, we lose our radiance.

This last week I visited a new member of National Presbyterian Church who is Chief of Radiology at the National Institute of Health. One of the labs we visited was marked to receive a new cyclotron for making radioactive elements that could be used to create radioactive isotopes, used in diagnostic scanning equipment or in radiation therapy. Some of the elements have such a short half-life of radioactivity that they must be used within a few minutes of their production. The cyclotron and the patient must be in close proximity to one another.

We Christians are like short-lived radioactive isotopes; we have very short half-life. Get us away from the worship of God with other saints and our radioactivity dissipates quickly and we lose our effective radiance. The circumstances of our writer's period intensified the need for maximum strength radiating from the lives of the believers. Christ is the radiance of God (see the section on *apaugasma* and *doxa*, 1:3), and we must constantly be in a worshiping relationship with Him and with other Christians.

Instead of forsaking the worship, let us instead encourage (*parakalountes*) one another and all the more so as we *"see the Day approaching"* (v. 25). Is that Day a day of heightened persecution or is it the last day of history which the early church thought was close at hand? That latter is less probable, I think, because much of the author's concern is for the coming time of persecution in which he wants his believers to stand firmly, not casting aside their faith and confidence in the face of severe pressure.

This concludes the three statements that make up the exhortation proper, which always precedes the warning and reason in our author's pattern of presentation.

A FEARFUL WARNING

26 For if we sin willfully after we have received
the knowledge of the truth, there no longer remains
a sacrifice for sins,

27 but a certain fearful expectation of judgment, and fiery indignation which will devour the adversaries.

28 Anyone who has rejected Moses' law dies without mercy on the testimony of two or three witnesses.

29 Of how much worse punishment, do you suppose, will he be thought worthy who has trampled the Son of God underfoot, counted the blood of the covenant by which he was sanctified a common thing, and insulted the Spirit of grace?

30 For we know Him who has said, "*Vengeance is Mine; I will repay, says the Lord.*" And again, "*The LORD will judge His people.*"

31 It is a fearful thing to fall into the hands of the living God!

Heb. 10:26–31

Here again is a passionate expression of our teacher's concern with regard to falling away. In a movement and reasoning similar to that of 5:11—6:20 he warns his readers that if they sin willfully after receiving the knowledge of the truth, there no longer remains a sacrifice for sins. *"Knowledge of the truth"* is expressed by a word that has the connotation of intimate knowledge as over against intellectual knowledge. The strong implication is that the knowledge is that which comes after the ministry of the Holy Spirit. That *"there no longer remains a sacrifice for sins"* indicates a desperate condition for the sinner. "No longer" implies that there was once a sacrifice reserved for the sinner. But after this type of sinning that sacrifice is withdrawn and he is without recourse to hope. Instead there is reserved a fearful prospect of judgment and fire that will devour those who stand against this knowledge of the truth. Not a happy prospect.

What sort of sin is that that deserves such punishment? Our writer describes it in inescapably clear terminology. *"Anyone who has rejected"* (*athetēsas,* "to do away with what has been laid down, to set aside, disregard") the law of Moses dies on the testimony of two or three witnesses. The directness of the verb "dies" is harsh and stark in this syntax. There is no qualifier such as "deserves to die" or "might die"; but simply "he dies," as though this was a foregone conclusion. *"How much worse punishment"* (*timōrias,* which can also mean "penalty" or "vengeance") will be deserved by one *"who has trampled the Son of God underfoot"*? The sin being implied here is not that of turning aside from or rejecting, but abusively and blatantly crushing with disdain none other than the Son of God. This does not appear to be a weakness of personality but a spirit of willful rejection.

The author further describes the sin as considering to be *"common"* the blood of the covenant by which this recipient of truth was sanctified. The phrase *"the blood . . . by which he was sanctified"* leaves little room for arguing anything other than the cleansing of conscience that is the mark of the new covenant in a worshiper's life. Calling the blood of Christ "common" (*koinon*) or unclean would be the ultimate insult, indicating utter derision or disdain. *Koinon* here would be in contrast to *hagion* ("holy, consecrated"), thus implying "defiled." In Matthew 15:11, Jesus says it is what comes out of the mouth that defiles a person. Acts 21:28 tells that a crowd of Jewish opponents of Paul claim he has brought Greeks into the temple, thus defiling it. Nothing could be more repulsive to the Jew. Evidently this is the sense in which our author is speaking.

A third characteristic of this rejecting spirit is the insulting or mocking of the Spirit of grace. Hebrews 10:29 is the only place this word, *enubrizō,* is used in the New Testament. In classical Greek, the word carries a meaning of insulting or mocking one regarding a matter. Evidently the writer has in mind the sneering derogation of a gracious work of the Holy Spirit as being tawdry and cheap, sentimental and not worthy of respect. When used in the medical field, the word connotes the irritating of an ulcer or, as a noun, the victim of outrage.

And what is God's response to this rejection of the most costly gift? Our teacher quotes Deuteronomy 32:35–36, which shows God's outrage and judgment upon those who have scoffed at the Rock of their salvation and stirred Him to jealousy and anger by going after strange gods and practicing abominations.

This section of warning closes with a chilling terseness: *"It is a fearful thing to fall into the hands of the living God!"* (v. 31).

A STATEMENT OF ENCOURAGEMENT

32 But recall the former days in which, after you were illuminated, you endured a great struggle with sufferings:

33 partly while you were made a spectacle both by

reproaches and tribulations, and partly while you became companions of those who were so treated;

34 for you had compassion on me in my chains, and joyfully accepted the plundering of your goods, knowing that you have a better and an enduring possession for yourselves in heaven.

35 Therefore do not cast away your confidence, which has great reward.

36 For you have need of endurance, so that after you have done the will of God, you may receive the promise:

37 *"For yet a little while,*
   And He who is coming will come and will not
      tarry.

38 *Now the just shall live by faith;*
   But if anyone draws back,
   My soul has no pleasure in him."

39 But we are not of those who draw back to perdition, but of those who believe to the saving of the soul.

Heb. 10:32–39

As in the previous passage of severe warning (5:11—6:8), our exhorter softens the sounds of judgment with a positive statement of praise and encouragement.

After the harsh warning and the tightly woven reasoning for the judgment, our writer plays the role of encourager; he reminds his people of their good days of early discipleship, when with a magnificent spirit they endured suffering themselves and identified with those who were suffering. He describes them as having been *"illuminated"* (*phōtisthentes*). You were marvelous! he says. In the midst of many afflictions (*pollēn athlēsin*—we get our word "athletics" from this word— "struggles, tough engagements") you *"endured"* (*hupemeinate*, "remained on top," from the root *monein*, "remain")—you did not go under.

This word brings to my mind an athletic event not many of us witness unless we are from logging territory. Log-rolling is a great thing to watch; the contestants display agility, precision, endurance— and somebody gets dunked! Two contestants take their positions on a section of a ten- or twelve-foot long log of considerable diameter. The goal is to stay on top while causing the opponent to lose his or her balance and fall off. The footwork is quick, and reactions must be immediate. The pace at which one must respond to the other's change of pace or shift of balance becomes dizzying. The victor fends off the challenge and stays on top! That is *hupomonē*—the ability to remain on top of the fast-moving circumstances and connivings of the enemy.

This kind of enduring had been difficult for the readers addressed in this epistle. They were not playing a game of sportful joy, but had been made the butt of ridicule and held up as spectacles of laughter (*theatrizomenoi*—to be put on stage as a comedy act against one's will, to be the recipient of raucous laughter). Reproach and suffering came at them from every direction. Some of it came directly to them; at times they voluntarily identified as comrades (*koinōnoi*) with those who had been so treated.

There is some doubt among various translations as to the exact wording of verse 34. Where our translation has *"me in my chains,"* as in some manuscripts, most others read "on prisoners." A few read "on chains," which is either an idiom meaning those in chains, or an errant copy. The point is not important; the emphasis here is on the readers having shown care and compassion even if such care implicated them. Moreover, they accepted with joy the plundering of their property. The Greek word means violent or illegal pillaging, robbery, or an act of seizure. Most probably the authorities turned their backs on the crime, leaving these victims with every reason to feel very angry or mistreated. Instead, they were joyful. Why?

During the destructive fire of Bel Air (Los Angeles) in 1960, in which some 465 homes were lost, several families who were members of our congregation lost their homes and all their belongings. Among these were Leonard and Marilee Picker. Leonard was one of Hollywood's very successful producers and his family controlled one of the large studios. His home was filled with valuable artifacts and awards from many years of film-making. Leonard had recently found Jesus Christ as the Messiah and referred to himself as a fulfilled Jew. His hunger for the Scriptures and theology had been insatiable, and he read voluminously. His way of gathering the congregation to his rotund body was so fatherly and loving that we called him our "thirteenth apostle." Now, in the third year of his new life in Christ, his home was gone and everything in it. After saving my own home which had started to burn, I joined the fire brigade and for two days tried to save homes, sometimes successfully, sometimes not successfully. On one of our runs to get ahead of the fire, we turned down Leonard and Marilee's street. I peered over the fire truck to get the earliest look at his home. It was just then going up in flames, engulfed—a raging furnace of destruction.

The next night we gathered at the church. The Sunday school tables had been piled high with emergency supplies of clothing, bedding, food, and such simple things as safety pins, with which Marilee held an oversized pair of trousers together. That was all she had. We ate, we sang, we testified to God's saving goodness and the dedication of those who had fought fires, for no one had died. Leonard stood up to make his statement. His face was alive with a radiance that was apostolic. With emotion clutching at his voice, he said, "I thank God for my life" (and with that he patted his ample forefront); "for my wife" (he looked tenderly at Marilee), "and for my family" (here he picked up Gina, his little daughter). "Three years ago I had my spiritual birth; yesterday I had my material birth; I was born free of material possessions!" Gratefulness filled his face; joy was in every pore of his body.

Agitated and angry, one young executive who had been coming up fast in the business world said to me, "What's he so happy about? Doesn't he know he's lost *everything?*" No, Leonard had not lost everything, certainly not the most important things; he still had Jesus and that was enough for him. He still possessed the enduring worth.

Our teacher saw this incalculable prize and he did not want his readers to risk losing it. Verse 35 puts it: *"Do not cast away your confidence, which has great reward"* (*misthapodosia,* from *misthos,* "wages or hire," and *apodidomi,* "to render, give back").

As a wise and experienced coach, he then puts his finger on the necessary ingredient. *"You have need of endurance"* (*hupomonēs,* the same word used in v. 32, translated "endured") *"so that after you have done the will of God, you may receive the promise."* The word used here for "receive" has the augmented meaning of carrying off *securely,* receiving *surely.*

Verses 37 and 38 are a quotation that he must have seen as a clear answer for those who asked about the timing of the gift and promise of God, "Why does it take so long for God to answer prayer?" He might well have responded, "Having done the will of God in obedience and having endured is like planting seed. Don't leave too soon or you may be departing just as the seed germinates and you may never see it. Some years are slower than others; wait a bit longer for the promise of God."

It is by such faith that the righteous live. But all too often we are like impetuous children, desiring immediate results. We have to learn that some things, like oak trees, take awhile to grow. If oak is the wood necessary for the building, then we must wait for the strength to come into its massive trunk. We can only optimize; we cannot hurry the process. Those who leave the scene before the process is completed are a deep disappointment to the keeper of the forest. He can see the growth and knows that things are on schedule. It is we, the overeager children, who grow weary.

Our writer urges his readers not to be among the impatient and assures them that they are winners. They are those who belong to salvation, forever!

CHAPTER FOURTEEN

The Character of Faith—
Basic Teaching for Perseverance

Hebrews 11:1–40

Chapter 11 of the Epistle to the Hebrews is one of the classic passages of the New Testament. The reason is not so much that its poetic language is equal to that of 1 Corinthians 13 or its impact as powerful as that of Romans 8. Rather its sheer weight of witness and its dynamic and unforgettable definition of faith penetrate the very core of the modern heart.

This chapter cannot be separated from the section just preceding. Our faith is based upon the perfect and sufficient sacrifice of Jesus Christ. It is that sacrifice, completed once for all time and for all people, which opens for us a way into the very presence of God in whose presence we can come with holy boldness, free of all fear of holy retribution, utterly confident of forgiveness in the face of God. Looking ahead, this chapter also becomes the launching pad of the next, regarding Christian discipline. The same God of love who has made His unique sacrifice for us also disciplines and brings us wholesome maturity by His own design and grace.

As chapter 11 closes, however, our author is talking about persecution as one of the outcomes of a life of faith. Not all the examples he uses are of victory and spiritual success. True, some of those who lived by faith conquered kingdoms, enforced justice, quenched raging fires, stopped the mouths of lions, escaped the edge of the sword, and become valiant in battle. Others had trials of mockings and scourgings, chains and imprisonment; they were stoned, sawed in two, slain with the sword. They were destitute, afflicted, tormented; they wandered over deserts and lived in caves and dens of earth. Yet, because of their faith, they shine as exemplars of endurance, perseverance, and courage. By faith, by faith, by faith—this phrase echoes again and again, line after line in this chapter. This faith must have been a powerful force, a well of refreshment, a stable platform of confidence upon which these saints could stand in every circumstance of life.

What was this faith?

Our author opens this faith drama with a definition that will be heralded by Christians forever. It will be mused on by those in the depths of discouragement; it will consume those with a voracious hunger for courage. Listen to the definition that will satisfy multitudes yet unborn.

THE SUBSTANCE OF FAITH

1 Now faith is the substance of things hoped for,
the evidence of things not seen.
2 For by it the elders obtained a good testimony.

Heb. 11:1–2

"Faith is the substance" (*hupostasis*). The Greek word here gives the sense of something foundational, basic, a concrete reality upon which other things are built. *Stasis,* the root of the word, means the place, setting, a standing pillar, that upon which other stones are placed. The prefix *hupo* means "under" or "below." Together the result signifies something solidly foundational, concrete in reality, something assured. Thus faith as defined by our exhorter is not an imaginary product of the mind fabricated out of its own philosophical needs or rationalistic dreams, but that which is firm, solid, of real existence. Faith is the solid certainty of that for which we hope, based upon reality and solid existence.

He continues: *"[Faith is] the evidence of things not seen."* The Greek phrase *pragmatos elegchos* is translated as the single word "evidence." Yet when the words are considered separately, they carry force and strength not usually associated with faith, which may more usually be seen as pragmatic reality. *Pragmatōn,* on the one hand, spreads out an idea of concrete reality, something that is critical, of consequence and of great importance—something foundational. *Elegchos* implies a thought or belief that has been cross-examined, questioned so as to be tested for validity or reality, brought to proof or placed under scrutiny for possible confutation. Faith, then, is based upon that which is tested and is crucial. And what is it that is unseen but is yet tested and important; is it not the power of God working through His government of all events in history, which from time to time experiences His mighty acts? This power may be unseen for awhile, perhaps, but we come to know it as ultimate and crucial, dependable, solid, foundational. Our faith does not create reality, but is based upon the reality of God's government and power. It is by this faith, turned loose in history by the faithful action of prophets and believers, that God has brought the miracles to bear upon nations and their history.

FAITH AND EPISTEMOLOGY

3 By faith we understand that the worlds were
framed by the word of God, so that the things which
are seen were not made of things which are visible.
Heb. 11:3

In verse 3 our writer indicates faith's place in epistemology, that is, in the structure or formation of knowledge: *"By faith we understand that the worlds were framed by the word of God, so that the things which are seen were not made of things which are visible."* The RSV words it: "so that what is seen was made out of things which do not appear." How do we know how the world was made? By scientific observation? No, for no one was there to observe. By laboratory experiment? Impossible, for in any experiment we must begin with that which is. Creation was out of nothing. By mathematical formulation? No, because all equations must finish with a balance; nothing can be added or subtracted from the sides of an equation without corresponding function on the other side. By what method do we then know how the worlds were made? Only through faith, given by revelation of God, beyond the proof or disproof of any person: "We know by faith that the worlds were created by the word of God." If that is what God has said in His communication with the prophets through the ages and we find Him dependable on all other matters regarding which He has communicated, then we believe—we know by faith.

All physical matter is made up of that which "does not appear." The basic particles of matter as we perceive them today are the protons, neutrons, and electrons that make up atomic nuclei. Put these into certain atomic relationships and build up enough of them in molecular structure and you have "that which is seen." Yet separated and unassociated, these building blocks are but energy—and unseen. Our author's statement is amazingly sophisticated in the light of contemporary understanding of physical matter.

Philosophically we are left in the air by creation. Infinite categories await us on either side of the argument. Either matter existed from all time (and that is an infinite idea) or it was made out of nothing (another infinite category). Logically and philosophically we are stymied. Only by faith can we hope to understand. We of faith are not embarrassed to say, "God created the heavens and the earth." Not to say that is to cast ourselves on some unknown, impersonal force that cares little if at all for what happens to creatures of this world. Our faith tells us that there is a Father and Creator Who cares after He has thrown the magnificence of the universe into its balanced structure. I would rather live in that faith than die in unbelief.

Moreover, faith not only gives us understanding as to the origin of existence, but also its meaning. Science can describe the atomic structures and can learn how to manipulate them, but it has proven itself tragically incapable of telling how to use such knowledge. Science can give us an atomic device and we view it in its glass case, its metal sheath burnished and gleaming with awesome quietness. We stand silent before it, knowing what can happen to a hundred thousand lives in a matter of infamous seconds. We are filled with a mixture of amazement at what we humans have wrought and at our stupidity in not knowing how to limit the use of such invention or how to control ourselves. It is faith that tells us how to use the dominion humanity has gained over nature, a faith born of the heart of a loving God and Creator, the only trustworthy object of our faith. Faith is not only to know; faith is a walk in God's world.

EXAMPLES IN FAITH—ABEL AND ENOCH

4 By faith Abel offered to God a more excellent sacrifice than Cain, through which he obtained witness that he was righteous, God testifying of his gifts; and through it he being dead still speaks.

5 By faith Enoch was translated so that he did not

see death, *"and was not found because God had
translated him"*; for before his translation he had this
testimony, that he pleased God.

6 But without faith it is impossible to please Him,
for he who comes to God must believe that He is,
and that He is a rewarder of those who diligently seek
Him.

Heb. 11:4–6

Our writer now leads us on to consider the lives of two men known
simply for their faith. Abel and Enoch pleased God, by their faith.
Abel offered to God a sacrifice more acceptable than his brother Cain.
Some have said this was because the sacrifice was one of blood, but
our author does not appear to support that thesis. At least, at this
point he is not talking about blood sacrifice but about faith. It seems
most probable, therefore, that the factor of difference in the comparison was that of heart, not of the sacrifice. Evidently Abel surpassed
his brother in that his attitude toward God was one of confidence
in God's graciousness. Cain's attitude, on the other hand, was one
of competitiveness that thought this graciousness had to be bought
by human effort or the sacrifice of a minimal offering after calculating
God's "price." To our author, the critical factor was the quality of
Abel's faith.

Enoch is described as having pleased God and so did not see death,
but was simply taken straight to God without the experience of physical death. The manner by which he pleased God was that of faith,
however expressed. His "walk with God" must have been one of
sensitivity to the mind of God and obedience to the mind and will
of God. In the thinking of our author, expressed in chapters 3 and
4, no one is going to obey God unless that person believes God knows
what He is talking about: that is faith. Moreover, because God has
a plan for every person and for His world, anyone who is not sensitive
to His will and who does not obey in faith is going to leave that
will of God unfulfilled. God takes no pleasure in such disregard.
Without faith in a God who created the world with order; without
faith in a God who provides for the children of His love; without
faith in a God who loves justice and hates lawlessness; without faith
in a God who makes a way, the only way, into the sanctuary of
His presence—without such faith it is impossible to please a God

who desires and demands that we believe these things about Him. To believe anything else or to think we can do these things without His aid is to deny the very character of God and try to play His role ourselves. That is the height of arrogance! No, without faith it is impossible to please God.

FAITH AND OBEDIENCE

7 By faith Noah, being divinely warned of things not yet seen, moved with godly fear, prepared an ark for the saving of his household, by which he condemned the world and became heir of the righteousness which is according to faith.

8 By faith Abraham obeyed when he was called to go out to the place which he would afterward receive as an inheritance. And he went out, not knowing where he was going.

9 By faith he sojourned in the land of promise as in a foreign country, dwelling in tents with Isaac and Jacob, the heirs with him of the same promise;

10 for he waited for the city which has foundations, whose builder and maker is God.

11 By faith Sarah herself also received strength to conceive seed, and she bore a child when she was past the age, because she judged Him faithful who had promised.

12 Therefore from one man, and him as good as dead, were born as many as the stars of the sky in multitude—innumerable as the sand which is by the seashore.

Heb. 11:7–12

In these verses our teacher gives us three examples of obedience that rise out of faith. Here again he shows the inseparability of faith and obedience. In this he concurs with other New Testament writers: there is no other way to be happy in Jesus but to trust and obey.

Noah, Abraham, and Sarah all exhibited obedience as a result of their faith. Moreover, all were characterized by an obedience that went beyond, or even contradicted, common sense.

Noah, in faith, received a divine revelation, heeded it, and built an ark, even against normal reason. Imagine, in a large field behind your home, constructing an ark that obviously could not be transported to water because of its bulky size. When Noah did this, friends and neighbors began to ridicule him. "Hey, Noah, what are you doing—building a boat? How are you going to get it to water?" Probably, raucous laughter mingled with their friendly or not-so-friendly jibes. However, when the waters came, the laughter changed to cries of anguish and pleading, finally fading away in the swirling waters of judgment. Noah's faith and obedience became judgment to those who would not listen or believe. His obedience was received as righteousness. It was obedience against all common sense.

Abraham, too, in faith, obeyed. His motivation was simple; he believed God when He said, "Go from your country and your kindred and your father's house to the land that I will show you." Abraham went, yet he did not have the slightest idea where he was going. It was against all common sense to leave the place of familiarity, the land and people that he had known and loved all the years, and go to a place that was unknown. When he reached his destination, he lived as a sojourner, not an owner or possessor, in tents of temporary nature. By faith he looked into the future toward a city whose buildings had foundation stones, a symbol of permanence of the promise of God, in comparison to movable and unstable tents. He foresaw that the builder and maker of that city would be God. He believed—and so was counted as righteous.

Sarah, his dear old wife, having long since gone through menopause, received the message that she was going to have a son. At first she laughed. "Imagine, I who am called 'barren,' I am going to have a baby! I guess the messenger doesn't know my female condition or doesn't understand about bearing children. Oh, these men!" However, the messengers persisted in their promises with an intensity and honesty that put aside all flippancy or doubt. She yielded, and a wave of belief swept over her whole being: "I *am* going to have a baby!" By that faith she received power to conceive, and she bore the promised child. At her age, to have a child was against all common sense. The promise came through obedient faith.

This combination of faith and obedience is a reminder of the theme of chapters 3 and 4 of the epistle: "Do not harden your hearts as your fathers disobeyed by lack of belief." Obedience rises out of the soil of faith to bear its fruit of obedience.

FAITH AND FUTURE

13 These all died in faith, not having received the promises, but having seen them afar off were assured of them, embraced them, and confessed that they were strangers and pilgrims on the earth.

14 For those who say such things declare plainly that they seek a homeland.

15 And truly if they had called to mind that country from which they had come out, they would have had opportunity to return.

16 But now they desire a better, that is, a heavenly country. Therefore God is not ashamed to be called their God, for He has prepared a city for them.

17 By faith Abraham, when he was tested, offered up Isaac, and he who had received the promises offered up his only begotten son,

18 of whom it was said, *"In Isaac your seed shall be called,"*

19 accounting that God was able to raise him up, even from the dead, from which he also received him in a figurative sense.

20 By faith Isaac blessed Jacob and Esau concerning things to come.

21 By faith Jacob, when he was dying, blessed each of the sons of Joseph, and worshiped, leaning on the top of his staff.

22 By faith Joseph, when he was dying, made mention of the departure of the children of Israel, and gave instructions concerning his bones.

23 By faith Moses, when he was born, was hidden three months by his parents, because they saw he was a beautiful child; and they were not afraid of the king's command.

24 By faith Moses, when he became of age, refused to be called the son of Pharaoh's daughter,

25 choosing rather to suffer affliction with the people of God than to enjoy the passing pleasures of sin,

26 esteeming the reproach of Christ greater riches than the treasures in Egypt; for he looked to the reward.

27 By faith he forsook Egypt, not fearing the wrath

of the king; for he endured as seeing Him who is invisible.

28 By faith he kept the Passover and the sprinkling of blood, lest he who destroyed the firstborn should touch them.

29 By faith they passed through the Red Sea as by dry land, whereas the Egyptians, attempting to do so, were drowned.

30 By faith the walls of Jericho fell down after they were encircled for seven days.

31 By faith the harlot Rahab did not perish with those who did not believe, when she had received the spies with peace.

32 And what more shall I say? For the time would fail me to tell of Gideon and Barak and Samson and Jephthah, also of David and Samuel and the prophets:

33 who through faith subdued kingdoms, worked righteousness, obtained promises, stopped the mouths of lions,

34 quenched the violence of fire, escaped the edge of the sword, out of weakness were made strong, became valiant in battle, turned to flight the armies of the aliens.

35 Women received their dead raised to life again. And others were tortured, not accepting deliverance, that they might obtain a better resurrection.

36 Still others had trial of mockings and scourgings, yes, and of chains and imprisonment.

37 They were stoned, they were sawn in two, were tempted, were slain with the sword. They wandered about in sheepskins and goatskins, being destitute, afflicted, tormented—

38 of whom the world was not worthy. They wandered in deserts and mountains, in dens and caves of the earth.

39 And all these, having obtained a good testimony through faith, did not receive the promise,

40 God having provided something better for us, that they should not be made perfect apart from us.

Heb. 11:13-40

A faith in the God of the future is the theme of this next passage. Those mentioned—Abraham, Sarah, Isaac, Jacob, Joseph, Moses and his parents, the followers of Joshua and Rahab, a Gentile harlot—were all futurists. In each case they died without having received what had been promised to them; they saw it afar off. The Greek verb translated *"not having received"* carries the notion of not having the promise in one's possession or pocket, as it were. As people of faith, however, they could see this promise afar off and were assured of it, embracing the vision of faith to their hearts, realizing they were merely pilgrims and strangers in the here and now. The desire was so intense, yet they sensed this was not God's timing. They put their lives on the foundation stones of faith in a reliable God upon which the future would be erected. Someday the building, the temple of faith, would be finished, and, according to verse 10, God Himself would be the builder (*technitēs,* "craftsman, artificer") and maker (*dēmiourgos,* "author, builder, maker, Creator"). It is interesting to recall our discussion on pp. 49–52 regarding Platonism and *dēmiourgos.* This is the only place in the New Testament where this word is used.

All the believers mentioned in this passage were to be the living stones of foundation upon which others would be laid. Thus they would be completed in those who would come later. We who have come later are those completing stones, giving the saints of old the joy and satisfaction realized by any pioneers who are able to look back and see their dreams fulfilled in later generations.

Each of these futurists looked into the future with eyes of faith and had some glimpse of the promise God had for them and for their children. They were unwilling to satisfy themselves with the short-term advantages that would have denied the long-term fulfillments. Many of them made the sacrifice of the quick gratification in order to possess the greater satisfaction of the ultimate promise. They did not jeopardize a future generation's resources or promises by craving immediate satisfaction of their desires. They left the promise intact for those who came after.

Abraham was told to offer up his son Isaac. We can only imagine the horror and anguish of his heart as he wrestled with the rationale of such a command. "But he is the son of promise, the one through whom God is going to fulfill His promise! Surely there must be some mistake. It's a bad dream; it's the silly pessimism of an old man who has waited so long. A foolish thought—I must get it out of my head. It can't be true!"

Still the command persisted. Abraham put aside his immediate gratification of having his son with him and in his mind gave him up to God—as our author says, believing that God "was able to raise him up, even from the dead." That is faith!—against all common sense. But who said the God in whom Abraham believed was at all common! In the very process of the sacrifice, God provided by other means, showing the importance of obedience but at the same time His gracious provision for our needs. When we act in belief, God gets into the act!

Isaac, looking into the future although no kind of demand was placed upon him to challenge the dream, blessed his two sons, Jacob and Esau. The covenant had been given to him as it had to his father, and he believed God. Jacob, old and feeble, living in the sojourn of simplicity, blessed each of the sons of Joseph. He looked forward to a day when the children would go to the land that had been promised to him, as it had been promised to his fathers Isaac and Abraham. When that happened he wanted his bones taken and buried in the land of covenant promise, "in the cave that was in the field of Ephron, in the cave that is in the field of Machpelah, to the east of Mamre." So clear and real was his vision that he knew even the place of his burial which would take place four centuries later. The Egyptians embalmed him over a period of forty days as was their custom and his final resting place was the land of promise (Gen. 49:29—50:3). He too was a futurist!

Joseph shared the dream of the future with his forebears. At his death he faced his brothers in all the honesty of a healing encounter, not hesitating to bring up their dastardly deed in selling him to the Ishmaelites. "As for you, you meant evil against me; but God meant it for good, in order to bring it about as it is this day, to save many people alive. Now therefore, do not be afraid; I will provide for you and your little ones. . . . I am dying; but God will surely visit you, and bring you out of this land to the land of which He swore to Abraham, to Isaac, and to Jacob. . . . And you shall carry up my bones from here" (Gen. 50:20–21, 24–25). He, too, like his father before him, trusted God for the promise of the future, for the land which they one day would inherit by the promise of God. Joseph was a futurist.

Moses also was a futurist, not willing to trade off the ultimate promise for the advantages that would have been immediate and powerful in the land of Egypt. He sensed that somehow he was to be identified with the people of his birth, even in their bondage and servitude. He saw no indication whatever that he was to be their victorious leader; he simply trusted God with the future of his life.

In this example of Moses our writer uses five illustrations of futuristic obedience. The first concerns his parents.

For his mother there might have been an immediate advantage of keeping her son. Her mother's instincts could well have overcome her faith in the future. For a mother to give up her child shortly after his birth, to take from her nurturing breast the child of love she had carried in her body for nine months and trust him to a frail basket on a mighty river, must have caused wrenching pain. Yet she trusted the future to hands of God whose love she trusted at least as much as her own for her son. Moses' parents refused to be cowered by the threats of Pharaoh; they defied the law of the land and set the pattern for their people for generations to come.

Moses himself, coming of age and seeing the suffering and pain of his people, refused to be called the son of Pharaoh's daughter. He must have experienced traumatic psychological tension. Imagine being raised in the court of Pharaoh, with all the stimulating advantage of education in science, architecture, military tactics, mathematics, and government. During those formative years, he had drunk of the sophistication and power of the Egyptian empire. He had grown up with princes and intelligentsia, in a heady atmosphere of power and prestige. When and how he became aware of his true native identity we do not know. At some time he must have seen the Hebrew people with eyes of belonging. Stories or cheap jokes about their fertility or customs would have become agonizing episodes that he buried inside. Dared he speak out or should he hold his tongue? So intense became this inward tension that he began to stammer in his speech, the problem growing until he could scarcely be understood. All the sophistication, all the education, all the military prowess and brilliance of that mind and spirit were bound with thongs of inner tension—a tension between being a son of Pharaoh's daughter or a son of Hebrew slaves. To identify himself with the Hebrews would mean letting go all the advantages he had known and the possibility of helping his people through the power that he would eventually have. Perhaps he dreamed of the time when he could release them from their bondage and elevate them to a respected position among the nations of the earth. Instead, he gave all that over, and chose to share the ill treatment with his own people.

Then one day, when seeing an Egyptian slavemaster beating a Hebrew slave, he could not restrain himself. In actions learned all too well in the gymnasium of martial arts, he suddenly and quickly killed the Egyptian. The break with Pharaoh was complete! There was but one course of action—flee to the desert and be lost from the eyes and reach of Pharaoh's justice. The resulting tension and anger he carried for years while keeping sheep on the backside of the desert of Sinai. Nevertheless, he saw there something worth more than the treasures of Egypt; our writer says *"he endured as seeing Him who is invisible"* (v. 27). The vision of God at the burning bush gave him the strength to make what many might feel was an unbelievable break.

By faith Moses believed that God indeed would send the angel of death upon the first-born of Pharaoh's land. In the face of such imminent death, he must have truly trusted God to pass over the homes of faith whose only indication was a few swatches of blood over the lintel and on the doorposts. Such frail barriers to the awesome power of God!

When crossing the Red Sea, Moses' heart and the hearts of the people must have hesitated more than a moment at the situation. It might seem that it was the wind that had blown the shallow sea to the south. Anybody familiar with the circumstances would have known that once the wind ceased, that water would come rushing back to engulf anything or anyone present in that massive swirling tide. How long would it take for the Hebrews to cross? Would the first make it and the remainder be lost in the sea? Evidently Moses computed all the possibilities but banked on what he considered greatest—the trustworthiness of God. Yes, the waters did come swirling back, but not until all the children of the Hebrews were safely through the shallows. Only when the armies of the Pharaoh tried to follow hard after, did those waters rush back, claiming those who stood in the way, chariot wheels amuck in the soft earth of the sea's bottom.

Rahab, by acknowledging the past actions of the God of Israel, could see what lay ahead. As a futurist she asked the spies to spare her and her family when they came into the land. She said in simple faith, "I know that the Lord has given you the land. . . . The Lord your God, He is God in heaven above and on earth beneath" (Josh. 2:9, 11). She lived in faith in the future and so became part of the bloodline of Christ.

The passage including verses 32–40 is one of the most passionate and dramatic statements in all of Christian literature. The rise of emotion in our exhorter becomes a swelling tide of rhetorical brilliance with the opening words, *"What more shall I say?"* He longed for enough time to flesh out the stories of Gideon, Barak, Samson, Jephthah, David, and Samuel. One can sense a flood of emotion aching for expression, but he must satisfy himself with a few closing paragraphs on one of his most fervent subjects—faith.

His heroes fall into two categories, those who knew victory before their deaths and those whose faith had to be futuristic because all the tragedy of life they endured in faith had its reward in later generations.

Through faith some subdued kingdoms. There was David; amidst great obstacles, from a paranoid king who sought his life to a son who sought his throne, David endured. He endured until the stretch of Israel's might stretched across expanses of land.

One of his court members struggled with the price of justice. Nathan had to tell the powerful and beloved king, popular and on a high roll, that he was guilty of adultery and murder. He could have lost his head, but his call for justice was heard by a penitent David. Fortunately Nathan lived to see the result (2 Sam. 12).

Others obtained promises through lively, indefatigable faith. Imagine, Abram and Sarai receive a promised and longed-for child almost a score of years after the original promise was made. How frustration and agony must have caused them to doubt, wonder, and take things into their own hands—which they did. After perhaps a decade of waiting, Sarai induced Abram to go into her handmaid and have the child by her. Not until fourteen years later did Sarah finally bear her own son! The fact of the matter is that the fulfillment of God's promises is not always the most important thing; rather, it is what happens to us in the waiting period. Abraham and Sarah became the paragons of faith for the community of believers through all generations. Their names will always be associated with faith (Gen. 12—21).

Daniel, in a determination some might call religious fanaticism, refused to bow to an ego-saturated King Darius. Full of remorse at the interdict he had signed in a moment of arrogant delusion, and having attempted all day to circumvent his own law, Darius poignantly expresses his hope that Daniel's God will deliver him. The courageous believer is sealed in the den of lions by the anguish-struck king. Darius then fasts all night, sleeplessly enduring the endless hours. When the first signs of dawn light the sky he scurries out of the palace, shattering all protocol by hurrying to the den. Every step on his dim path intensifies the rising surge of feeling within him. Letting go all his noble, kingly behavior, he cries out in a tone of anguish, "Daniel, servant of the living God, has your God, whom you serve continually, been able to deliver you from the lions?" (Dan. 6:20).

Is God able? Immensely! Daniel was saved and Darius converted. Just read the song of praise Darius raises to God in Daniel 6:26–27. If your soul languishes in the face of seemingly overwhelming odds, read it and trust in a great God!

Prior to this Daniel and his renamed companions escaped the desperately hot fire Nebuchadnezzar had planned for those who would not worship him. After this first encounter with political power gone out of control, some might have breathed a sigh of relief and determined not to pay that price again. But not Daniel. Faith in almighty God should be proportionate to the object of faith; there could be no diminution of faith even as there was no diminution of God. He was willing to face a fiery furnace (Dan. 3:1–30).

Gideon saw the power of God without the power of the human sword (Judg. 7). Elijah (1 Kings 19) and Elisha (2 Kings 6) saw victory without the bloodshed.

Moses in his weakness found both strategy and strength to continue serving God (Exod. 18, Num. 11). Weak as they were in the moment of fatigue and extremity, God showed Himself in various ways to meet their faith hunger. David's faith in the power of God to win a victory over Goliath put a Philistine army in disarray (1 Sam. 17).

The widow of Zarephath who hosted Elijah received her son back in health after breath had gone out of him. Elijah's faith in the healing power of God and his urgent prayers were the avenues of God's might (1 Kings 17).

Not all men and women of faith had the rewards of faith in their grasp during their lifetimes, however.

"Others were tortured, not accepting deliverance, that they might obtain a better resurrection" (Heb. 11:35). Here, I cannot help thinking that our author has in mind the martyrdom of Paul, which probably took place just one or two years or even a few months before the writing of this epistle. If Paul had played the game a bit more politically, he doubtless could have had his freedom (Acts 25:12; 26:32). If, as tradition has it, Paul was beheaded in A.D. 67 or 68 and this epistle was written in A.D. 68 or 69 as we have argued (pp. 29–30),

then the memory of his death still burned as a fresh, hot fire on the hearth of his mind. The persecution may well have been going on in the empire since A.D. 64 when Nero proclaimed holding the Christian faith a crime worthy of death and falsely accused and imprisoned Christians. He killed them in all sorts of imaginative ways in the circuses of Rome, even dressing them in animal skins to be ravaged by hungry lions. Gawking, shouting mobs crowded the arenas to watch the carnage. With their almost insatiable appetites for violence, they were not worthy of these simple believers, who in their destitution appeared so frail and powerless. Yet these martyrs turned not only stomachs but the souls of Rome. They fled to the caves of the wilderness and wandered across the deserts on their way to distant lands to preach and find safety (vv. 35–37).

These latter Christians died without having possessed the promise. In spite of their empty-handedness, they perservered in faith, knowing that faith's reward is not always given now. Revolutionaries over the world have died for future generations. Is that any less true of the saints? Theirs was a foundational faith, faith upon which others built. Their perfection, their completedness, is not in their own experience but in ours. In Romans 4:9, Paul states that God "reckoned" (an accountant's word, meaning "it is credited") righteousness to Abraham. At times we are credited with resources that cannot be withdrawn until a deposit is made. When these saints see us walking into the bank of God and coming out with our hands full of the abundance of God's grace in Jesus Christ, they know that their completion has come as well. They rejoice to see our day, for our day becomes their day of rejoicing in the appropriation of the grace of Jesus Christ.

This futuristic faith has been more than any persecuting power could control, superior to any pompous ideology that has claimed the right to rule the world. Long after such demagogues have been defeated, humiliated, broken, and forgotten, the lives of the believing saints have been remembered in the songs, histories, pageants, and hearts of one generation after another. Maybe they died without receiving what this world considers the rewards and possessions of victory, but they do not die unattached. They are tied to later generations by the cords of God's living community of faith. They are brought to completion by those who march on the roads they built with the stones of their faithful actions; they have their joy as saints consciously with Jesus Christ, looking back upon the lives marching after them. They are aware of their faith being perfected and completed by the next band of believers. In God's perfect unity, they are being perfected in us. What a glorious responsibility we share to complete the lives and the faith of those who have paid the price of faith before us!

I am thinking of a group of young German theological students who after World War II had bicycled to northern Italy to participate in an ecumenical work camp in the Alps. They had grown up during the dreaded days of Hitler's Germany, knowing nothing but the demagoguery that led that historic nation into such tragic defeat. But no sooner had the acrid war clouds of fighting between the Allied and Axis powers blown away, giving hope of their once again being able to breathe the air of liberty and freedom, than they were stifled by the oppression of a Communist government. Once again they were betrayed by some of their own countrymen who were willing to sell their souls for a bit of power or security by cooperating with the new regime. These young men knew nothing but oppression.

At the camp, they told us stories of their fathers. Christians, these men had each been taken by the secret police. Not one of the young men knew the circumstances of his father. Yet each continued his studies in order to become a pastor ministering to the community of the faithful.

One of the men told the story of his New Testament professor who was taken into custody by Communist authorities. Wanting to break down the leadership and make it subservient to Marxist ideology, they subjected this professor to the diabolical process of brainwashing. They would let him sleep only two or three hours a night; his food was kept from him until he almost died of starvation and then he was fed just in time to "save" him. He said that, strangely, he appreciated the efforts of those who fed him back to some strength and even felt kindness toward them. He was tortured by having a hollow steel cylinder placed over his head and struck at random intervals with a steel hammer, so as almost to make him deaf. His cell was only $1\frac{1}{3}$ x $1\frac{2}{3}$ meters in dimension so that he could not stretch out or exercise. His light, which was kept on at all hours, was recessed into the concrete ceiling and covered with a steel mesh so that he could not get at it. He had no idea of day or night, or of how many days he had been incarcerated. All they wanted from him was a "confession" that he had participated in teaching a religion that "was an opiate of the people."

His response was one of strength and refusal to cooperate. They asked him time after time how he could say that the life he had known with Jesus Christ was not a sham and an opiate. Then the fatigue and confusion of starvation began to take their toll. He knew he was close to the breaking point; certainly God would understand.

Then on one occasion when he was left to himself for a short period of cherished rest, his cell was filled with a light far more brilliant than that of the electric light bulb. He saw no figure, but knew that God was present in the form of this light. He heard no sound, but understood the message: "I will never leave you nor forsake you. I will give you power for whatever comes. You will be utterly sufficient."

It was as though he had had a full night's sleep. His body was refreshed; his mind renewed as having been with loved ones for a long and therapeutic period. Passages of the Greek testament he had memorized came back in a rush of clarity and brilliance. Truths from the Word that he had never perceived before flooded over him with a powerful energy.

When shortly his tormentors came, he not only stood up to their questions, but actually felt an overwhelming love for them, and even preached short sentences until they forced him to silence. He knew the victory would ultimately be God's. He felt he could see years or decades into the future when this ideology would be seen for what it was—a Godless materialism. He was absolutely convinced it could not meet the hungers and desires of the people and would be thrown aside. He said so.

A few days later he was suddenly released. He could hardly believe he was walking through the streets of his town with those he loved. To his students and those to whom he preached, he was a firebrand of apostolic power! Having glimpsed the future through the eyes of faith, he conquered kingdoms and sent burning torches to set aflame the dry kindling of God-hungering hearts. He was multiplied in scores of his students, ministering with such power as to confute the authorities.

Recently the bishop of Uganda, Festo Kivengere, came to us in Washington, D.C. As that magnificent man of God stood, I felt as though a tired Western church was hearing a dynamic new word from one who had been sent as our missionary. How desperately we needed him in our church, and what his communion in Africa had. The historical tables of missionary activity had reversed.

He spoke of his countrymen who had suffered at the hands of Idi Amin. Many had been killed, many tortured. Yet as they were placed before firing squads, they spoke of God's love to their executioners. Smiles wreathed their faces and their songs to Jesus filled the stadiums or the fields where they were martyred. Waves were converted in their stead so that if the present rate of Christian growth continues in that continent, 300 million of 500 million by the year 2000 will be baptized Christians.

Those who died had one common belief—they were going to be with Jesus immediately upon their earthly death. Some even thanked their murderers for sending them home to Jesus. Their future was secure; they could see beyond this life to that which Christ has promised His faithful. They were indeed futurists—like the great cloud of witnesses who had gone before.

Now they add to that great cloud of witnesses sitting in the stadium of eternal history and shouting encouragement to those of us who run our races. God grant that we can hear their shouts. May we too be the futurists of faith!

CHAPTER FIFTEEN

An Exhortation to Perseverance

Hebrews 12:1–29

Let Us Run with Endurance

> 1 Therefore we also, since we are surrounded by
> so great a cloud of witnesses, let us lay aside every
> weight, and the sin which so easily ensnares us, and
> let us run with endurance the race that is set before
> us,
>
> *Heb. 12:1*

The twelfth chapter of Hebrews is again one of the great classic passages, this time on the Christian life. Like the preceding chapter, it will always be held close by those of the faith. One does not come to any familiarity with the New Testament without coming to cherish this section on discipline. Not that all of us thrill at the idea of discipline! Yet deep down, like teenagers chafing under it, we know it is absolutely necessary, and we even long for it.

Our author has included this passage for a very definite reason. As he looks into the future, he sees the high probability of persecution coming down heavily on the lives of his readers. As one who loves them, he desires that they be ready and fit for the trauma. We can sense that he does not wish to indulge them in sympathy, but to stir them to stand as did those who have gone before. Do they think they can get off with any less commitment or cost than the saints who earlier bore their witness? No, what was required of the witnesses of the past will be required of this generation.

The setting is a great stadium of spiritual athletics. The stands are filled with the great athletes of the past who have run their races and completed their events and are now eager to encourage the new contestants. Notice, they are alive, aware, and present. No mere sense of historical memory is expressed here, but the picture of an active, watching throng shouting encouragement to those now struggling in their own events.

Abel is there, having offered a sacrifice in the attitude of faith which pleased God. There was no self-trust in his sacrifice.

Noah is sitting beside him; having heard the command of God to do that which was ridiculous in the eyes of his neighbors, he obeyed in the simple faith that God knew what he was talking about. That mindset of the spiritual athlete is so critical to success.

Abraham is there with Sarah, his wife. The promise given to them was totally unreasonable by human understanding of physiology, but when God persisted in His promise, they believed Him. That great old saint left the land of his fathers and went out to a land whose location he did not even know, and he did not demand of God an explanation or map. He trusted Him. That is the attitude of the spiritual champion.

Close by was Enoch, whose simple life was one of walking with God. Some folks are not known for their awesome feats, but just for the quality of their personal lives. That is the quality that marks the athlete of the Spirit.

Isaac, Jacob, and Joseph were in the author's mind as athletes who had looked to the tape at the finish of their race and were so confident of its reality that they blessed their children in the light of God's promise.

Moses caught everyone's attention. His massive frame and intense eyes gave him that charismatic countenance that draws the breath of others in seeing it.

Now comes the moment of our race. The call for the race is given; the athletes begin to prepare themselves for the event. It is evident that a great deal of training has gone on. As warm-up suits are laid aside, lean and conditioned muscles witness to months of intense discipline. Our writer encourages those who read his exhortation to "lay aside every weight." The Greek word for "weight" can mean body bulk, excess weight. For spiritual athletes that can be a case of too many irons in the fire, too many dissipating interests, too many branches of good things that suck the vital energy from the very best. Jesus said that God, the Vinedresser, prunes the best branches of any suckers that they may bear all the more quality fruit. The word can also mean weight in the sense of an encumbrance. Those warm-up togs now must be discarded. Protective warmth is fine for preparatory periods of spiritual growth, but there comes a time when these pleasant weights must be laid aside and we expose our bodies to whatever conditions prevail as we run the race.

The word may also mean a spirit of overconfidence and arrogance. Many a great team with championship potential has taken the field in an attitude of haughtiness only to receive a drubbing at lesser hands. The idea that a certain contest is a "pushover, a breather, an easy day" anesthetizes a team into complacency. That is the making of an upset! When we let down our concentration on the basics of the Christian life and become distracted, we are in for a sudden and shocking surprise. Many a great saint has been caught off guard by a sloppy attitude toward relationships, disciplines of preparation, or commitment to excellence, only to find the situation lost and the opportunity gone.

The writer to the Hebrews says "lay aside" (*apothemenoi*) such weights; they have no place for the Christian disciple who wants to compete in the race that Jesus has laid out for him. Christ's demand and design will require everything we have in ourselves and much more. There cannot be any extra weight. In order to "win," every ounce of human and divine energy must be directed to the race. Anything less will cause us to fall behind the intentions and designs of our God. In a day like this, where the world teeters on a fine edge of tragedy, we must be all we can be for the purpose of salvation and ministry. Anything less will be a burial of our talents in the soil of dissipation and indulgence. One day when our Master returns, we will all give an accounting. May that be a glorious day for all involved! "Well done, good and faithful athlete!"

We are also told to lay aside the *"sin which so easily ensnares us."* Runners are careful to wear no clothing that fits too tightly or binds the movement. Just so, we spiritual athletes are to have no habits that hamper movement, no dissipations that ensnare us so easily. The Greek word here (*euperistatos*) is not used anywhere else in the New Testament. Neither is it found in the LXX nor in the classical writers. Perhaps our author is coining a word for his own intentions. Its meaning is somewhat questionable. (1) It may mean "easy to be put off" (Chrysostom). This does not fit with passage, however. (2) It may stand for "well-befriended" or "popularly supported." This could well be the meaning. Many friends encourage us to keep on with things that really hamper our effectiveness as Christians. The encouragement to keep certain things that are actually weights detrimental to spiritual athletics is their acceptability in the culture which we as God's people too often accept. Affluent life styles in the midst of a world of hunger and poverty often leave us falling short of the witness we should be making, losing the race to other ideologies that are willing, at least in promises, to pay the price. We fail to show the world the redeeming and caring life modeled by our Master because we carry the weight of honestly believing that we deserve our affluence, or that it is quite all right for Christians to live this way. After all, don't most of our friends? In comparison to an affluence-oriented society, we don't come off so badly. Only one problem, we don't win the race for allegiance of heart and soul to our Master. (3) The third meaning, "easily besetting," comes clear when we break *euperistaton* into its components: *eu,* "easily"; *peri,* "around, about"; *staton,* "standing position." "Easily surrounded"—how quickly some actions or habits become addictive. They come so easily, establish themselves so tenaciously but effortlessly. Oh, the power needed to divest ourselves of their clinging tendency! This too could well be the meaning of the author.

How easily we are ensnared by sin, that self-centered orientation that adds weight to the spiritual athlete! We are to put it off by the power and authority of Christ. This truth applies as much to nations as to individuals. So quickly we become indulgent in matters of national security and those things "in the interest of" our native land. But we need to see that, in the long run, we dissipate the energies that would make us truly a great nation and that would answer some of those human hungers for justice and life's simple necessities. If we were to do this, there would be a far greater security not only in our nation, but in the peace of all nations. True, there are many causes of war, but not the least of them is starvation and injustice. If we will not move in to give what aid we can out of the abundance God has given to us, then we cannot be surprised when other nations' ideologies promise to meet these needs and gain control. God has not only supplied enough for our needs, but also for the needs of others (2 Cor. 9:8–14). If He places in our hands resources meant for others and we use them for ourselves, what can He do but judge us, not only at the end of history, but now? Is this not a form of spiritual embezzlement? He designated the wealth for others, gave the accounting and management to us, but we kept it for ourselves. What would a moral God have us do? Is there not a clue as to the nature of our race in Isaiah 1:16–17?

"Wash yourselves, make yourselves clean;
Put away the evil of your doings from before My eyes.
Cease to do evil,
Learn to do good;
Seek justice,
Reprove the oppressor;
Defend the fatherless,
Plead for the widow."

We are to *"run with endurance the race that is set before us."* The Greek word translated "race" is *agōn,* from which we get our word agony. It signifies a wrestling match or race in which endurance and determination must overcome the aching desire to quit. In a race such as the quarter mile, there are moments toward the end of the race when the body cries out to let up. Pain starts in the calf and works up through the hamstrings to the gluteus maximus. At times it is so intense it feels like a burning fire. Agony is the best way to describe it. A wrestler knows the same pain when struggling against a powerful opponent who seeks to crush him to the mat by sheer weight and relentless hold. It would be so easy to let up and let a fall be declared, but the champion heart fights through, waiting for that opportunistic moment of lost concentration or of a shifting of weight that allows an explosive hold-breaking surge.

Paul describes his efforts to bring others to their full maturity as the agonizing of an athlete, but he said, "I do it with all the might that He mightily inspires within me" (Col. 1:29).

JESUS, OUR EXAMPLE

2 looking unto Jesus, the author and finisher of
our faith, who for the joy that was set before Him
endured the cross, despising the shame, and has sat
down at the right hand of the throne of God.
3 For consider Him who endured such hostility
from sinners against Himself, lest you become weary
and discouraged in your souls.

Heb. 12:2–3

For the Christian disciple there is only one way to run this race successfully and that is to look to Jesus, whom our author describes first as *"author"* (*archēgon*) and then as *"finisher"* (*teleiōtēn*) of our faith. *Archēgos* can mean founder, leader, or pioneer, a prince or ruler. The meaning here is that of founder, the first, even the designer of this race. As a leader or pioneer, Jesus is meant to be followed. He is not the one and only, but the first of many. He has set the course and we are to follow hard after Him.

He is also the first one to finish the race, the perfecter in terms of having completed it. The word *teleiōtēs* is used nowhere else in the New Testament, the LXX, or the classical writers. Again, is our author coining a usage? If so, it is one more indication of this creative and facile mind, which we made mention of in the Introduction. Jesus not only designed the race, but He was the first to complete it and break the tape.

As pioneer Jesus set a number of firsts; He designed several facets of the race He has called us to run.

First, Jesus set the pattern of identifying with those in need. This was made clear by our author in chapter 2 in which he thrusts the great Creator and Eternal One down into the stream of a suffering and soiled humanity. Jesus walked among the sinful, the sick, and the excluded, forever setting the example for His followers.

Second, He claimed that His own life was the essential base for life itself. The Father had given Him life, and now He had the authority to give it to whomever He willed (John 4:13–14; 5:26–27; see also p. 18). He described Himself as the Vine and the believer as the branch. There was no way the branch could live or bear fruit except by abiding in the Vine (John 15:1–8). The only way we as disciples can hope to run and complete that race is to abide in the Vine even as Christ abided in His Father.

Third, Jesus set the pattern for our race by accepting social outcasts and ministering to them without being repulsed by their outward behavior. He did not consider them untouchable or unclean but rather persons whose inward needs had to be met before they could ever change their outward behavior patterns (Luke 7:36–50; John 4:1–30). If we are to be His disciples, we too must be more sensitive to the inward needs of those whose behavior is considered bizarre, wrong, or repulsive by society. If we constantly turn away, there is little hope that any of these will ever find the redemption of the life-giving Christ.

Fourth, Jesus set a difficult portion of the race, that of loving one's enemies. In this He pioneered a whole new form of patient construction. He knew that love was often necessary to break down the patterns of hostility that had grown up over a long period of time, whether between two parties or as a result of their heritage passed on to them. Patience over a long period of time, laying the foundations of loving deeds, made possible the recall of some lost sinners.

Some years ago, during the building of the Bel Air Presbyterian Church, I experienced an example of patient foundation-laying. The site for the church was high in some spots and low in others. The tops needed to be knocked off the hills and put into the valleys. However, as the contractor began his work, he discovered the hill to be made of sandstone schist, a very tightly compacted rock that would not yield even to the largest of bulldozers with the single tooth designed to rip up compacted earth. Dynamiting became the order of the day, and we dynamited time after time! Huge boulders had to be carted away, for they could not be put into the fill.

At the same time, a breakwater was being built in Los Angeles Harbor, and our site was a happy hunting ground for the contractors. They came with large, low-bed trailers which were loaded with one or two of these boulders at a time and taken to the harbor. There the boulders were loaded onto huge barges, and then lifted by cranes, lowered into the waters of the bay, and set on the bottom. Can you imagine how many of these boulders are needed for such a project? Thousands went down into the water, and for years I saw absolutely no evidence that any headway was being made. It seemed so frustrating and pointless. Then one day as I drove by I could see some of the boulders staying above the surface. Slowly the breakwater was completed and the disturbing wave patterns were changed, making a quiet harbor.

I have thought since then how much like redemptive love that process was. So many persons have destructive wave patterns that keep the harbors of their lives from the quietness necessary for normal traffic. Only those who are willing to put stone after stone into the lives of others—patiently, perceptively, carefully—will see the ultimate success of changed wave patterns. Jesus set the example for us.

Fifth, our Lord set the example of servant lordship. Other rulers had used their lordship to lord it over others, but Jesus set His lordship *under* those He served in order to hold them up to their highest potential. Servant lordship or leadership determines to be a resource for another's discovery of his or her own God-created identity, for developing that identity and finally, for offering a place for the emerging identity and strength to be used in the Body of the church. The servant leader does not fear the growing strength of another, but encourages it to its maximum, recognizing that the potential of each person has been created by God for the sake of the kingdom. Any frustration of that design is to frustrate the will of God. No disciple wants to diminish the effectiveness of God's kingdom, for the goal of every believer is to press the kingdom forward as far as possible. Each person who claims the name of Christ also commits herself or himself to the furtherance of every other person so that the kingdom may be as strong as possible.

While a student at Occidental College during the years immediately following World War II, I was a member of the track team. All international track and field meets had been suspended for the duration of the war, and there were no Olympics. However, when the lights went on again all over the world, so did the desire for international competition, in particular, the Olympics.

Our track coach at the time was Payton Jordan, a world record holder in the 100-meter on grass. Still a trim athlete, he was also an internationally recognized coach. He had a way of making champions, and runners came from all over the world to train under him. I can still remember seeing him stride around the infield with another runner, his blond hair blowing in the wind, his blue eyes intense with interest and concentration, shouting instructions and encouragement to his athletes. He would take long minutes to explain the finer points of a race, the stride, the strategy, the timing necessary for winning. Encouragement and edification radiated from this coach's heart. No wonder champions loved to train under him. Truly, he was a servant to their emergence even if that meant their shattering his world record. The important thing was the new generation, the strength of the team. God give us Payton Jordans for the sake of the kingdom.

All too frequently, those in senior leadership in the church look with fear or anxiety upon those who are rising in strength. Will their job be threatened? Will someone run off with more of the love of the congregation than they can stand to lose? Will they have to share the authority and the credit? Yes, all of these are possibilities, but the bottom line is the effectiveness of the kingdom, maximum productivity to the glory of God.

These are but a few of the characteristics of the race Jesus has set for us to run. Not only did He set the course, He was the first to finish it and to break the tape! Our author implores us to run this race with perseverance, our eyes fixed on Jesus as the pioneer that we are to follow.

Why did Jesus run this race of servanthood and suffering? His motivation for this great effort was the joy that was set before Him, out in the future. Jesus too was a futurist. He could see beyond the immediate suffering and cost to a future of redemptive blessing for all humanity. In His inmost soul He knew He was the fulfillment of the ancient covenants of God. When God promised Abraham that not only would he have sons and those sons would have a land of promise in which to dwell, but that in his descendants all the nations of the earth would be blessed (Gen. 12:3), Jesus knew He was to fulfill that covenant. The expectancy of that fulfillment flooded Him with joy (Ps. 22:22–31).

When God promised through Jeremiah a new covenant, Jesus knew He was to be its fulfillment. Look for a moment at that covenant, stated in Jeremiah 31:31–34. It had three characteristics: (1) It was a covenant of the inward and internal, not external: "I will put My law in their minds, and write it on their hearts." (2) It was a covenant of intimacy with God: "I will be their God, and they shall be My people. No more shall every man teach his neighbor, and every man his brother, saying, 'Know the Lord,' for they all shall [intimately] know Me, from the least of them to the greatest of them." (3) It was a covenant of forgiveness and forgetting: "For I will forgive their iniquity, and their sin I will remember no more" (pp. 148–51).

Looking into the future at the blessing His suffering would bring, Jesus put aside consideration of the pain and humiliation He would have to endure on the cross. In the public eye, the cross was a symbol of repulsion and degradation. It was despised and abhorred by decent people. Cicero said that the cross should not even be mentioned in cultured society. Indeed, anyone who hung on the cross was cursed.

And yet Jesus despised its shame. The Greek used here means "to look down on or think little of." The shame was simply not important to Him. Comparing that rejection and degradation with the blessing that would come through it for all nations, Jesus put it aside as of little account and endured the cross in loving redemption.

"Consider Him" (v. 3). We are asked to take a hard, analytical look,

make a complete analysis, and do it once and for all. Westcott emphasizes the decisive nature of this consideration. We might call it a determinative analysis—one that determines how we live. No other uses of this term are made by New Testament writers although it is used commonly in the classical Greek. This analysis calls us to look not only at the nature of His suffering, but also its outcome. When He endured the hostility which occasioned the cross, He won an ultimate victory that has enduring effect. As we saw above, He was able to look into the future and see the realization of this victory. Just so should we look at the outcome of Christ's suffering and see its effect.

Our author's purpose in asking us to make this consideration is that we not grow weary and faint with the relentlessness of the battle. Knowing that ultimate victory will be ours as it was Jesus', our author is hoping that we the readers will also be able to stand the short-term suffering, remaining on top with perseverance, because we see the future result. This insight is given by the Holy Spirit whom Christ has promised will "lead us into all truth," a truth that allows us to see what lies ahead.

Christ knew the hostility from sinners against Himself because He judged their religious and social systems, found them wanting, and lived life as God would have Him, irrespective of their laws. Such lack of respect drew their anger and hostility, for their laws had become their highest allegiance. The work of their minds and their hands had become the idols they worshiped. No wonder they were hostile!

As we stand against the same sort of laws and idols, we too can expect hostility from idolators. The author hopes that this realization will ward off the weariness of the struggle, that they the readers, and we also, will be able to ward off not only the growing weariness but the progressive discouragement. The Greek word used here for "discouragement" also means to unstring a bow, relax, or let down. We might paraphrase that in modern idiom and say that we should not unstring our bows, call it quits, or give up the battle.

Surely this is how we feel at times. As those working for justice in the establishment, we become weary with the resistance to change. As pastors attempting to bring spiritual depth and insight to congregations that are just playing church and treating it as a club for members only, we are tempted to shake off the dust from our feet and take another charge that they "will appreciate us and respond." As those seeking to build new images in the minds of the emotionally troubled whom we counsel and in whom we see little or no improvement, we are tempted to give up, only leaving the counselee with one more experience of rejection and failure.

These readers had other problems awaiting them. Our author gives an idea of what these problems might be, and they were not light ones. Persecution of a far heavier sort awaited them. They had already experienced the plundering of their goods; they had been ridiculed and made a spectacle of—either they themselves or vicariously through friends who had been so treated. But more was coming, as a perusal of the historical situation that I feel probably surrounds this writing may show.

PERSECUTION AHEAD; DISCIPLINE NEEDED

4 You have not yet resisted to bloodshed, striving against sin.

5 And you have forgotten the exhortation which speaks to you as to sons:

"My son, do not despise the chastening of the LORD,

Nor be discouraged when you are rebuked by *Him.*

6 For whom the LORD loves He chastens,

And scourges every son whom He receives."

7 If you endure chastening, God deals with you as with sons; for what son is there whom a father does not chasten?

8 But if you are without chastening, of which all have become partakers, then you are illegitimate and not sons.

9 Furthermore, we have had human fathers who corrected us, and we paid them respect. Shall we not much more readily be in subjection to the Father of spirits and live?

10 For they indeed for a few days chastened us as seemed best to them, but He for our profit, that we may be partakers of His holiness.

11 Now no chastening seems to be joyful for the present, but grievous; nevertheless, afterward it yields the peaceable fruit of righteousness to those who have been trained by it.

Heb. 12:4–11

Very probably our author sincerely believes that persecution and bloodshed may well lie ahead of his readers. "In your struggle against sin," he says to them, *"you have not yet resisted to bloodshed."* "Not yet"— does that mean it is soon to come? Possibly. Under what circumstances?

It has been my premise that this epistle was written before the fall of the temple at Jerusalem (see Introduction), but after the persecution of Nero had begun. Its full effect has not reached these believers, but its approach is imminent. In the past they have known some suffering, perhaps at the hands of the Jews who took strong exception to the Gospel as portrayed by Luke in his account in Acts. Most likely our writer perceives that it will be Christianity's fate to be charged with criminal impiety—not believing in the gods of Rome. It is possible that word has reached his ears that Christians have died in the circus in Rome and that it will not be long until Christians in other parts of the empire will experience the same fate. Theirs might well be a "resistance to bloodshed."

If the above be the case, then preparation is necessary in order to keep the faith firm to the end. Only those who so keep the faith will be saved. For their sakes and the sake of their salvation our author is concerned, but also for the sake of the Gospel which he does not desire to see belittled or denied. His severe warnings to his readers of the possibility of apostasy unnerve us who have been raised in a Calvinistic theology. However we interpret those passages, there is no doubt of our author's concern. He firmly believes that God wishes these Christians to be strong enough for the occasion, and He determines to prepare them for it through His discipline. Our author sees this as preparation.

Whether we translate verse 5a as a question or a statement of fact ("And you have forgotten," NKJV, or "And have you forgotten," RSV), it is evident that our writer has concern regarding his readers' reaction to the discipline of God. He reminds them of the teaching of Proverbs 3:11–12:

> My son, do not despise the chastening of the Lord,
> Nor detest His correction;
> For whom the Lord loves He corrects,
> Just as a father the son in whom he delights.

We might paraphrase this section: "Do not treat lightly the training of the Lord." The Greek word for "despise" means "to treat lightly, to disregard" or "to think unimportant." All too many Christians both then and now, have a blasé attitude about discipline of the spiritual life. We consider it a holdover from a pietism that we have rejected as narrow and stifling. We are too often like a football team that considers blocking and tackling already learned and unimportant, only to find themselves coming apart in a tough ball game and the score mounting against them with shocking rapidity.

The word translated "chastening," *paidiea,* has wider meaning than "chastening" or "punishment." It also means the training up of a child, a teaching, preparation for life, an art or science, or an instruction. The main emphasis is upon preparation for life. Chastening or punishment is only a small part of preparation.

In scholarly circles we ask the question "What is your discipline?" We are not asking, "What is your punishment?" Rather, we want to know, "What field of study or what art are you studying?" The emphasis is upon the learning of a skill, the preparation for a given profession. The same word is used in athletics. Discipline is that process by which we are taught and by which we learn. In flying we speak of an "air discipline" which stands for an attitude of care and professionalism that refuses to accept sloppy or careless procedures. Instructors inculcate this discipline into their students, knowing that their safety and the safety of their passengers is going to depend on it.

In similar fashion the writer of this epistle is convinced that his readers' future solidarity in faith is going to depend upon this teaching of the Lord. Therefore, he is urging them, "Do not treat lightly this training of the Lord. To disregard or look upon it as unimportant is foolish and dangerous. Do you not understand how critical His discipline is?"

God's motivation for this discipline is His love—love for His people and love for His kingdom. Every believer is a child of God. With that child God has made a covenant of intimacy. He longs for a full relationship with that child as any good earthly father longs for a full and loving relationship with his child. For a child to fall or fail is agony for the Father. Out of His love He wishes to ward off such tragedy.

The same is true for His kingdom. He loves His kingdom, and, knowing it is the salvation of all peoples, He wishes it to move ahead toward its goal without dissipation or frustration. Every member of the kingdom who is not performing up to par is a loss for the kingdom.

Not to be disciplined by a father is an indication of lack of love.

It takes energy to discipline. The task is fatiguing. Many a father does not discipline because of the cost. Not to pay that cost is to say to the child, "You are not that important to me. You are not worth it." He may use busyness as an excuse; he may plead even the demands of the kingdom of God. The result is the same—loveless neglect. There is no product more important to any nation or culture than that of human beings. Not to put the best of materials into those humans is to produce an inferior product that will not stand up under the competition of the modern world, nor hold up under trying circumstances.

When fathers and mothers spend the necessary time and energy to discipline children with fair and consistent training, in spite of momentary flareups and resistance, there is loving respect. When we as parents pay more attention to the flareups and the cry of resistance than to the call of the future, we deny our children both a sense of belonging and the opportunity to reach a mature and strong adulthood. If that is true with our earthly parents, how much more true is it of God? Admittedly, our human discipline is sometimes less than highly motivated or effective, but God's discipline is for our ultimate good, without qualification. The result of His training is holiness, a likeness to God. There is nothing more beautiful!

"Now no chastening seems to be joyful for the present, but grievous; nevertheless, afterward it yields the peaceable fruit of righteousness to those who have been trained by it" (v. 11).

I remember how painful and agonizing were the first weeks of football practice at college. Twice a day we suited out in full uniform, exercised strenuously in 108-degree temperature with smog being compacted against the mountains behind the college. Every breath was torture; we waited expectantly for even a wisp of air through our helmets, which we were not permitted to remove. Not allowed to drink, we sucked on wet towels and held slices of lemons between our teeth to soothe our dry throats. After a long siege of scrimmaging, hoping to be dismissed to the locker room, the whistle of the assistant coach would call us to the goal line where in groupings according to our positions we raced fifty yards a dozen times. With the last of our energy expended, we would half stumble, exhausted, into the locker room. Although it was normally lighted, we could not see because of the fatigue. We inhaled sections of cool oranges, showered off the sweat and the fatigue, and collapsed on a dorm bunk, hardly capable of rising for dinner.

At times we would have gladly hung the coach from the flagpole by his thumbs. But he knew what he was doing. He had watched the films of the teams we would be playing. He knew every position, their strengths and weaknesses. He had assessed our resources and potentials and knew his only hope was in our depth, speed, timing, and endurance. From past experiences he knew how much collegians could take. Later I thought he had it figured to the teaspoonful of energy!

The season progressed and we notched one victory after another. The championship was ours. Then came a New Year's Day bowl game—and that was ours too! Instead of hanging him by his thumbs from the flagpole, we carried him off the field on our shoulders. He had studied the game and he knew the season. We were ready— through discipline—and looking back on it, we loved it!

Is God any less perceptive or capable in His strategy? The fruit is indeed sweet—the peaceable fruit of righteousness to those who stayed out for practice.

The Need to Press On

12 Therefore strengthen the hands which hang
down, and the feeble knees,
13 and make straight paths for your feet, so that
what is lame may not be dislocated, but rather be
healed.

Heb. 12:12–13

At those moments when we thought surely we would collapse to the grass (and how good it would have felt to lie down!), we would hear the coach's raspy voice, "C'mon, you always have one good play left!" One good play—he was right; with some spunk and determination, there was always one good play left.

In the power of the Spirit there also is always one good effort remaining. Paul said that when he was fatigued and agonizing under the toil, he could do the task in the strength that God mightily inspired within him (Col. 1:29). Few Christians have known the difficulties and fatigue that Paul experienced in his ministries (2 Cor. 4:7–18; 11:21–29). Given impossible tasks to perform and awesome obstacles to overcome, he could cry out, "I can do all things through Christ who strengthens me" (Phil. 4:13). Whether adrift at sea on a bit of wreckage or stoned and left for dead, when he despaired of life itself, he discovered a well of strength that was sufficient for his needs. Instead of staggering through life, weaving under the load, his feet found a straight path. Limbs sore and bruised, he did not have to stop at the side of the road as a cripple, but was healed as he went on his way.

Bed rest is the worst thing one can do for certain kinds of injury. Lie dormant and inactive, and strained or damaged tissue will become stiff and immovable. Active strength brought to bear on life's difficulties is the way of the disciple. Thank God for His sufficient strength!

In the field of psychotherapy, it is evident that many neurotics attempt to escape pain by their neurotic action. In fact, what they are doing is putting off the pain to a later date, when most likely it will be far worse than at the time they sought to escape it. All life has in it necessary pain that can be used for strengthening if we will submit to the struggle, leap into the arena, and fight the beasts. We may even discover they were not as powerful as we thought. The joy is in having the victory behind, then marching into the future with a clear slate, knowing we are stronger and more ready for the next encounter. To put off the necessary pains of life, to take detours and alternate byways that take us years out of our way, is to live life in a very costly manner, having few resources left for even a low level of existence. Instead, "to take the pain up front," to get it over with, is to be free to enjoy the leisure that comes after the real battle is won. One of God's disciplines is immediate obedience, getting the task done early, meeting the suffering head-on at the earliest proper moment. Why put off for tomorrow anxieties that can be met right now? What a burden and pall to put on the beautiful days ahead. Take the strength for the weak knees today, lift the drooping hands now in the strength of the Lord, and sing the song,

> Strength for today and bright hope for tomorrow,
> Blessings all mine, with ten thousand beside.
> Great is thy faithfulness, Lord, unto me![1]

THE DYNAMICS OF PEACEFUL RELATIONS

14 Pursue peace with all men, and holiness, without which no one will see the Lord:

15 looking diligently lest anyone fall short of the grace of God; lest any root of bitterness springing up cause trouble, and by this many become defiled;

16 lest there be any fornicator or profane person like Esau, who for one morsel of food sold his birthright.

17 For you know that afterward, when he wanted to inherit the blessing, he was rejected, for he found no place for repentance, though he sought it diligently with tears.

Heb. 12:14–17

"Pursue peace" boldly sets out the next theme of peaceful relations. The dynamics are several: first, seek out peace and reconciliation; follow hard after them. This is a guideline not only for those we love, but for all people with whom we are in relation, including those we designate as enemies or opponents.

The exhortation is clear throughout the Old and New Testaments. Isaiah counsels us to seek peace (1:17) through justice. The psalmist instructs us to "seek peace, pursue it!" (34:14). Jesus tells His disciples that the forgiveness of God is limited to those who in turn forgive their neighbors (Matt. 6:14). With any person with whom there has been a falling out, a loss of peace, relational debris that is not cleaned up, we are to seek peace. Not to do so is to leave a board with a rusty nail through it on the floor of a heavily trafficked shop. Sooner or later someone is going to step on it and be injured.

Almost as a parenthesis, our writer includes *"and holiness."* He probably means that we are not to seek peace with the wicked just for the sake of "peace." That would be shouting, "peace, peace," where there is no lasting basis for peace; like engaging in an illusion and a charade. Only on the basis of integrity and honest foundations do we have that vision of God with which saints are blessed.

"Without which no one will see the Lord." the word used for "see" is *opsetai*—to see with perceptive insight, with an "aha!" sort of understanding. Our author is not talking about the physical act of seeing (*blepō*), nor just a theorizing, academic sort of seeing (*theoreō*). Instead the meaning is that of thrilling perception. This comes only to the eyes of the pure.

Who may ascend into the hill of the Lord?
Or who may stand in His holy place?

He who has clean hands and a pure heart,
Who has not lifted up his soul to an idol,
Nor sworn deceitfully.

Ps. 24:3–4

Now the exhorter spurs his readers to look diligently. The Greek word used here is one which can also mean "overseeing." He desires that we watch for three things, each of which he introduces with the phrase "lest any" (*mē tis*).

1. *"Lest anyone fall short of the grace of God"* might mean one or both of two things: (a) to fall short in accepting the grace of God's forgiveness, or (b) to fall short in granting the grace of one's own forgiveness. If we do not diligently seek the peace with another and thus have unforgiven material in our soul, a barrier to the forgiveness of God exists and we fall short of realization of that grace. The covenant of forgiveness is expected of us just as God gave it to us—as grace, undeserved. If we insist that another person meet our conditions for forgiveness, then our forgiveness is not gracious and we deny as well the grace of God to us. "If you do not forgive [others] their trespasses, neither will your Father forgive your trespasses" (Matt. 6:15).

2. *"Lest any root of bitterness springing up cause trouble."* This second item to watch for in the search for peace is bitterness. This emotion has spilled over from one life to many others all too often in the Christian body, causing trouble. The unforgiveness mentioned above is the result of failing to pursue peace, and the residue becomes a root of bitterness, producing its bitter fruit time and again.

In one of the homes to which we had moved in Los Angeles I had a persistent problem of a weed that grew rapidly and pushed up its ugly stalk and leaves right in front of a bedroom window. Each time it would grow, I would chop it off, hoping it would become discouraged and die. Not so. I went deeper and cut off the stalk well below the surface thinking surely I had done mortal damage to the tap root. Not so. Finally, in angry desperation, I got my round-nosed shovel and dug deeper, and deeper, following the root more than two feet below ground level. The hole appeared so ludicrously deep that I called one of the children to help me, and together we shared in amazement as we had to go deeper and deeper. Finally, four feet below the surface, I found a large, ugly bulbous root. We had obviously reached our target. I dug it out, making sure there were no other tentacles of growth. We then salted the hole to discourage any further growth of some unseen portion. That was the end of it.

Roots of bitterness can go very deep into our lives so that periodic prunings will never suffice. Only the major therapeutic surgery of forgiveness will get out the ugly source. If not, that stalk of bitterness will continue to grow throughout our lives, disrupting the beauty of the relational landscape. Such roots cause many to be defiled by false accusation, rumor, or innuendo. And all this stems from unforgiveness. How can God forgive when there is such a root of bitterness?

3. *"Lest there be any fornicator or profane person like Esau"* (v. 16). Something of a problem exists in the wording here. Esau is not described in the Genesis story as a fornicator. Is this some other sort of person or is our author speaking of Esau metaphorically? To say that he is speaking of some sort other than Esau appears to do violence to the Greek syntax. If we are to say that the term stands as a description of Esau, then I would suggest that our author is speaking metaphorically. The word *pornos* can mean a male prostitute or a fornicator. It is possible to think of Esau prostituting himself to his passionate desire for food, so that he was willing to give a long-term promise for the immediate gratification of a single morsel of food offered by his opportunistic brother. He gave up what had great and lasting value for something momentary. Even though Westcott denies the application of the word to Esau, I think it bears considering. The immorality of the act was to depreciate a valuable tradition that meant a great deal in his social structure. He simply waved it away with blatant disregard.

The word *bebēlos,* translated here as "profane person," certainly describes Esau. He profaned the worthy birthright by treating it lightly, which is of concern to our writer in whatever context it occurs. As Calvin says, his depraved lust dazzled his eyes and blinded him. Moreover, his culpability was demonstrated in that, after he had waved off his birthright, he yet sought its advantage in the blessing which went with it. It is this double action that takes us back to the consideration of the theme of "bitter root" above. The same idea of root of bitterness is mentioned in Deuteronomy 29:8–19. In fact it is highly probable that our writer had in mind the very phraseology of Deuteronomy when composing this passage we are considering. "[Beware lest there] be among you man or woman or family or tribe, whose heart turns away today from the Lord our God, to go and serve the gods of these nations; [lest there] be among you a root bearing bitterness or wormwood; [one who,] when he hears the words of this curse, . . . blesses himself in his heart, saying, 'I shall have peace, even though I walk in the imagination of my heart.'. . ."

Notice the doublemindedness; wanting both at the same time—the covenant of God that limits other covenants and the serving of other gods.

Esau might well have been in our writer's mind as an example *par excellence* of such doublemindedness, prostitution of allegiances and profaning. He turned away from the inheritance for a bit of food and yet wanted all the advantage of the inheritance. For earthly satisfaction he turned away from heavenly things and thus profaned the most beautiful.

So many Christians demonstrate the same doublemindedness. They want all the immediate gratification of the world about them, giving up true piety for immediate satisfaction because everyone around them is doing such things. Then they want the advantages of spiritual blessing meant for those who have submitted to the training and discipline of the spiritual coach and have run patiently and perseveringly the race that Christ has set out for them. They want the glory but not the fortitude or the discipline.

In the words of Jesus, such persons are trying to serve two masters (Matt. 6:24). They want to satisfy the master of indulgence and immediate gratification which the society around them teaches, but they want also the sweet and peaceable fruit of righteousness that comes to those who are trained by Christ. To live in that sort of duplicity is to be torn by inward strife which Christ describes as darkness (Matt. 6:23). The only one who experiences the radiance of joy and light is that one who chooses a single goal with a single eye (*haplous*, not multiformed, but single), and holds firm to the end.

Our author thoroughly agrees. Several times he speaks of the necessity of holding firm our confession to the end, not wavering with doublemindedness (Heb. 2:1; 3:6; 6:4–8; 10:23, 26–31, 35).

THE DREAD AND THE JOY

18 For you have not come to the mountain that may be touched and that burned with fire, and to blackness and darkness and tempest,

19 and the sound of a trumpet and the voice of words, so that those who heard it begged that the word should not be spoken to them anymore.

20 (For they could not endure what was commanded: *"And if so much as a beast touches the mountain, it shall be stoned or thrust through with an arrow."*

21 And so terrifying was the sight that Moses said, *"I am exceedingly afraid and trembling."*)

22 But you have come to Mount Zion and to the city of the living God, the heavenly Jerusalem, to an innumerable company of angels,

23 to the general assembly and church of the firstborn who are registered in heaven, to God the Judge of all, to the spirits of just men made perfect,

24 to Jesus the Mediator of the new covenant, and to the blood of sprinkling that speaks better things than that of Abel.

25 See that you do not refuse Him who speaks. For if they did not escape who refused Him who spoke on earth, much more shall we not escape if we turn away from Him who speaks from heaven,

26 whose voice then shook the earth; but now He has promised, saying, *"Yet once more I shake not only the earth, but also heaven."*

27 Now this, *"Yet once more,"* indicates the removal of those things that are being shaken, as of things that are made, that the things which cannot be shaken may remain.

28 Therefore, since we are receiving a kingdom which cannot be shaken, let us have grace, by which we may serve God acceptably with reverence and godly fear.

29 For our God is a consuming fire.

Heb. 12:18–29

Our author is untiring in his use of opportunities to contrast the old covenant of the law and the new covenant of the Gospel. Thus, in these final verses of chapter 12, he embarks on a stark comparison of the dread and fear associated with the giving of the first law and the joy and festive atmosphere of the giving of the Gospel.

The elements of fear include, first, a mountain that can be touched.

Some scholars argue that perhaps the word "not" (*mē* in the Greek) has been left out by the author. None of the texts show the word, but the possibility of this passage's being a parallel to Exodus 19 certainly raises the question. The mountain in Exodus could *not* be touched; thus the element of fear. Any person or any beast that touched the mountain was to be stoned or pierced with a javelin, but not touched. Calvin accepts the text without question and emphasizes the distinction between that which can be touched and that which is vapid or metaphysical. The aspects of the theophany—the fire, the darkness, the whirlwind, the voice—were all terrifying. The fact that they were physically real made them all the more fearsome.

The "blackness" (*gnophos*, "darkness, gloom") has the sense of glowering. The "darkness" or gloom (*zophos*) conjures up an eeriness of the underworld. The "tempest" (*thuella*), "whirlwind, cyclonic wind" coupled with the blackness, the darkness, and the fire (which might have been lightning in multiple, simultaneous flashings), could indicate a severe storm similar to a tornado. Those who have been close to such a severe storm would quickly recognize the glowering darkness, the suppressing gloom and awesomeness of such a storm with its cyclonic wind. To be in the presence of such a phenomenon is terrifying.

In the midst of this experience the sound of trumpets and the sound of a voice that brought to mind the voice of creation added to the dread. The term *phōnē rhēmatōn* brings to mind the words of the author in describing how the world was created, by the word of God (*rhēmati tou theou*). So frightful and awesome was this display of God's power that the people begged God speak to them only through Moses. The experience was hardly conducive to intimacy.

In contrast to this experience of dread is that of the Gospel. Not only do the terms used in this section all purvey the feeling of confidence, assurance, and festive joy, but there is also the dramatic contrast of two mountains. Mount Zion was for the Jew the symbolic term of the everlasting reign of the Messiah-King, the holy hill of God where God provided for the sacrifice in Isaac's stead, the location of God's ultimate victory. Here obviously the mountain of Sinai with all its dreadful associations is being compared to the mountain of hope and prosperity.

Zion is then closely associated with the next two phrases, *"the city of the living God"* and *"the heavenly Jerusalem"* (v. 22). In each case the former concept of the secure habitation of the believer is reinforced with telling redundance, springing out of an emotional state approaching ecstasy on the part of our author. His heavenly vision of the resources God has provided for His people is so clear that it cascades like a magnificent waterfall over all who believe.

In a manner reminiscent of 2:1–4, the teacher exhorts his readers not to decline or refuse the One who is speaking. Repeating the reasoning for his warning, he alludes to the judgment that fell on those who refused to obey the law as it was given under awesome circumstances at the mountain, an earthly setting. Now the speaking is from heaven, making it all the more important. The voice is the same, that of God. But this time there is a word of future judgment; God will shake not only the earth but also heaven. Most probably our writer has in mind Haggai 2:6, alluding to the shaking of the nations to bring the stolen treasures back to the Temple, to restore its magnificence. The purpose of the shaking in this instance, however, is not the restoration of a temple of an earthly kingdom, but something more in keeping with 1 Corinthians 3:12–15, in which Paul speaks of the ultimate evaluation of everything before the Lord at His coming. We are reminded of Ephesians 1:10, which states that all things will be gathered together, harvested, in Christ, and only those things of Christ will stand. The *"things that are made"* (Heb. 12:27), meaning of human origin, are implied as passing away, shaken through the sieve; the things that cannot be shaken, that is, that are not of human making, will remain as evidence of their godly origin and making.

That which cannot be shaken, which is not of human manufacture, is the kingdom of Jesus Christ. Having received it, or since we have received it, one of two statements can be made, both of which fit the context and spiritual truth. However, a variant reading here gives an option of interpretation. The received text is in the subjunctive, indicating an exhortation, "Let us have grace." The alternate reading, from fewer manuscripts, but very good ones including the Chester Beatty Papyri P46, a third-century document, uses the indicative, "We have grace." Calvin prefers this second reading as stronger and more suited. Whether spoken of in the indicative or hortatory, the "grace" is the vehicle by which we may serve God in a manner pleasing and acceptable to Him in a kingdom that is unshakable and immovable. Yes, we are invited to do this in the grace, but we do it with reverence, devoutly, circumspectly, and in no way flippantly; in fact, we do this with a godly fear. The reason is simple. The God we are serving is a consuming fire. He extends intimacy and grace, but the other side of His personality enacts judgment and fire for that which does not please Him.

This is an interesting tension in the Christian faith. On the one hand, we enjoy that intimacy of father and child spoken in Jeremiah 31 and Hosea 2:20–23. On the other hand, we always live in deep respect of the moral order God has created and in the design He has for each of our lives. We do not treat that design lightly, but constantly search for it, ask for it, and pursue it. Just the other day, my wife, Colleen, said to me, "There is one thing I fear, and that is being out of the will of God." The resources that are given to us, the grace of God that moves mountains from our pathways in miraculous power, the enthusiasm and perseverance come to a sudden stop when we are out of the will of God. The Old Testament so often speaks of "being cut off." Exactly; and once we are cut off, it is to wither and to be cast into the fire as unproductive (John 15:6).

With this rather severe thought, the writer to the Hebrews concludes this section of his exhortation and moves on into a random list of exhortations in chapter 13.

NOTE

1. "Great Is Thy Faithfulness," Thomas Chisholm, 1923.

CHAPTER SIXTEEN

A Flurry of Community Exhortations

Hebrews 13:1–25

We come at last to the final section of exhortation in the epistle. In a manner similar to that of Paul, our exhorter finishes his "word of exhortation" with a flurry of community memos (compare Rom. 15:30—16:33; 1 Cor. 16; 2 Cor. 13:5–14).

AN EXHORTATION TO PERSONAL MORALITY

1 Let brotherly love continue.

2 Do not forget to entertain strangers, for by so doing some have unwittingly entertained angels.

3 Remember the prisoners as if chained with them, and those who are mistreated, since you yourselves are in the body also.

4 Marriage is honorable among all, and the bed undefiled; but fornicators and adulterers God will judge.

5 Let your conduct be without covetousness, and be content with such things as you have. For He Himself has said, *"I will never leave you nor forsake you."*

6 So we may boldly say:
*"The LORD is my helper,
I will not fear.
What can man do to me?"*

Heb. 13:1–6

"Brotherly love" (*philadelphia*) is used in four other places in the New Testament: Romans 12:10, 1 Thessalonians 4:9, 1 Peter 1:22, and 2

Peter 1:7. The root word from which it is derived is *adelphos,* which is used 30 times in the Book of Acts and 130 in the Pauline epistles. The LXX uses it for the Hebrew *ach,* which means brother, relative, or co-religionist. Perhaps one of the most definitive uses occurs in Acts 13:26 as Paul is addressing the members of the synagogue in Pisidian Antioch: "Men and brothers, sons of the family of Abraham." The Jews considered themselves the sons of the patriarch and thus the chosen people of God. This sense of chosenness produced a camaraderie among Jews that led them to speak of one another as brother. Their common heritage through Abraham and the prophets, their shared status as recipients of the mighty acts of God, created a ground in which the rich fruit of nationality found deep rootage. (Compare Paul's passionate desire for his brethren by race in Rom. 9:3.)

Jesus used the term *adelphon* for both the suffering people of the world ("inasmuch as you did it to one of the least of these My *brethren* . . . ," Matt. 25:40) and the disciple band ("Go and tell My *brethren* . . . ," Matt. 28:10; "go to My *brethren* . . . ," John 20:17). He also used this term to describe the design He had in His heart for the relationship among the disciples, which certainly was not realized during the days of His ministry (Matt. 23:8, Luke 22:32).

What does this word mean to the Christian community of our writer's day and for us of this season? I think of three applications. First, we Christians do not look at the world with cool disdain or reserved sophistication. Walk the streets of New York. Notice the attitude and look of the passersby. For the most part they seem distant, cold, as if they believe that any one of them might turn in a moment and take advantage of another, given a convenient opportunity. Perhaps the people of New York are people-tired. The Christian has an opportunity to radiate an engaging warmth even though this may be ridiculous to the ambient society. A friend of mine, who was accustomed to greeting life and strangers with enthusiastic warmth and pleasure, told me with pain of a sensitivity group member who ordered him to wipe the silly smirk off his face. I thank God that he never stopped smiling, for I could name scores who have been blessed by that hospitable radiance. We could paraphrase a popular song and say, "People who enjoy people are the most refreshing people in the world."

Second, "brotherly love" calls Christians to love one another in spite of their differences. There is nothing of a more bonding nature than our common acceptance by Jesus Christ. National Presbyterian

Church has a Sunday morning study group called the Wrestlers. They wrestle with the issues of the day from a biblical point of view. And do they wrestle! The moderators of the class bring in speakers to represent the various sides of an issue that is currently "hot" in the life of the church: abortion, peace, women's place in the church and society, prayer in the schools, refugees, the Mideast, nuclear disarmament, and many others. Individual group members feel intensely the partisan stand they take, because many of them are pouring their very lives into the polemic struggle for this or that side. And yet when the series of weeks on any given topic is over, they walk out arm in arm or periodically have a great social night of food, fun, and frolic. What a model they give for others. Many of our most recent converts have come to Christ because of what they have seen in this group, both in the depth and honesty of how the issues are handled, but also in the love and acceptance that the group obviously has in Christ.

Third, the brotherly love of which our teacher speaks must certainly be a parallel to the love of Jesus for the suffering of the world. I have a dear conservative friend who is downright right-wing and often calls me a "bleeding heart." That's all right. Christ's heart bled too, literally. Moreover, the Christians first attained the name "Christian" in Antioch where it was used derisively to mean "little Christs"! You bet! *"Let [this] brotherly love continue."* The Greek verb is *menetō,* from *monien,* "to remain," from which we get our word "monument." Let brotherly love stand unmovable and uneroded by the weather of history.

The source of this brotherly and sisterly love is our birth into the family of God through the redemption of Jesus Christ. It has something of the same dynamic as Jews all being considered to be siblings because of their common heritage in Abraham, but it goes far beyond. The experience of redemption is so radical that the human personality is transformed (Rom. 12:2; Eph. 2:1–10) and drawn into a family fellowship that covers the world and includes every believer, irrespective of race, nationality, color, economic condition, or political party. Calvin speaks of it as the "common bond of adoption." Paul expresses it in saying that when we cry out, "Abba, Father," the Spirit is bearing "witness with our spirit that we are children of God" (Rom. 8:16) and that we are "no longer strangers and foreigners, but . . . members of the household of God" (Eph. 2:19). Ephesians

1:5 and Galatians 4:5 also speak of our relationship as children of God.

Whether our writer feels pressed to encourage his readers in brotherly love because they may be tempted to turn against one another in times of persecution or in the midst of theological debate, we do not know. We do know this: he was deeply concerned that brotherly love continue.

"Do not forget to entertain strangers, for by so doing some have unwittingly entertained angels." The word for "entertaining strangers" is *philozenias.* Notice the phonetic similarity to *philadelphia* of the previous verse. This kind of near repetition is characteristic of our writer, whose rich, seemingly inexhaustible vocabulary can be used in such effective rhetorical fashion not only to give a euphonious sound but to create a contrast of meaning. Here the contrast is between the love for brothers and love for the foreigner. *Zenia,* "hospitality," is derived from *zenos,* "foreigner," or, used as an adjective, "strange, unusual, foreign." We are not to forget to entertain such persons. The verb translated "forget" comes from a root word that means "to escape notice, to be hidden or forgotten."

It is so easy for us to fail to love the unusual; we are embarrassed by evidences of strange culture, unsure of ourselves in the presence of unfamiliar behavior, turned away by an unfamiliar race, nonplussed by our ignorance of another language. It takes a little something extra to engage in the entertainment of the foreigner or stranger. The something extra is the love of Christ that reaches out to the outsider and includes him or her. It draws that person into the inner circle, where, to our amazement, we discover an absolutely delightful and lovable individual who brings a unique blessing into our lives. Indeed, the stranger could be an angel, a messenger of God introducing His specially designed blessing which we would never have known if we had not loved the foreigner.

For the second time in this verse, the author employs in the Greek for "unwittingly," *elathon,* the device of contrasting similarity. The word stands in rhetorical contrast to the Greek for "forget," *epilanthanesthe,* an intensified compound with the root *lanthanō.*

Now our author moves to another category of the strange and unusual: the embarrassing—the prisoner. This person is embarrassing for other reasons—association with the unpopular and impious as seen by Roman law, or the blowing of one's own cover while trying to live the faith incognito. Whatever the reason, our exhorter instructs his readers to remember the prisoner (*desmios*, "one in chains") whether he has been fettered for his faith or his criminal action, and to imagine ourselves *"as if"* chained with him. It is so much easier in one sense to go to the one persecuted than to the errant. Fear of association or of being "conned" can keep a lot of us away from those in prison.

In visiting Lorton Prison here in the Washington, D.C., area, and in fellowshiping with those who have been released or who are in an experimental release program, I was at first amazed and then reminded that these are human beings whose guidance mechanisms have been knocked out of line. I could see in them an inner core of potentiality, waiting to be discovered and brought back to full design. When that happens, some of God's most exciting and lovable people emerge in the victory of Christ.

"As if chained with them. . . ." If we could see ourselves there (and perhaps we might if we had been caught), humility would flush away our pride and remind us that there "but for the grace of God, go I." Our repulsion is swept away in a stream of insight that is able to discern the injury and deprivation that caused the bizarre behavior. Or perhaps our imagination fantasizes the circumstances of our standing up for our faith in the face of hostile opposition that has political power, and we wonder if we could do it.

"Marriage is honorable among all." One senses a desire to use the imperative form of the verb: *"Let* marriage *be* honorable among all." No doubt, this meaning is implied. The word for "honorable" can also be translated "highly valued, precious, costly, or dear." It brings to mind not only "the honorable estate of marriage" but also the cost of making it work. Marriage, like any other covenant relationship, is not cheap; it "takes a heap of doing!" Nevertheless, it is built into the very core of the human psyche, and the very costliness of it makes it both frightening and difficult, but also tremendously rewarding.

The costliness of marriage is in its covenant nature. Having been made by God *imago dei*, "in the image of God," we find that, in marriage, that means taking the initiative in covenant-making, and risking rejection. At times the covenant of marriage appears unilateral—when one of the parties appears to disregard the relationship or treats it cheaply; when love is not requited; or when little comes back in response to the love that has been offered. There are times when marriage must persevere and make new covenants when an old one has become threadbare or has been broken. Marriage must build into the partners affirmations that become internalized so deeply and thoroughly that they become an essential part of the personality. Marriage is costly because of the intimacy it demands—in time, in communication, in sharing dreams and agendas, pains and struggles, in physical tenderness and verbal expression. Intimacy costs. It costs our privacy, our self-centered scheduling, our secrecy of musing, and our individualistic economics. The covenant of marriage demands forgiveness so complete that the forgiver forgets and embraces again without any reservation. Yes, marriage is costly.

But oh, what value there is in that which is precious, for which a high price has been paid! Whether our author meant to make a declamatory statement or an exhortation is a question we could discuss at some length. It *is* honorable and *let* it *be* honorable!

Moreover, *"the bed [is] undefiled,"* which is a socially decorous way of saying "intercourse is untainted." The word translated "undefiled" comes from a root meaning "to taint or pollute" and in a moral sense "to defile"; a prefix adds the meaning "without." *Koitē*, "intercourse, bed," has a root meaning of "having in common" and in this circumstance implies the deepest sort of sharing or commonality, that of bonding. Paul has said that intercourse is in fact becoming one flesh with another (see the teaching in 1 Cor. 6:16–18). The one flesh in marriage is not just a physical phenomenon, but a uniting of the totality of two personalities. In marriage we are one flesh spiritually by vow, economically by sharing, logistically by adjusting time and agreeing on the disbursement of all life's resources, experientially by trudging through the dark valleys and standing victoriously on the peaks of success, and sexually by the bonding of our bodies. In intercourse, which is the expression created uniquely for marriage, the male and female fibers interwine in complementation, creating a living fabric that cannot be undone without serious damage to the living fibers. When that happens, they are left scarred and therefore lacking in suppleness, circulation, sensitivity, or strength. Scar tissue is not good tissue. Let *koitē* be undefiled and untainted, undefiled and beautiful as God designed it.

Fornicators (*pornoi*) and adulterers (*moichoi*) God will judge. Both of these taint and defile the awesome creation of God. Through all its media, modern American culture as well as many others disengages *koitē* from the other facets of one-fleshness and claim the physical experience to be the end and goal of romantic relationships. Now we are reaping the results in uncontrollable disease, whether the long-known venereal kind or the more recent Acquired Immunity Deficiency Syndrome. Is this what Paul meant when he said those participating in promiscuous sexual activity bear in their bodies the marks of their own sins (Rom. 1:27)? God's judgment can be manifested in spiritual, physical, emotional, social, or psychological forms.

Broken marriage and the family disintegration that goes with it are taking a tremendously costly toll on our society. Children from such homes are very often only partially matured human beings, lacking major components of preparedness for life. Children need so desperately both father and mother as critical resources in discovering personal identity, sexual orientation, social and communicative dynamics, and imaginative production. Denied these resources, they come off the assembly line with important parts missing. Some are without the drive train of motivation; some lack clear sense of identity and the cargo they are to carry; others have no guidance mechanism and career down the highways at high speed, out of control. Society spends massive amounts of time and energy towing in these dear offspring of a broken society for major repair or recall.

Marriage is honorable, highly valued, precious, costly, dear to a society—and high priced. Let it be of high priority! If not, we will discover what other civilizations have discovered: we don't break God's laws; they break us.

"Let your conduct be without covetousness" (v. 5). Here for a third time our exhorter and preacher uses a word containing *philo,* this time *aphilarguros. Philo,* of course, is love; *arguros,* "silver," therefore "money," sets the basic tone of the word; the prefix *a* signifies the negative, *"not* a lover of money." *Tropos,* "style, or way of life," here translated "conduct," again presupposes the imperative verb in this hortatory passage. The sentence could read: "Let your life style be nonavaricious." Calvin rightly observes those who crave affluence are never satisfied; the search goes from sufficiency to overabundance to avarice which is never satiated. The reason, of course, is an inner hunger, one that possessions (*arguroi*) can never fill.

There is a content that dissipates the driving hunger for acquisition of endless wealth. Such hunger is manifestation of spiritual immaturity, an unconsciousness of the provision of God. In a very sound psychological rationale, our writer then quotes the Lord (Deut. 31:6, 8; Josh. 1:5): *"I will never leave you nor forsake you."* Where God is, there is sufficient resource. If God's presence is perpetual, then so will be the necessities of life. Therefore, the crucial necessity is our abiding relationship with God (John 15:1–8), not material possessions. The latter are important—no argument—but they are serendipity or the fruit of God's abiding presence. So we may boldly say, *"The Lord is on my side"* (Ps. 118:6). Here our author, as is typical, quotes the LXX rather than the Hebrew. *Boēthos,* Greek for "helper," comes from a verb that means in military usage, hasting to the cry for reinforcements, or, in nautical terminology, a frapping or the tightening of a tackle to hold something secure against the storm. If the Lord is such a helper, what can the howling adversity of a hostile humanity do to us? We are held secure against the storm by an anchor that will not slip (Heb. 6:18–19).

The Dynamics of Christian Community

7 Remember those who rule over you, who have spoken the word of God to you, whose faith follow, considering the outcome of their conduct.

8 Jesus Christ is the same yesterday, today, and forever.

9 Do not be carried about with various and strange doctrines. For it is good that the heart be established by grace, not with foods which have not profited those who have been occupied with them.

10 We have an altar from which those who serve the tabernacle have no right to eat.

11 For the bodies of those beasts, whose blood is brought into the sanctuary by the high priest for sin, are burned outside the camp.

12 Therefore Jesus also, that He might sanctify the people with His own blood, suffered outside the gate.

13 Therefore let us go forth to Him, outside the camp, bearing His reproach.

14 For here we have no continuing city, but we seek the one to come.

15 Therefore by Him let us continually offer the sacrifice of praise to God, that is, the fruit of our lips, giving thanks to His name.

16 But do not forget to do good and to share, for with such sacrifices God is well pleased.

17 Obey those who rule over you, and

be submissive, for they watch out for your souls, as
those who must give account. Let them do so with
joy and not with grief, for that would be unprofitable
for you.

Heb. 13:7–17

"Remember those who rule over you, who have spoken the word of God to you."
For "remember" our author uses an alternate word to the one he
used in 13:3. There his word was *mimnēskesthe* ("bring your knowledge
into line with, remember"); here he uses *mnēmoneuete* ("call to mind,
remember"). The former is probably an older form. Characteristically,
he has reached into his expansive vocabulary for a nuance of meaning.
His readers are to remember "those who rule over" them (*hēgoumenōn*)
which might more naturally be translated "those who have led" them,
from *agō*, "to lead." They are the ones who have spoken the word
of God to the hearers. He continues: *"considering the outcome of their
conduct."* Anatheōrountes is a compound verb which was common especially in later and Koine Greek. The root is *theōreō* ("to theorize, analyze, see"), to which has been added the prefix *ana*. In this compound
it has the ring of "again" or "anew"; thus, "look twice, consider
carefully." They are to consider the outcome of their conduct (*anas-
trophē*). This last word, again a compound with rhetorical similarity
to *anatheōreō*, has the sense of turning back or around, going in a
different direction. (The word for "repentance," *metanoia*, similarly
denotes a changing of mind.) Evidently they have had a turning
around to a new life style and conduct that has borne good fruit of
example. Mimic that faith! our writer exhorts.

Now comes a verse that at first appears to stand in absolute indepen-
dence: *"Jesus Christ is the same yesterday, today, and forever."* But does it
stand alone? Perhaps not. Think of it this way. If these readers are
being called to a remembrance and mimicry of their leaders and this
might lead to persecution, what reason is there for their hitching
their wagons to such falling stars? But if the star which they follow
is not really falling, but holding firm against others which are, in
reality, the ones that are falling, then theirs is the victory and the
stability. Jesus Christ is not going to change. Our author is really
pointing to what he has said throughout this epistle: "Do you not
remember the dozen or more characteristics of the Son? What more
could you want? What Christ was in creation, He is now and always
will be! Reality does not change. Do not follow after the transient

and the false. Hold firm to Him, to the confession of your hope without wavering, for He who has promised is faithful." (Note especially 10:23; 2:1–4.)

Several characteristics can be observed in the example of their leaders.

• They had been open to the work of Christ in their lives; they had been submissive to His redemption and His grace.

• They had gained perception of the truth of Christ out of their discipline of study of the word.

• They had exhibited courage and boldness in its preaching.

• They had shown perseverance in living out the Gospel until abundant fruit was the evidence of their maturity.

In our day there is probably no better example of this last characteristic than that of Mother Teresa of Calcutta. I had been asked by Senator Hatfield to a luncheon in his senate office to meet her. It was my deep privilege to spend a few minutes with her privately, and it was an unforgettable experience. Very obvious was her great modesty and humility. Her plaintive eyes, the often prayerful clasping of her hands, the slight stoop of her shoulders, more of humility than of age, were all statements of nonverbal language. But from that little woman radiated a power and authority that left me in awe. "Not by might, nor by power, but by My Spirit, saith the Lord" (Zech. 4:6) was being lived out right before my eyes. I was conscious that I was experiencing the power of a life that had submitted itself to Jesus completely, that had bowed its knee to Him daily in long hours of agonizing, concentrated prayer born of sheer desperation. Discipline, piety, and self-effacement were mixed with the power of Christ's Spirit to produce a very powerful potion. Afterwards, I asked my wife, Colleen, "What am I going to do with her?" The answer was simple; remember her and follow her example.

Let us consider verse 17 here rather than later, for it is in the same vein as verse 8: *"Obey those who rule over you, and be submissive, for they watch out for your souls, as those who must give account. Let them do so with joy and not with grief, for that would be unprofitable for you."*

The word translated "obey" is *peithesthe.* In the active the word means to persuade or prevail upon, and in the passive or middle voice, to be persuaded, to listen to or obey. Thus, this is not blind obedience to which our teacher refers, but obedience after thoughtful consideration that results in persuasion—all the stronger base for obedience. Those of us who demand obedience without reason, although that is necessary at times of childhood or emergency, are likely to get chameleon Christians who change orientation every time some golden-mouthed authoritarian happens along. Again, as in verse 7, the exhortation is to "obey those who have led you or rule over you; submit, obey!" The word stands alone and simply. The reason is straightforward; those leaders have been watchful, vigilant concerning the souls of the believers. So, very realistically, the author asks the readers to make this an enjoyable task for the leaders so that they may not be grieved. The Greek word here paints a colorful picture—*stenazontes*, to groan inwardly without external expression. What a description of some pastoring tasks. When that happens, nobody wins! It is downright unprofitable, for both leaders and learners. When the fun has gone out of ministry, a lot dies with it. On the contrary, it can be great joy to lead and grow in the guidance and power of the Spirit.

Verse 9 most likely follows right along in our writer's mind as an example of how to mimic the conduct of his readers' teacher/leaders. The example has to do with inconsistent teachings (*poikilais*, "many-colored, variegated") and foreign doctrine (*xenais*, "strange, foreign"). The teaching foreign to the Christian faith was that of foods having some spiritual value or abstinence from them some saving virtue. Such legalism has no place in the Christian's piety because the grace of God is all that can bring salvation and true piety to the human heart. Nothing else has any profit or value. Evidently our author is concerned about the same teaching as Paul in Romans 14. Another way to make the point might be to say, "Some walk around (*peripatountes*) in these profitless rules; don't you!"

The foods spoken of here might well have been the foods the Jews were either forbidden to eat by cleanliness laws or those special foods preserved for only the priests to eat. No one but priests could eat the portions brought as sacrifice and set aside for them (Lev. 7:7–21). The priests were to take their portions from the guilt offering and the sin offering after other portions had been burned with fire to the Lord. Our teacher tells us that we have an altar from which those who serve the tent have no right to eat. Notice the implication here that every believer can do what only the priest of the old covenant could do, eat from the food on the altar. Does that indicate that all believers are priests? It certainly appears to. Some have claimed that this section was a covert allusion to the eucharist. Most likely it is a reference to the sacrament of the Lord's Supper, but it does not seem at all covert. To eat the bread and wine as symbols of the sacrifice of Christ's body offered upon the heavenly altar is the satisfying food of the Christian, an all-sufficient sustenance for witness in life.

The author now speaks of the sacrifice of Yom Kippur, the flesh of which was taken outside the camp and burned there. The one who took it out was considered unclean and had to wash with clean water before he could come back into the camp. He was a reproach of uncleanliness, not to be touched by anyone until he was washed (Lev. 16:23–28). The sin sacrifice which had been identified with the sins of the people by the laying on of the hands of the priest was a fountain of uncleanness.

So it was with Jesus the Savior. When He identified with us in taking the sins of the world into His own body, He became unclean, a repulsion, a scandal in the eyes of the secular world, foolishness to the Greeks, and an abhorrence to the Jews. He has been thrust out of the dwelling places of many a religion, culture, and heart. If our greatest desire is to be accepted by other humans and included in their society, then the Person of Jesus Christ just may be a millstone about our necks. He has been excluded by many as a *"reproach"* (*oneidismos*, "disgrace, a matter of reproach," v. 13). Were those first readers ashamed that the great Messiah could not bring off the liberation from the Romans? "A dead messiah, hah!" With hostile eyes and raucous voices the masses could well have ridiculed the people of the Way: "Risen from the dead in power, is He? Then why do the Romans still take our flocks? Why are dirty Gentiles carrying off our wealth to a pagan caesar who thinks He's God? Jesus Christ on the right hand of power—for God's sake and for the sake of our children, we would like to have some of that power here on earth! He's a disgrace to Almighty God!"

Even today do we not share that same reproach? Those who want political liberation now and have no time or stomach for gradualism, no patience to work for a servant leadership in lands where arrogant oppressors rule, ridicule a soul-saving Christ. Those who see the uselessness of hoping for justice without a radical change of the individual human heart belittle the struggle for justice of those who sweat in the fields and labor in the streets. The answer is to go to that Christ outside the city; to be ready to bear the disgrace and reproach with Him, knowing that there is a power that is more lasting and pragmatic than any partial human answer.

Verse 14 shows why it is so foolish to trust the human dynamics of violence or individualistic religion. There is no lasting city here among the fickle hearts of humanity. There is no way to build a strong building with weak timbers or rotten bricks. No rearrangement of bad eggs will ever make a good omelette and no social reorganization will ever make a strong church without the renewing power of the Spirit. There is no way a new believer can be nurtured away from the tempting world without years of intensive discipling until he or she thinks, acts, and reacts according to the manner of Jesus Christ.

The continuing city we seek, the city of God, will come to this world only insofar as there are masses who have been redeemed by the cleansing of their consciences and toughened by discipline to stand against the torrent of a world gone mad. That city may only appear with the victorious coming of Jesus Christ somewhere in the unknown future, but that is no reason for us to stop working for every bit of it we can here. "Thy Kingdom come, Thy will be done on earth as it is in heaven" is still the fervent prayer of every true disciple. Ours is a realistic hope, not based on a false hope of humanity's innate goodness, nor upon a cynicism that is absolutely sure "people is hell." Ours is a hope both here and in the future: to build enclaves of Christian love in order that people may see and take hope, in spite of imperfection; and to wait for that city of God which will be only when Christ comes a second time, not to deal with sin but to save those "who eagerly wait for Him" (9:28).

In verse 15 our author touches on one of the most powerful dynamics of the Christian life: praise. When discouragement tethers our feet to the stakes, when fatigue numbs our spirit, when relentless circumstance hounds us moment by moment and day by day, the mature disciple discovers that praise both produces and releases energy. If only we could understand this, we would not wallow in the mire of self-pity and whine our way through the dark valleys, whimpering pathetically like spoiled children. By His power and grace, let us continually, through all circumstance and through all time, bring forward this sacrifice of praise and offer it upon the altar of our hearts. Praise will rise like a sweet incense before God; it is the praise of our lips rising like magma in the heart of a volcano that cannot be restrained in erupting to His name. It is the fruit of agreement and concurrence with God which we translate in giving thanks or praise.

Lest we make the mistake of thinking that such verbal and worship-ful praise is the completion of our witness, our exhorter quickly reminds us that worship must not be an excuse to forget good works and to share. Isaiah so clearly coupled worship and justice (Isa. 1:12–20), pointing out that justice and righteousness are also sacrifices which are pleasing to God and demanded by Him. They can never be the reason for our salvation but they are the proof of it. Without good works for which we were all created (Heb. 9:14; Eph. 2:10), there is every reason to doubt the validity of one's claim of salvation.

A REQUEST FOR PRAYER

18 Pray for us; for we are confident that we have
a good conscience, in all things desiring to live
honorably.
19 But I especially urge you to do this, that I may
be restored to you the sooner.

Heb. 13:18–19

"Pray for us" is a plea from a person who obviously has great insight into the gospel and is mature in faith, able to communicate that faith in clear perception and to urge maturity out of his own strength. Now he asks for prayer. That may seem odd to us, that the greater should ask from the lesser; or, to turn that presupposition around, does not the superior pray for the inferior? Such a belief has kept many of us from praying for others, thinking prayers flow downward from spiritual authority and maturity to those underneath and less mature—"Who am I to pray for you or anyone else? That sounds like superiority."

What a gross misconception. The power and superiority belong to God, not to any of us. It is not out of our resources that we pray prayers of intercession, but out of God's inexhaustible grace. The point we should remember is this: God has created us as interdependent people interacting in a community that functions like a body. Each part of the body has its abilities, which it offers to the whole; yet each part is dependent upon the other members of the body for its supply of strength. My thumb has certain functions which only it can accomplish, and yet it is dependent upon blood vessels to carry food, nerves to transmit commands from the brain, and skeletal structure to support its action. It is not a matter of superiority or inferiority as Paul indicates (1 Cor. 12:14–26), but of interdependence.

So it is with prayer. God has created us, whether in society or the church, as interdependent. Each of us is a creation of Christ (Gen. 1:26 ff.; John 1:1–3; Col. 1:15–16) with a purpose in Christ's kingdom. God has given us responsibility for one another and will not take the responsibility away. If we do not carry out our task, then it goes undone. If God were to rush in and fill in every nonperformance, we would become a totally irresponsible society overnight. He will not let that happen. His grace is like a great reservoir held behind a dam. Floodgates have been built into the dam so that water can be released on command. If, however, the command is never exercised, if we do not open the floodgates, the resources do not flow to our fellow members of the body.

The writer to the Hebrews recognized this dynamic. He knew that some portion of needed resources would not flow if his readers did not release the power of God through their prayers.

He feels right in asking this; his mental computer must have been rushing through its memory bank to see if there were anything that would have made this request invalid. He could find none. As he said, *"we have a good conscience"* (v. 18); of that he and his companions were confident. In all things they sought to live honorably (cf. v. 7). Their motives were clear; their consciences allowed them good nights' sleep.

He had yet another reason for their prayers; he wished to be restored to them. A thought of imprisonment comes quickly to our mind, but this is probably not his situation, as he says he hopes to come with Timothy if he arrives in time for an imminent departure. Some other cause for which he sought relief must have detained him, perhaps sickness.

A BENEDICTION

20 Now may the God of peace who brought up our
Lord Jesus from the dead, that great Shepherd of the
sheep, through the blood of the everlasting covenant,
21 make you complete in every good work to do
His will, working in you what is well pleasing

in His sight, through Jesus Christ, to whom be glory
forever and ever. Amen.

Heb. 13:20–21

What appears to be an irenic benediction in pastoral language becomes, with deeper consideration, a shout of apostolic encouragement
to be about the mandate of Christ. The term *"God of peace"* brings
to mind three different thoughts: (1) a consciousness of warfare with
a hostile and persecuting world on the outside; (2) a painful awareness
of the struggles and tensions within the church, as some might be
turning away from Christ in the midst of persecution's pressure; and
(3) the peace of redemption and reconciliation expressed in Romans
5:1, an ending of the warfare with God, a submission to His plan
in Christ, and acceptance of the forgiveness as foretold in the new
covenant of Jeremiah 31:31–34. We are looking at a God who always
takes the initiative in peacemaking and we are the blessed respondents.

"Who brought up our Lord Jesus from the dead" is a translation preferred
by B. F. Westcott (*The Epistle to the Hebrews*, p. 448), rather than "brought
again" as in KJV and RSV. The former places its emphasis upon
the victorious nature of the resurrection over the powers of darkness,
Satan, and sin. With the city of Jerusalem under siege and the forces
of the enemy pressing from every side, it is understandable that the
writer should emphasize the victorious character and power of God.
Anagagōn, translated "brought up," carries the idea of leading up in
a personal and dynamic fashion, not just an ephemeral and mystical
power working out in space somewhere.

The phrase *"our Lord Jesus"* is common in Luke's Book of Acts, in
contrast to the fuller title "the Lord Jesus Christ" which only a few
variant manuscripts indicate in this spot. The Lordship of Christ made
manifest in the power of the resurrection brings forth an image that
even as God brought Him up from the dead, so Christ leads us forth
into the world to accomplish His will, an idea the author will develop
considerably after the next phrase.

The title *"that great Shepherd of the sheep"* carries with it at least two
concepts. The first is that of a caring, searching, finding, redemptive
shepherd. To know that the most important One cares for us and
takes the initiative to come after us when we go astray must have
been of great comfort to those sheep of the flock who were in jeopardy
by their own waywardness or by virtue of the hostile enemies that
stalked them. The second concept is that this shepherd is also King,

which is reminiscent of Psalm 23 in which the shepherd leads out into justice and righteousness for His own name's sake. It is native to His personality; He must lead His sheep both into safety and into righteousness. This concept of caring is foundational to the emphasis on justice. There can be no willingness to risk the adventure of building the kingdom in the face of opposition without there being a sense of security in the hearts of those being asked to "move out." The evangelical experience of a redeeming shepherd is a necessary prerequisite to the accomplishment of the apostolic mandate.

The idea of Christ Himself being our shepherd is reminiscent of Ezekiel 34. God, judging the self-centered shepherds who have taken very good care of themselves and are living off the fat of the flock, declares that He Himself will be Shepherd to the people, making a covenant with them, enabling them to dwell in security, blessing them with showers and rich pasture and providing them with prosperity. Moreover, the Good Shepherd laid down His life for the sheep in accordance with an everlasting covenant.

Now notice the author's movement from security to the strategy of the kingdom. In verse 21, four important phrases follow regarding the ministry of his readers: (1) *"make you complete"*; (2) *"in every good work"*; (3) *"working in you"*; and (4) *"what is well pleasing in His sight."*

The Greek phrase translated *"make you complete"* paints a picture of making repairs, putting in order, mending or restoring implements that will be used in some task. My forebears on my mother's side were all Mennonite farmers. After the autumn harvest, there was little relaxation on the farms. The corn was plowed under so that it could be composting during the winter, and the stock still required care. But as important as anything was the repair and mending of the equipment so that it would be ready at the first hint of spring. In later Greek, the term used here, when referring to persons, has the sense of training and discipling, of getting them ready for battle. Primarily a military term, it was also used in a culinary sense, to mean getting a dish or plate ready to serve. There is no doubt that our author had not only the personal relationship of the believer to God in mind, but also the apostolic tasks of the building of the kingdom. What was the purpose of this preparation?

"In every good work" answers the question. Just as our exhorter stated in 9:14 that our consciences are cleansed from dead works to serve the living God, so here he indicates the purpose of shepherding— good works.

"To do His will" indicates that the good works are not nice little Boy Scout deeds drummed up for the sake of earning religious merit badges, but rather these good works are critical building blocks for the kingdom of Jesus Christ, which is the purpose of Christ's coming: "I shall build the kingdom and the gates of hell shall not prevail against it." Our good works have both a high humanitarian motive and also a zealous motivation to accomplish the task which takes preeminence over all other tasks, building the kingdom.

"Working in you" leaves no doubt as to how or by what methods God will build this kingdom; it is through committed disciples. You! Christians are the subcontractors without whom the kingdom cannot be built.

A story is told of the saints of heaven questioning Jesus upon His entry there. "What plans do You have for the continuance of Your enterprise?" they asked. "I have left it in the hands of My apostles," He responded. A ring of realism encircled the retort: "But what if they fail?" Christ's answer was simple and poignant: "They cannot fail; I have no other plan."

"What is well pleasing in His sight" presupposes that God has a strategy that is very important to Him. If that strategy is not fulfilled, He will be very disappointed and judge those who have failed (Matt. 25:31–46). If that strategy is carried out, He will be very pleased. We are to do those things that will be part of the Great Plan, and there isn't time for much else in a disciple's life. His plan is a mandate to His church and includes the whole gospel to the whole person in the whole world. "Blessed is that servant, whom his master, when he comes, will find so doing" (Matt. 24:46).

There is only one way in which we disciples will be able to fulfill this ministry, and that is by Jesus Christ. The phrase *"through Jesus Christ"* is not euphemistic rhetoric, but a perceptive recognition that He is the Vine and we are the branches, and that without the Vine the branches bear no fruit. "Without Me you can do nothing"— that is a given dynamic in the kingdom of God.

"To whom be glory forever and ever" shows close agreement with Paul and is one more indication that the author may well have been in the Pauline school (Eph. 1:3–23, Col. 1:15–20). Even our death in persecution for the name of Jesus becomes a moment of victory, for in laboring and dying for the kingdom we are a portion of the ultimate success of the One before whom every knee shall bow and every tongue confess that He is Lord to the glory of the Father.

An Appeal

22 And I appeal to you, brethren, bear with the word
of exhortation, for I have written to you in few words.

Heb. 13:22

"*I appeal to you*" (*parakalō*) introduces a short postscript using the
same word as in verse 19 where he "urges" their prayers. Compare
this word with *paraklēseōs,* "the word of exhortation," which follows;
the latter describes well the whole document, both a teaching and
goading epistle which has been the vehicle for our teacher's deepest
concerns and most urgent thoughts. Therefore, he begs them to "bear
with" this writing, literally to hold it up as though on hands of
prayer (*anechesthe,* middle voice of *anechō,* which means lifting up as
in prayer, holding up, keeping constant to). The request is not so
much being patient with, but rather sustaining the adhering to. "*I
have written to you in few words*" may be an indication of how much
more the author might have had in mind on a subject so important
to him and resplendent with yet many other facets which he felt
he could not have written in full. Certainly the letter is not short,
so he must be comparing its length to what it could have been had
he written his full mind on all aspects of the subject of the priesthood
of Jesus Christ. There is evidently some self-consciousness on his
part—not over the need to apologize for the length, but rather for
not having said enough. He is like a professor who is so filled with
his subject that he must beg pardon for not saying it all. That is
probably to the relief of his students. What if he had written it all!

Postscript

23 Know that our brother Timothy has been set
free, with whom I shall see you if he comes shortly.
24 Greet all those who rule over you, and all the
saints. Those from Italy greet you.
25 Grace be with you all. Amen.

Heb. 13:23–25

The Timothy mentioned here might well be the Timothy of the
Pauline entourage; there is no indication to the contrary. The style
of referring to Timothy differs from that of Paul who invariably

speaks of any companion in the gospel as *Timotheos* (or any other name) *ho adelphos*, whereas our author uses the phrase *ton adelphon hēmōn Timotheon*, a reverse order. Evidently he has been set free from prison or from a charge brought against him, even as Paul sought to be set free of charges by appealing to Caesar. Our writer is intending to travel with him to see the readers of this epistle if circumstances allow him to come before long. We have no clue as to what circumstances might make his arrival date unsure except the normal uncertainty of travel in those days.

It is only normal protocol as well as Christian concern for leadership that our author should send the greetings of verse 24. *Aspasasthe*, "great," is a salutatory term that was commonly used in letters of the day, just as we commonly employ a complimentary closing like "sincerely yours." In return he is saying that those from Italy greet the readers. In both instances, he uses the same word, in appropriate forms.

It is uncertain whether the reference to Italian Christians means that some have sent greetings by letter or personal courier or whether they are present in person. Some have argued for an Italian origin of this epistle, but that cannot be determined simply on the basis of this passage.

The words of the final verse have a simple and beautiful lilt in both the Greek and our translation—*hē charis meta pantōn humōn, "grace be with you all."* It is very similar to the blessings given at the end of Paul's letters. Paul at times expands the blessing in a variety of ways, but the core remains the same. He may add "of the Lord Jesus Christ" after "grace" or say "your spirit" rather than "you" at the end of the phrase. None of the other New Testament writers uses a similar style.

Once again, in this period of history, the church of Jesus Christ in the Western World needs to be revitalized in its apostolic fervor. There is no way that can happen without a clear understanding of Jesus Christ, His Atonement, the cleansing of the human heart from sin, and in our living as disciples in fulfillment of the apostolic mandate.

I trust this epistle, a magnificent document of that apostolic First Century, will be pulled from the dusty shelf and come alive in the mind and heart of the church. Share your excitement with your disciple companions, that they too may give praise to God for the single perfecting sacrifice of Jesus Christ our Savior and Lord.

Bibliography

Bruce, A. B. *The Epistle to the Hebrews.* Edinburgh: T. and T. Clark, 1899.

Brunner, Emil. *The Mediator.* Philadelphia: Westminster Press, 1947.

Calvin, John. *Hebrews.* Calvin Commentary Series. Tr. J. Owen. Edinburgh: Calvin Translation Society, 1853.

Cullmann, Oscar. *Christ and Time.* Tr. Floyd Filson. Philadelphia: Westminster Press, 1950.

Danby, H. *The Mishnah.* London: Oxford University Press, George Cumberlege, 1933.

Daube, David. *The New Testament and Rabbinic Judaism.* Jordan Lectures, 1952. London: Athlone Press, 1956.

_____. *The Apostolic Preaching and Its Developments.* London: Hodder and Stoughton, 1936.

Dods, Marcus. "The Epistle to the Hebrews," *Expositor's Greek Testament,* vol. 4. Grand Rapids: Eerdmans, 1951.

Eusebius, Pamphilus. *Ecclesiastical History.* Tr. C. F. Cruse. London: Henry G. Bohn, 1851.

Josephus, Flavius. *The Works of Flavius Josephus.* Tr. W. Whiston. London: George Virtue, 1841.

Kirkpatrick, *The Book of the Psalms.* Cambridge University Press, 1951.

Luther, Martin. *The Works of Martin Luther,* vol. 6. Philadelphia: A. J. Holman Co. and Castle Press, 1932.

Macintosh, H. R. *The Doctrine of the Person of Jesus Christ.* 2nd ed. Edinburgh: T. and T. Clark, 1912.

Manson, T. W. *The Church's Ministry.* London: Hodder and Stoughton, 1948.

_____. *The Servant-Messiah.* Cambridge University Press, 1953.

Manson, W. *Jesus the Messiah.* Philadelphia: Westminster Press, 1946.

_____. *The Epistle to the Hebrews.* London: Hodder and Stoughton, 1951.

Moffatt, James. *Hebrews.* ICC. Edinburgh: T. and T. Clark, 1924.

Philo Judaeus. *The Works of Philo Judaeus.* Tr. C. D. Yonge. London: Henry Bohn, 1854.

Robinson, T. H. *The Epistle to the Hebrews.* London: Hodder and Stoughton, 1933.

Suetonius, G. Tranquillus. *The Lives of the Twelve Caesars.* Tr. Thompson, rev. Forester. London: George Bell and Sons, 1890.

Taylor, Vincent. *The Atonement in New Testament Teaching.* 2nd ed. London: Epworth Press, 1945.

_____. *Jesus and His Sacrifice.* London: Macmillan and Co., 1951.

_____. *Forgiveness and Reconciliation.* 2nd ed. London: Macmillan and Co., 1952.

Westcott, Brooks F. *The Epistle to the Hebrews.* London: Macmillan and Co., 1899.